# 'RUSTICUS'

## Diary of a Modern
## Countryman

# 'RUSTICUS'

## Diary of a Modern Countryman

Illustrations by John Hill

**BRIAN P. MARTIN**

SWAN·HILL
PRESS

First published in the UK in 1997
by Swan Hill Press, an imprint of Airlife Publishing Ltd

**British Library Cataloguing-in-Publication Data**
 A catalogue record for this book
 is available from the British Library

ISBN 1 85310 752 2

Typeset by Hewer Text Composition Services, Edinburgh
Printed in England by Hartnolls Ltd, Bodmin, Cornwall

# Swan Hill Press
an imprint of Airlife Publishing Ltd
101 Longden Road, Shrewsbury, SY3 9EB, England

To my wife, Carol

# *Acknowledgements*

By far the most important help to me in writing my 'Country Scene' column was my wife, Carol. Not only has she shared my love of the countryside and wildlife for so many years, accompanying me on innumerable walks and field trips, but she has also been a great source of inspiration. Furthermore, she has acted as my 'chief scout', bringing to my attention many incidents and trends which I might otherwise have missed, and has acted as an invaluable 'sounding board' for my ideas and comments.

Second, I am grateful to my two sons, Spencer and Ross, for sharing my love of the outdoors, for acting as 'spurs' when the mind was willing but the body 'reluctant'; and for getting me involved in so many things which I might never have known about.

Third, I must thank the editors and staff of *Shooting Times & Country Magazine*, with whom I worked closely over many years; in particular Tony Jackson for his initial encouragement and for giving me the opportunity to start writing the 'Country Scene' column.

In addition, I am grateful to the many readers of *Shooting Times & Country Magazine* who gave me their strong support and frequently wrote to me to share their original – and often fascinating – observations of wildlife and country ways.

Finally, I acknowledge the great country commentators and poets of the past, especially W.H. Hudson and Thomas Hardy, who have acted as major sources of inspiration.

# Contents

# Introduction

As a schoolboy I kept books in which I described and illustrated my observations of wildlife and the countryside. These included everything from detailed measurements of the dead animals I found to notes on rare birds and butterflies encountered. Furthermore, there was some account of local change in human society. Even then, in the 1950s and early 1960s, I was sufficiently moved to make strong comment on the way so-called 'progress' was shaping 'the great outdoors'. In those days I did have fairly easy access to relatively unspoilt places as I lived on the edge of a town, but the odd thing was that none of my family was even remotely involved in country activities. My only significant influence came from a few schoolchums, kindred spirits with a taste for adventure.

Anyway, throughout my childhood I 'lived for nature', for birdwatching, bird's-nesting, butterfly and beetle collecting, and later for shooting. My 'museum' contained everything from the skull of a razorbill which I found washed up on the shore to a tiny dried hummingbird which an old lady gave me in a Swan Vestas matchbox. And it was nothing for my mother to throw her hands up in horror at finding a heron's wing drying under the sideboard or an orphan tawny owl snoozing in my bedroom cupboard.

At first I had no idea how all this interest in nature would shape my life. In any case, I had no thought for the future when every 'free' hour was spent rooting around for owl pellets and bones under bushes. Then, one day when I was ten or eleven, my teacher asked each member of my class to write a 'composition' on 'my favourite hobby'. Not surprisingly, I decided to expound on birdwatching, and I suppose it was because I wrote with such passion that my piece was chosen to be read out to the class as a fine example.

Soon after, the same teacher suggested that we all wrote a poem. Again not surprisingly, I wrote one called 'The Owl', and to my delight this too was singled out for special praise. However, this did spark a little jealousy, which surfaced one day in class when Alison Trout (sic) poured ink all over my drawing of a heron. Undaunted, I decided to add a third verse to my poem and submit it to *Birds Illustrated Magazine*, which, along with the very authoritative *British Birds*, I then subscribed to. To my astonishment and delight, the editor published the poem in June 1959, when I was aged eleven. From then on I knew that I wanted to be 'a writer' and that 'nature' would be my main subject.

However, when I was studying for my zoology, botany and chemistry A levels (the plan was to study biochemistry at university) I suddenly got 'itchy feet' and left school. My slightly older, outdoors chum suggested that I should join him in hospital administration, so I did. Unfortunately this meant a lot of studying for exams concerned with boring things such as economics and law, so my opportunities to 'get out' were restricted. For a while, wildlife and writing had to take a back seat as a career had to be established and a 'living' earned.

Inevitably, after a few years the old interests resurfaced and I started to submit articles to various magazines. Once again, I got off to an encouraging start when my very first effort – a profile of a local gamekeeper – was published by *Gamekeeper and Countryside Magazine* in 1972. A few years later I was given the opportunity to start and edit a weekly, regional health-services newsletter and – much as I liked it – I began to wonder if I was in the right job.

At the age of twenty-nine, I decided that if I wanted to be a writer after all I had better act quickly. So I simply wrote to three magazines close to my interests and asked for a job. The editor of *The Countryman* quarterly had just taken on an assistant and therefore did not require anyone, and when I went for interview at the *Health and Social Services Journal* I decided that it was too boring. Fortunately, *Shooting Times & Country Magazine* liked what I had already written and were set for expansion, so in August 1977 I was taken on as assistant editor. It was, of course, a fortuitous appointment, but it did seem remarkable that I still happened to have a photograph of me reading the *Shooting Times* in 1962, when I was a schoolboy subscriber!

At first, 'BB' (Denys Watkins-Pitchford) wrote the 'Country Scene' page every week, but then editor Tony Jackson invited me to alternate with 'BB' on a fortnightly basis. But, as I would often write other features for the magazine, we decided that I should have a 'Country Scene' pen-name, so that my name would not appear twice in the same issue. I found the name Rusticus while looking up the derivatives of country-related words in my Latin dictionary and my first piece under that nom de plume was published on 13 December 1979. It was not until the following year that I was shocked to discover that, by complete coincidence, in the nineteenth century another writer had not only used the pen-name Rusticus but also lived in the same area as me! (see account in June)

I am proud to say that my fortnightly contribution continued without interruption until 30 December 1993. Sadly 'BB' died in October 1990, so for just over three years I continued alone with the 'Country Scene'. I had left the magazine in December 1990 in order to concentrate on writing books, which I started doing in 1984.

My fourteen years of 'Country Scene' gave me a wonderful opportunity to record and comment on a period of almost unprecedented change in the countryside. It was a time when the 'green revolution' really got going, when the general public started to have great concern for the environment. Global issues such as the 'greenhouse effect', acid rain, sea pollution and destruction of the ozone layer became everyday topics of conversation. Meanwhile, in Britain we were also increasingly concerned with subjects such as hedgerow loss, peat extraction, intensification of farming, the ending of stubble burning, public perception of fieldsports, and European Community Directives.

At the same time I wanted to describe how all these universal matters related to the ordinary 'man on the ground', so at every opportunity I tried to 'illustrate' points with example. And in doing this my work for *Shooting Times*, which took me all over the British Isles, proved invaluable. I established a very knowledgeable network of contacts within the farming, conservation and sporting communities and was in an excellent position to comment on the nitty-gritty of country life across the land. Simultaneously, I could record the impact of historic events such as the introduction of The Wildlife and Countryside Act in 1981 and 'The Great Storm' of October 1987.

However, I did not want my page to be full of 'serious stuff'. I also wanted it to be a celebration of country life, one to reflect the romance and adventure of the seasons. To achieve this, I often wrote in the field, not trusting anything to memory for even a few hours lest some important detail should be overlooked. I hoped to make every outdoors element come alive, and at the same time I sought subjects with which many readers could identify.

For this book I have chosen 'Country Scene' pieces covering the entire period, from 1979 to 1993. In length, they range from entire articles to short extracts. In portraying the magic and character of the English countryside, they reflect both the reassuring nature and unpredictability of the seasons.

While often writing evocatively, I became very much aware of what I call 'the cycle of nostalgia', in which there is always a new yesteryear for every generation to hold up as 'golden'. Indeed, on reflection I now see how much I have drawn on

11

my own 'idyllic' childhood. However, while I love old country classics such as Gilbert White's *Natural History of Selborne*, I am also aware that much of their appeal and apparent romance masquerades beneath the charm of archaic language. Indeed, even prose written as recently as the Edwardian period can please us without necessarily saying or meaning much. Yet I have no doubt that all the successful old country commentators were simply writing in the style of their day. With this in mind, I have had no hesitation in 'painting pictures' in often very modern language. If things continue to change as quickly as they have done recently, I expect that within only a few generations the language of my 'Country Scene' will appear as quaint as White's. All that really matters is that it contains the truth and stimulates our descendants to care for nature as we have done.

*Brian P. Martin*
*Brook, Surrey, 1996*

# January

## Discovering the Countryside

Few months harbour the mystery and wonder of January. Now those troglodytes of 'Glitz City' may be forgiven for thinking that the land lies fervourless in hibernation. The façade is barely skin-deep and even persons completely unskilled in nature detection can easily discover the great treasures of midwinter countryside. Mere idling along lanes may begin insignificantly as post-Christmas exercise born of New Year resolutions, but end in fascination and far greater awareness of outdoor life.

Some people find the desolation of deep countryside unnerving on grey January days without whisper of wind or apparent movement of man or beast. Yet is that so surprising when most of their lives are spent in bright society? Thrust into woodland ways, many folk soon miss their usual companions. Yet most of their grandfathers knew times when the countryside, not the town, was the hub of human life.

I used to wish that I lived way back, when nature held dominion over most of the land, when no wire scarred the skyline and only a curl of cottage smoke marked the valley now killed by concrete. There, surely, would be real room to spread your wings, abundant wildlife, unrestricted sport and a true sense of belonging to a local and satisfied community free of hard-sell advertising. But that phase passed as I discovered the importance of variety in both nature and human activity, and the learning process was accelerated through study of those great chroniclers of yesteryear. They proved that, like poverty, all wildness is relative and an expression of the general spirit and understanding of the day.

1989

## Gone to Roost

On one of the few icy mornings this month I found a blackbird stiff with death in the hedge bottom. Its sooty plumage and crocus

13

bill were as perfect as ever as it lay on its back, clenched claws and brittle legs fending off the invisible executioner. One frost too many had silenced the songster whose body once pulsed so fully in tune with the idyll of English summer.

Just hours before I had watched him enter his garden holly retreat along with a few sparrows and finches. Now I cupped the chill bird in my hand and thought how sad it was that his eyes had closed for the last time in the season of emptiness rather than the fullness of summer, for which he was an unrivalled herald. Yet I knew this was but an everyday incident and that blackbird was only one of millions which perish in this undignified way every winter.

I was reminded of the pathetic corpses I regularly used to find beneath a great starling roost in Hampshire. It was a very secret and undisturbed place, but then it was on Ministry of Defence land and, as a young explorer, I should not have been there.

Each evening I stood fascinated as the dusky legions poured in from every direction, stomachs full after a hard day's foraging. At first they settled on bushes and small trees in surrounding fields, cluster upon cluster of silhouettes charged with almost tangible energy, chattering excitedly in the fire of sunset. But almost as soon as every twig in sight was drooping under the weight of birds some unseen conductor waved his baton and the entire army took wing for a remarkable encore. It was as if their swirling, aerial dance as one body was carried out entirely for my benefit and I could scarcely believe that there were no other witnesses.

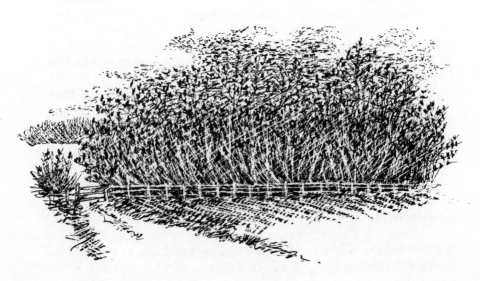

Why people paid good money to watch the paltry shows of men while this great spectacle was entirely free was then one of life's mysteries in my child's mind. I cannot imagine how many times I stayed there till every single bird was still in the depths of the black wood and not one voice was to be heard.

1988

## When Eggs Froze

At last we have been able to drag the 'new' sledge from its three-year exile in the broom cupboard. What exhilaration – even for my rusty frame! Yet this brightly painted snow-glider was no better than a simple sanenwood tray or even just an empty fertilizer bag which we brought into use to avoid waiting for 'turns'. My neighbour swears by two old car bumpers as runners. However I cracked my tray on a rut too narrow.

Recently there have been many very sad stories concerning tragedy, even death, as a direct result of the big freeze-up, and I do hope that any reader connected with such serious mishap will bear with my romantically biased image of snow. Like most people, we have had our problems.

When the latest snowstorm struck I was rambling around the woods, where we already had about five inches of level snow, and was amazed at what little notice some wild creatures took of the conditions. Pheasants, for example, continued to feed in the late afternoon on an open field – goodness knows what on – in a most ferocious wind which blew snow horizontally and so hard that I could not look into it. And in and around the more sheltered parts the wrens and tits fed on, searching out every scrap of energy-giving food to stand a chance of surviving the exceptionally low temperatures of the nights ahead, when Jack Frost would lay his artwork even on the inside of our bedroom windows.

That night the combination of gale and heavy snow snapped many a branch from trees across the land and I was so concerned about some particularly attractive garden junipers, about twelve feet high, for they were bent double, that I went out in the blizzard every hour or two to shake the snow from them. Unfortunately, the only handy handle long enough to do the job was that of the cobweb brush and its flimsy dowelling soon snapped as I tried to press the trees upright again.

15

With such low temperatures one has to think twice about what is left outdoors. Even pintas have frozen on the step, and eggs in the henhouse have solidified before we could take them in. Luckily it was so cold that even when scuppered power lines meant we were without electricity for twenty-six hours, the food in the freezer (luckily in an outhouse) showed not the slightest degree of defrosting.

And all this just a few days after I had seen a peacock butterfly skimming a lonely Hampshire hill, in a temperature of just 6°C in thin sunshine.

1982

## Bad Start to the New Year

One species for which I need no scientific aid in classifying is the collared dove. To me, at least, this twentieth-century colonist of Europe has always been simply a pest of the first order, one which fouls grain stores, takes valuable livestock food, increasingly competes with indigenous species of wildlife and often keeps me awake with its incessant, boring coo. Its only saving grace is that its flesh is very good to eat.

But this year I have already had reason to despise the collared dove even more. On staggering down from bed at noon on New Year's Day (not typical I hasten to add!) with a monumental hangover from festivities which finished at 5 a.m., I found the kitchen full of feathers. Under the table was the source of this infection – a collared dove collared by our young cat, Percy.

Now hoovering with a headache was all I needed to start 1993, but then I suppose us humans of the household were to blame in that if we had been up to feed the cats at the customary hour, then Percy would not have gone a huntin'. Now if only I could train him to kill collared doves but not tits and finches.

1993

## Winter Mixture

Our change to cold weather came overnight, when rain clouds blew off to leave a high and frosty heaven and drips frozen to

16

every sealed bud which hid a promise of spring. Beneath my boots a deep, frozen carpet of chestnut leaves creaked as new leather.

No one season exists in isolation from the other three, especially in unpredictable Britain. Even now, in mid-January, when deepest winter crackles the grass with frost, there are clear signs of *all* the seasons. Our spinning Earth is a swirling ambiguity of cloud, current and climate, and in Britain's tempestuous corner there is certainly no clear demarcation of season.

Even now, in this snowscape, we have woodland leaf litter with fruits and nuts lingering on to remind us of autumn. The first flowers, such as aconites, prove that there will once again be renewal of life, and signal a rush of spring growth that is already building and swelling beneath the protecting mantle of snow. The brilliant yellow gorse still brightens the way, commonly being found flowering in every month of the year. And on those mild January days when hard winter relaxes its grip, blackbirds and thrushes may offer a little tremulous song to remind us of far-off summer.

After the first snow, before those penetrating frosts set furrows hard as rock, I came across a woodland glade where some hungry creature had been scraping out the mould. The objects of its attention appeared to be white eggs, but they were really stinkhorn fungi in their subterranean embryonic stage, apparently the only form in which they are edible.

Another important wild fruit now is the ivy berry, and many fill the crops of woodpigeon. These birds are quite good at finding a warm roost, but far from excellent. Many get right into the thick of ivy or conifer but others seem surprisingly content to sit out the freeze in thin cover. Shelter from the wind is most important, for that can increase the chill factor tremendously. Thus birds such as starlings, which seem stupid in contenting themselves with a building ledge, are not so daft after all. They probably have very good shelter, not to mention the fact that the temperature in towns is often several degrees higher than in the surrounding countryside.

1985

## Conservation Hope

After all the excesses of Christmas, when the balloons have shrivelled, tree needles litter the carpet and the fairy's white dress is tainted with cigar smoke, many of us face the overdrafts and reality of the new year with some concern. Yet in one area at least I believe there is cause for optimism. That is in the relatively new field of wildlife conservation and the interdependent area of countryside management.

The 'Global 2000' report to the president of the United States estimated that between half a million and two million species of plants and animals could become extinct over the next twenty years as a result of habitat loss or pollution. Greatest concern has been over tropical forests, where between a half and three-quarters of all species exist, but which are now being cleared at an unprecedented rate.

Unfortunately, most of the tropical forest lies within the so-called 'developing' countries, where people simply do not have as much time as we do to detach themselves from pressing everyday problems of financial survival in order to consider the fate of other living things. Thus, quite understandably, the more caring of 'advanced' western societies increasingly began to co-operate internationally and now try to lead, chiefly by example. At last, in March 1980, a World Conservation Strategy was launched and it has been extremely encouraging to see many of the developing countries among those attempting national plans.

In Britain, of course, we are also forced to abide by constraints imposed by the European Economic Community and new legislation must take account of fresh Directives as well as national opinion, custom and international convention. At the moment hardly a day passes without us reading about the Wildlife and Countryside Bill which is now going through Parliament and has been called the most significant piece of legislation of its type of our generation. It is certainly a milestone in Britain's formulation of a national conservation policy and enhances the belief that 1980 has been the year in which many problems have been identified, while 1981 should be the year in which many of them are solved.

The Wildlife and Countryside Bill is a long and complex document covering many areas of country life, and because of this I can see some danger in the long term of not being able to see the wood for the trees. It is a good start but we must not be fooled into believing that it is anything like a complete answer, especially now, when society is undergoing such rapid change.

This Bill is nothing more than a legal tool of society *today*. Its real success and the success of any subsequent legislation will be in how much it anticipates the whims of society *tomorrow*. In deciding which species shall proliferate, man has set himself up as a pompous king of natural selection and is bound to find himself in a tangled web. Because of the complexity of natural systems every move is bound to have repercussions and it is a little daunting and humbling for mankind to realise that he will *never* have comprehensive legislation concerning natural orders. All we can do is to try to obtain *flexible* controls, at least in order to handle varying populations. We can legislate for man's actions but we cannot legislate for long-term variance in animal and plant populations through climatic change.

Thinking of populations, I was reminded of how many people are too ready to assume and accept basic parameters for living when assessing conservation strategy today. They accept that the human population will continue virtually unchecked and that urban sprawl is a fact of life. Untrue! It is *not* inevitable that a particular habitat will *decrease* in any country and that pollution will *increase*. It is a matter of priorities and the price society is prepared to pay. This Bill, commendable as it is, is not really concerned with such major issues of principle but more about important secondary issues such as which species will be protected, where and when they will be protected and which areas are the best to protect them within. Where is the clearly defined long-term strategy? We need bold thinkers and visionaries more concerned with the ideal countryside of 2081 than with dilly-dallying about how many lesser spotted tit babblers visit the bird table today.

Meanwhile, in conservation we need a base line and I suppose the easiest way out is to say that a minimum acceptable population of a species is one which is naturally viable – able to procreate and sustain itself within those areas which man deigns to set aside for it. Today it is assumed that every living thing from rats to ragwort deserves a niche and must be protected at any cost. Beyond the level of mere continued existence it would take a brave man to suggest that, for example, we should have more parrots than crows because they are prettier and more nightingales than sparrows because they sing more sweetly.

At the moment it is regrettable that it seems as if we must prove that a species is endangered before affording it special protection within the law. Surely this is the antithesis of English justice. In any case where there is strong doubt about whether or not to protect a particular species we should err on the side of safety and impose protection, not forgetting of course that so long as society accepts hunting in principle, the converse should apply and the list of quarry species should be added to as seen fit. But even when we have decided *what* to protect we can only legislate for *human* action. We cannot fine the climate or disease.

19

Naturally, most conservation thought occurs with the premise that concern comes only after man's welfare. Indeed, that is often the only way to win popular support for a crusade, for truthfully terms such as 'pest' and 'natural resource' are ugly and have been invented to succour man's ends, chiefly in gaining financial advantage. But is man capable of accepting the existence of all species simply for their own sake? I think not at the moment. We have a long way to go in issuing blanket licences to live. For example, why not exterminate all rats now? What good do they do? Oh, I forgot, man has a vested interest in using them for laboratory experiments and the fact that owls eat them is only of secondary importance. Unfortunately I feel that it will be a long time before we completely forget about the weak arguments of *justification* of any particular existence. Even the arguments about removing links in the ecological chain (no matter how important) constitute weak pandering to justification. Man is far from mature. Unless the existence of any creature or plant directly threatens his survival and there is no foreseeable solution to the problem he should not be so pompous as to seek to control its population level unduly. However, in practice it is not so bad for we generally bumble along from one cull to the next without any long-term national or global plan. By all means harvest an edible natural or artificial surplus. After all, the presence of dog teeth confirms that we are all meat eaters!

Regarding the Wildlife Bill, it has been suggested that the actual mechanics of exercising control will remain or become difficult in some instances, but that should be no deterrent as we cannot bury our heads in the sand: we must at least try to solve identified problems, even within a very sad budget.

There are so many principles involved in conservation and this present Bill, but they have been and always will be hampered by nostalgia and its ensuing prejudice. Perhaps that's not a bad thing. What probably will change is the order of the chicken and the egg. So far, from a conservation viewpoint man has mostly considered the countryside in terms of various habitats which must continue to be represented in order to sustain the various species found in each. But it is possible that growth of nostalgia will see the increased preservation of land for its value as scenery, and the fact that the bee orchid or Dartford warbler is found there might become secondary. Some people might be more interested in rocks than wildlife. But should we ever abolish nostalgia and introduce a national scenery plan we might get into a right pickle.

1981

## *Bats and Spiders*

Not surprisingly, the more ugly species which inhabit this planet
have had rather a raw deal in terms of conservation effort to date.
But at last the weird and the frightening have such a dedicated
band of champions that they too regularly make the news.

For example, in 1986 birds must share the headlines with bats
for this is National Bat Year. A recent issue of *Bat News*, the
guiding light of Bat Groups of Britain, states: 'It is intended to
encourage public interest and awareness of bats and to raise funds
for their conservation'.

I think awareness is the key word, for bats generally 'work
unsocial hours' and can quite easily live in and about an abode
for centuries without the occupants even being aware of them.
Sadly, because of this, roofs have frequently been treated against
rot and worm without the owners realising that bats were present.
This has led to many unnecessary bat deaths and, in recent years,
some well-publicised prosecutions. Such cases were readily taken
up by the popular press because they were seen as bizarre and likely
to capture the public imagination, but at least this has served the
conservation effort well in bringing bats to the fore.

Another group of animals which has scared the faint-hearted for
centuries is spiders, but they too are now the focus of specialist
conservation groups, both on a species basis and as part of food
webs. But had someone told me that it was possible for a British
spider to become as tame as a robin I would not have believed him.
Yet such an unlikely occurrence took place in my home – twice!

Over many weeks a house spider took to trotting across our
sitting room about our feet while we lounged each evening. At

first the slightest movement of the foot or tremor of floorboards would send this large spider scurrying away to safety beneath the furniture. But gradually he was less and less easy to impress and in the end he actually seemed to prefer our brightly lit company to the dark, dusty backroads of low life. We called him Fred.

One day Fred was not there. He never returned, but soon afterwards a larger spider appeared. Had she eaten Fred? Whatever the case, she too soon became very tame and we christened her Freda. Visitors had to be dissuaded from trying to put the boot in whenever she tiptoed out for company, and furniture had to be moved with care for fear of squashing the friendly arachnid.

Sadly, even in such a sheltering environment, a spider's life is indeed fleeting and one day Freda was there quite inert, feet up among the fly wings and beetle cases. It was as if a friend had departed.

1986

## End of Burning

I am pleased that the Government has decided to ban straw burning from 1992. Of course there are objections on economic grounds but these pale into insignificance compared with environmental concerns. Social considerations such as black smuts on washing are generally relatively minor, but smoke hazards to road traffic have been considerable and the destruction of hedges and wildlife has been very significant indeed. I expect many farmers are now wishing that they had taken more trouble in controlling their fires.

Between now and 1992 every economic avenue will be explored to minimise the impact of the cessation of straw burning. I hope that this will not lead to any new problems and that disgruntled farmers will have increasing concern for the wider environment. The Government is to be congratulated on making a rare move which does not appear to be primarily profit-motivated.

1990

## Tamed by Hunger

How tame the songbirds are now! In the hushed woods the bee-like wren whirrs across the track just inches away from my crushing

22

wellies. He perches sideways on a stump, head cocked and thin bill poised to seize any morsel of suspended animation lurking in cold hollows. Further on, a robin is attracted to one of those mysteriously unfrozen puddles which gathers the perpetual seepage from adjoining clay-cap pasture. And there, a dozen blue tits fidget through the ice-tinkling dusk towards some secret, warmth-giving communal roost. But now, when the ground is bitter with stones and ice daggers pierce the heart of every wild roost, there is sudden interest in nestboxes, garages, haylofts and barns as temporary sleeping quarters.

1982

## Talking Trees

One of the great joys of the January landscape is the architecture of trees, from the bold grandeur of old oaks in the pheasant covert to wind-shaped and stunted hawthorns atop the open moor. Summer may bring them leafy splendour, but now, with only their rattling bones, they are the talkative companions of every hunter and wayfarer. The pigeon shooter listens to the wild music of beech towers while awaiting the roost flight, and the pheasant Shot is intrigued by creaking oak and ash as he anticipates the whirr of wings. Duck shooters dream among pond-side willows while rabbit stalkers are fascinated by the riot of roots above the warren. How sad then that this ancient framework of nature is in jeopardy.

First we lost the majority of our elms to disease. Then came the hurricanes of 1987 and 1990. And now many survivors are in very poor shape following the summer droughts of 1989 and 1990. Air pollution and the heavy snows and strong winds of December 1990 have exacerbated the situation.

The Forestry Commission's 1991 monitoring programme, involving a study of 9,000 trees across Britain, has revealed that the proportion of trees in the healthiest category dropped from 15% in 1990 to 6% in 1991. Many people are justifiably worried about the effect on our trees of climatic change, brought on by the much-publicised 'greenhouse effect'. The previously most vigorous trees appear to have suffered most because those with a lot of leaves or needles need more moisture than those with less foliage.

23

Now, as I write, another big wind is moaning meanly down the chimney, subduing the blue-tinged flames which flare from my birch fire. Outside, the garden bench has been tossed over like matchwood and I am fearful that more precious trees, already weakened by wind and drought, will tumble. But then, it was ever thus, and as long as I play my part in renewing the forest I need not feel guilty in burning logs. Not only are trees a valued, sustainable crop but also an inspiration the year round.

1992

## Coastal Contrast

I do miss living within a mile of the sea. I miss the foghorns booming out on still nights, especially the ships' chorus to greet the new year, and the clouds of seagulls soaring in lazy spirals to gorge upon the ants which flight on thundery afternoons. I miss the tang of the salt air, the intrigue of shoreline flotsam and jetsam and the music of yacht rigging in the jetty breeze. There were ragworms for digging, cockles for bucketing, mullet for spearing in moonlit shallows and pools for prying in. Above all there was the crashing of surf on shingle.

Then, in the orchid days of some years, the migrant clouded yellow butterflies swarmed in over the dunelands where linnets and goldfinches danced in the shimmering sea breezes. The new hovercrafts droned across the Solent to the Isle of Wight while basking picnickers sought shingle territories free from tar to watch the great ships funnel past to Portsmouth or Southampton. Only the sandhoppers and wasps on the cucumber sandwiches and in runny ice creams dispelled the idyll.

But while one can never completely satisfactorily go back, memories can be heightened by contrast and, on occasion, re-glimpsed. For me a love of the coast and the occasional shoreline wildfowling trip today increase my awareness and appreciation of the special qualities of the inland country scene.

1980

## Fireside Reflection

Wildfowlers, gameshooters, roughshooters, anglers and bird-watchers all have one thing in common: from time to time they get extremely cold. I know this only too well because I have been in all their shoes at some point. Yet for me, at least, the fanaticism which sometimes numbs the senses is warmed as much by the prospect of a fire at the end of a day as by the sport itself. And now, in the greyness of winter, those reviving, reflective flames are never far from my mind.

There can be little doubt that the coastal wildfowler is the hardiest of all hunters. Not only does his best sport abound in the bleakest months of the year, but also he is regularly abroad after dusk and before dawn, when the mercury sinks lowest. Furthermore, he must endure the greatest wind-chill factor in the most exposed parts of the kingdom, all the while staying utterly inactive and often wet in some muddy pit. No wonder wildfowling is primarily a young man's obsession.

When I think back to my fowling heyday, when even iced estuaries warranted no excuses, I realise just how much the pub fire at the end of each outing meant to me. But then I was biased because in those days not only was my father a landlord, but so too was the pater of my best shooting pal, who lived in the same road.

It is quite remarkable that you can become so cold that any movement is an effort, let alone being able to slip the safety catch or feel the trigger. Yet as soon as the prospect of action looms your temperature soars. If the whistle of wings in the half-light is worth ten degrees, then the sight of wigeon heading straight towards you inspires true fever.

For the wildfowler who takes relatively few shots, the fireside inquest is a must, and the closer the pub the better. Straight into the ale, straight into the stories and straight into some good old-fashioned tucker such as steak-and-kidney pie. After the thrills and chills of evening flight no marsh man wants to lounge in a long bath – good as it is – for then the spark is gone. No, that is more in keeping with the end of a refined pheasant-shooting day, when generally older bones need more careful nurturing and Burgundy beckons more than beer.

But sometimes, usually at an 'away match' when staying at an hotel, things go awfully wrong despite the best of intentions. The assembled company is of two minds and you and Fred are still bloodstained at the bar going over every shot when Harry and Horace materialise in the foyer, all squeaky clean and pink-skinned from a deep, hot soak. You have completely forgotten that you promised to dine with them at eight and the horror on Harry's wife's face shows that you will never be forgiven. All you can do is apologise and blame the soporific effects of a stiff drink and 'that wonderful fire'.

After wildfowling, I consider sea fishing to be the coldest outdoor pursuit. This, too, necessitates staying in more or less the same position for hours on end while exposed to inevitably strong winds. Winter days on the briny can be real bone-crackers, and even in other seasons you can get chilled to the marrow. But I love it, especially when a good fire awaits you ashore.

Probably the world's best combination of sea fishing and warming fires is in Ireland. I cannot think of anything more invigorating than a day at sea followed by a peat fire. What can be more heart-warming than the twinkling lights of quayside cottages from which peat smoke drifts and pervades everything as you unload your catch at dusk. And if it's raining – which it always is in south-west Ireland – the intoxication is even greater as the scented smoke wafts heavily in low layers that you can almost cut with your filleting knife.

Of course, I share the concern about the over-exploitation of peat and I welcome recent pressure on firms such as Fisons to find alternative composts. But I do feel sorry for folk whose families have known no fuel other than peat. It is the elixir of the mountains and I can imagine many an uplander pining for it, should he emigrate to the lowlands.

They always used to say that when you went into an empty cottage you could tell when the owner was coming back by the way the peat fire was left. If the woman of the house had cooking to do on her return the fire would be strong below but well battened down, with some thick, dry peats on top and wet ones laid flat over all. But if a shepherd was alone and unlikely to be back until the next day, the peats would all be laid close and flat round a little fire and smothered in with a thick layer of damp peats. Sadly, we have no local peat to burn in Surrey, but when I wend my way home from a mid-winter pheasant shoot I am always heartened by the curl of wood smoke that rises up from my chimney to meet the first star.

1993

## The Reawakening

Even as January departs, mistle thrushes, wrens and dunnocks deliver old favourite melodies to our back doors and the bright bullfinch groups are especially conspicuous as they clamber about the bare trees searching for the earliest buds.

The 'fair maids of February', the snowdrops, also known as

'Candlemas bells' or 'purification flowers', crowd among the quaking grasses or in cherished borders where the soured surface cracks in drying winds to reveal a rich, chocolate brown. The trout-fisher is already inspecting his tackle and dreaming of prime brownies pulsing in the net, while the student of salmon has long had his holidays planned and tickets reserved.

On inland waters there is a great air of expectancy. Ice may seal the shallows and few creatures stir, but that inexorable reawakening fills fur, fin, feather and flower alike.

Predators are frequently more obvious now, not just because they have no canopy to lurk behind but of necessity many must range more widely at this time to get sufficient food. Harriers frequently turn up unexpectedly, wavering across the marsh like huge, displaced moths. Merlins (few that there are now) often desert their moorland to search marsh and coast for waders, and peregrines too range out from their cliff and mountain fortresses to seek duck, waders and pigeon in a surprising variety of lowland habitats.

Lambing approaches its peak now and I cannot help regretting the widespread disappearance of the 'folding' system in which a flock is confined within portable hurdles on an arable crop such as roots or kale, and the sheep are moved on as the food is consumed. There is no doubt that land manured by folded sheep used to do much to sustain a wealth of wildlife, including our 'little brown bird', the native English partridge.

1986

## Surviving the Storm

I am surrounded by demented dancers which writhe to an unspeakable moan summoned from the bowels of the universe. They are the trees in the garden and on the skyline before me, thrashing and crashing their pathetic limbs as I watch this monstrous storm from the relative safety of my window. Hitherto calm, graceful giants, now they move on a 'high' while a vicious low wreaks havoc across Britain. 25 January 1990 will certainly be remembered.

At the end of my garden is a tall spruce which had been a rather fine specimen before last summer's almost unprecedented drought left it with a fatal, spiralling crack all the way up its trunk. Amputation of the main member was essential in the interests of safety, but now I am saved at least part of the tree surgeon's bill as the storm snaps the trunk in two and deposits the top in my neighbour's garden.

Now the wind peaks and every latch rattles, every casement quakes, as artificial structures rely on sheer strength rather than 'give' for survival. But even the whippiest trees are thwarted by this impish blast. As I watch, a large cypress, shallow roots already stressed by the drought, leans dramatically at 45 degrees in a sustained high gust. This it should survive, but just as I think the wind could not increase any more a secondary gust is inspired by the hounds of heaven and the tree falls, crushing shrubs and trellis, its jagged limbs stabbing into the soft earth.

Soon the cyclone swirls to allow the onslaught to commence from the north-west rather than south-east, so that 'muscles' are stretched in different directions. As a result, weakened nails pop like corks and garden fences start to collapse. More trees topple, bits of strange roofing appear as if by magic and the garden furniture is rearranged.

Yet, at the height of the holocaust, when neither man nor beast should be abroad, small birds continue to fly about in search of sustenance. How do these specks, weighing little more than a large leaf, have the confidence even to take off in such an aerial maelstrom?

Well, these little songbirds tend to have relatively short, rounded wings which are highly manoeuvrable and able to make use of subtle variations in air currents. They also seem to have an uncanny ability to sense imminent lulls between gusts of wind, just like pedestrians waiting to cross a busy road.

Very strong winds restrict the height at which small passerines can forage successfully but the reduction in wind speed can be very pronounced in the boundary layer close to the earth's surface. This, in turn, varies with the degree of shelter afforded by local habitat. Bare islands always offer a rocky ride, but even within a forest the buffeting of wind can be considerable, with large-scale wind eddies forming within clearings.

What a great shame it is that we let all this wind go to waste in Britain, when on land it could provide at least 20 per cent of our current electricity needs, and offshore windpower – sneeringly classified as 'longshot technology' – could yield three times as much. We do, as they say, 'have the technology', and it is certainly economically viable – in 1987 the appropriately named Watts Committee on energy estimated that land wind power costs only 2.26p per kilowatt hour.

Now, as darkness falls and the candles are lit, we must fear for the contents of our freezer yet again. We expect to be 'off' for at least several days because, understandably, small rural communities get low priority in the restoration of power.

And it's all very well having the freezer contents insured, but tell me how you can replace the brace of grouse *you* shot in the autumn, the rowan berries *you* gathered to accompany the grouse, the magnificent brown trout which a more privileged friend gave you, and the fruits ready for sloe gin production. Then there's that lovely reserve of sea fish which you built up, not to mention your basic stock of pheasants and other game, and special puddings such as my favourite home-made rum and raisin ice-cream.

I suppose, as usual, we'll end up going to the limits of defrost before rushing the relicts to the nearest friend still on power. I tell you, I'm going to the library to sort out plans for an ice house.

With increasingly frequent failure of electricity, gas, water and telephone services through freak weather in recent years, many of us, especially in rural areas, are learning to be at least a little self-sufficient again. Good stocks of candles and paraffin are par for the course in any household, and – without gas in our area – think how cold we would be now without our wood stove, which also conveniently cooks all that defrosted food.

But perhaps the most welcome item in my home-survival kit of recent black years has been the battery-powered radio, broadcasting local stations. Not only does this provide the housebound, sick and elderly with an important lifeline and companionship but also the very latest information on blocked roads (due to fallen trees, blizzards, etc), traffic chaos and school closures for those who must go out. Local radio has certainly become an invaluable aid to modern country life, but I do wish that DJ would refrain from chanting 'Welcome to the After The Storm Show'.

1990

## Lonely Landscape

I was thinking about bird numbers last week, when I strolled along the South Downs Way, near Cocking in Sussex. The old man's beard lay gently about the face of winter, in so many garlands upon trees and bushes it looked as if Mother Nature had been practising the art of Christmas decoration. And for her lights she had set rose-hips in every hedgerow. This was indeed a quiet and kindly landscape, though apart from the passage of a pigeon scarcely a bird moved.

As I surveyed the Sussex hills I wondered how accurate our general impression of bird species' abundance is. Presumably those creatures with sensory perception superior to man's hide away more quickly as we blunder along and thus give the illusion of greater rarity.

1989

## Early Flowers

Throughout much of January there was a distinct softness in the air which drifted up from the south-west to mellow around the wood stack and draw early flowers out of the moist earth. From winter's deathbed the miracle of regeneration gladdened the heart as the veil was lifted to receive the gathering light.

Daffodils bloomed in many a southern garden while rhododendrons adorned town parks to deceive the observer into believing that winter had ended. Snowdrops and primroses, too, filled local papers and TV programmes with the usual rivalry for earliest sightings. Apart from one primrose, our first garden flowers were the highly poisonous aconites, whose yellow starred the earth from the 22nd, after the required temperature of about 10°C had been maintained for some days. I am always amazed how these gems just pop up and expose their bright faces on the first warm day. These flowers are surrounded by leaf-like bracts and only when the flowers have faded do the real leaves appear.

Today the commercial grower cannot afford to rely on the whims of climate and must employ every artificial aid available to keep in the black. In the same week in which the aconites appeared in my garden a grower from Warsash, in Hampshire, put the year's first English tomatoes on the market at £1 a pound. His whole incredible operation is controlled by a computer which even regulates the temperature in the glasshouse after allowing for outside temperature in association with wind speed. Carbon dioxide is fed around the plants, which grow only in water containing essential nutrients, and a vibrating stick compensates for the activities of the bee.

There are wild flowers, too, in January – the white chickweed and yellow groundsel, both eaten by pigeons and sparrows, as well as the occasional dandelion. While they bloom the last leaves drop from the oaks as mallard begin their queer and unexpected winter courtship.

1981

# February

## Dangerous Waters

I had hoped that February would wring the sponge, but it has started off as dismally as January. Go away sodden mildness and come back cold, frosty weather with blue skies, cotton-ball clouds and a distant prospect of spring. Yet there is light at the end of the tunnel for today (1 February) I have seen rooks repairing their storm-tossed nests. Such optimism from mere birds without science or philosophy, only the ancient instinct to trust their future to a few clusters of sticks suspended for all to see in the most turbulent run of air we have had for years.

I, for one, have had enough of water in this soggiest of seasons and now look forward to a good old-fashioned drought. But there is water and water, and all of it has been in the news of late.

In an age when E numbers and additives are threatening to oust TV trivia such as Eastenders small talk, it is not surprising that water is coming under the microscope. Five million Britons drink water which breaks the limits for nitrates and now, not before time, the Environment Secretary is considering far-reaching controls on our water supply. The EEC is getting tough on the quality of drinking water and farming is under scrutiny.

The problem lies chiefly where cereal growing is intense, where the massive application of nitrogen to boost crop yields results in nitrates being leached out by rain into rivers, streams and still-waters. Yet much of this could be so easily avoided as ADAS report that some 70 per cent of farmers are putting on too much nitrogen and most would suffer no loss of profits if they cut back. On the contrary, they would save a bit on chemicals. The application of a crushing one and a half million tons of nitrogen compounds per annum has brought about a massive 40 per cent increase in crop yields. A 50 per cent reduction would reduce the yield by about 10 per cent, but profits by only 50 per cent.

Some areas have a special problem with spring source water and a high water table where cereal growing is intense. A few have gone over to bottled water as high nitrate levels have been linked with the 'blue baby' syndrome. However, there appears to be no link with stomach cancer. In fact one study found a higher

32

incidence of the disease in areas with *low* nitrate levels.

The south-east produces a huge amount of cereals in its relatively dry climate so, not surprisingly, Anglian Water reports 23 water supplies which exceed the EEC nitrate limit of 50mg per litre. Denitrification would cost Anglian Water £70 million immediately and £5 million per annum to keep up. Alternatives to this costly process include special protection zones, but simply sticking to the code of good agricultural practice would help enormously.

There would appear to be no easy way to effect a total clean-up. Yet again we are suffering from too many people demanding too much of the land. Its regenerative powers are not limitless and it is about time man got his act together and replaced greed with sympathy. There must be plenty of cash to tap as already millions of people are worried enough to be duped by those slick adverts promoting bottles of 'wonderful well' or 'super spring' water. Still, if it keeps them happy . . .

I am sure the rooks must be laughing at us from their uncomplicated world of wind and sky and glorious freedom.

1988

# Sharp Lesson

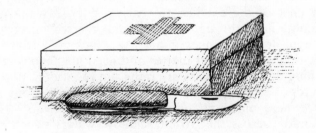

Christmas is forgotten but many presents remain. A gleaming new penknife gave a sharp lesson to a whittling nine-year-old Number One Son – blood everywhere, but only four stitches in the back of the hand this time. However, it did instil a healthy regard for knives and we did find out where the new hospital is. This was at 2 p.m. on a Sunday and six-year-old Number Two Son, who was forced to accompany us, was most concerned that he might miss his girlfriend's birthday party at 3.30 p.m., especially as he was one of only two boys invited. Imagine his horror when he saw six people ahead of us in the casualty department, ranging from a firewood chopper with a bandaged thumb presented like a lollipop, to a fully kitted soccer player with mud and broken leg.

1981

## Dicing with Death

Once again, this morning some courage was needed to leave the warmth of my bed, yet not for me the stifling atmosphere of central heating. I scratched a hole in the Jack Frost and peered through a frieze of icicles to watch the poor birds pathetically poking about for yesterday's overlooked crumbs. Natural food is scarce but death commonplace now in the country scene of late winter.

Yet who would suspect that man, too, in this age of 'minimum standards' and 'high tech' would succumb to this latest 'big freeze'? Who could even guess that otherwise healthy individuals might fade away through hypothermia in our capital city? Then there has been the recent spate of incidents in which both children and adults have fallen through ice to their deaths.

Fearful for the safety of my own children, repeatedly I stress: 'Stay away from the pond'. Yet how vividly I remember my own reckless youth when, for example, I walked half a mile across a frozen inlet of the sea just to reach a good fowling ground. Another time I fell through pack ice into the sea in retrieving a shot wigeon. Being a non-swimmer I was lucky to survive.

Yet skating is a different matter and need not involve any risk of drowning if the conditions are right and the water chosen with care. Outdoor skating remains popular in some of our eastern counties, where many people seize every opportunity to glide with abandon across the frozen, shallow waters which abound there. And if conditions were right in my youth, I used to seek out a frozen meadow splash which was shallow enough to offer no more of a threat than a crack on the head if I tumbled.

1985

## Barn Magic

One of the things I like best about visiting different shoots all over the country is the great variety of old buildings in which lunch is taken. Sometimes I have been lucky enough to savour silver service in architectural grandeur surrounded by ancestral portraits. On other occasions I have enjoyed the black-beamed, stone-floored antiquity of rambling farmhouses, the bustle of the pub, the charming simplicity of the keeper's cottage, and once even a large garage. But best of all I like dusty old barns and outbuildings where you do not have to take your boots off and there is at least a little room for species other than man.

Somehow, if I can look up from my soup and see an old swallow's nest on the rafter above, as you can in our shoot 'dining room', I feel more in tune with nature. The mouse scurrying across the grain sacks; the cornered sparrow desperately trying to exit; the fluttering butterfly roused from hibernation; and even the hole at the bottom of the door chewed by generations of rats make my day that much more natural.

Sadly, we have lost so many of our old barns as farmers are forced to address ever stiffer competition and that 'bottom line'. Now, instead of the delightful stone or timbered building which was the home of owls and blended perfectly with the landscape, we have the 'eco-box', with precise control of temperature and humidity.

Today the word barn is commonly used for any farm outbuilding, but strictly speaking it is one which stores grain or fodder. The word derives from the old English 'bern', which meant 'barley house', barley being the main crop of Anglo-Saxon farmers.

The traditional barn was a long, rectangular building with large doors opposite each other in the centre. This enabled a corn wagon to enter one door, be unloaded on each side and leave through the other door. Not only was this easier for the horses, but also it enabled a number of wagons to rush the harvest in before the weather broke.

The wooden floor was very strong in the middle of the barn because that was where the men threshed the corn with flails. The ends of the barn were used to store the threshed straw, hay, sacks of grain and root crops. Machinery was often housed in lean-to sheds built alongside the barn. The thatch on a traditional downland barn was high-pitched, rounded and deep, sweeping almost to the ground. Inside it was always uniformly cool, neither cold in winter nor hot in summer – ideal for stock or storage, but also a wonderful refuge for the wayfarer.

There is something very special about the atmosphere of an ancient barn. As a lad I loved the peace and coolness there on a parched, hot day tramping around the countryside. I'd clamber high among the sacks and beams to take my rest with only mice for company. As I ate my sandwiches and slaked my thirst with lemonade, I marvelled at all the old farming equipment mouldering in dark corners. Sometimes shafts of sunlight pierced the walls to catch the eyes of a white owl as well as the shimmering dust of centuries.

Now those carefree days are long gone and many of the old buildings have been replaced, collapsed beyond repair or developed as trendy 'conversions'. The owl and his retinue have been evicted in favour of economy and sterility. But at least on my shoot travels I can still enjoy a taste of how it used to be.

1993


## Message in a Bottle

Whereas October is the month of gathering darkness, February is that of increasing light. And this year our emergence from the months of blackness was especially sudden as weeks of unending gales and grey rain evaporated before a gentle southerly.

On the first clear night of the month the owls certainly made their presence known, making good after their enforced hunting lay-off. How difficult it must have been for predators which rely so much on hearing to detect their victims and whose very soft plumage is easily waterlogged.

It was 11 February when my daily arrival home from the office was first greeted by two tawny owls as I turned into the drive beneath the stars. As I locked the car, one of the hidden hooters called from the great oak skeleton hunched over the brimming pond and I paused before it as if to acknowledge an old friend. Then I saw the silhouette fly silently out towards another bird calling nearby. Inevitably it is on such a calm, frosty night that they first break their midwinter silence.

Always among the year's earliest breeders, owls even beat the traditional Valentine's Day pairing, when legend has it that all birds select a mate. The truth is that most breeding seasons are as variable as the weather and very few books acknowledge the considerable differences among individual birds and between north and south.

The sudden sunshine brought an explosion of life, nowhere more evident than along the town river where, like bears from their dens, men ventured out to parade their finery along with the courting ducks. But whereas the green-headed drake mallard pursued his mate with insensitive, unbridled ardour, the pale-faced beau led his loved one gently by the hand (in public at least!) beneath the budding willow.

Rivers often yield treasures other than the natural wonders we all admire. They have long been centres of human activity – for transport and sources of food. Their sporting and amenity value has been recognised much more recently, perhaps in an attempt to compensate for our estranged, modern lifestyle.

As a result, the swirling waters have claimed many a valuable: recent finds including axe heads, bone tools, iron spears, bronze shields and even Victorian pistols. There have been spectacular discoveries too, such as a chest containing 20,000 silver pennies lost by the Earl of Lancaster when he tried to cross the flooded river near Burton-on-Trent centuries ago. But to me everyday objects which reflect life from generations past are equally interesting. And now the cast-offs and disposables from the age of craftsmanship are eagerly sought as collectables in an era when rubbish really is rubbish.

Today the litter lout is vociferously condemned – and rightly so, as there are regular rubbish collections from every door and waste bins are universally provided. However, not so many decades ago there was no refuse collection and few public dumps so men tossed all and sundry into the most convenient hole, whether it was at the bottom of the garden or in the local pond or river. Indeed, some people saw rubbish disposal as an easy way to fill in mosquito-ridden swamps or dangerous chasms.

Obviously anyone living out in the country well away from public dumps had to make his own arrangements for much longer, especially with transport so difficult. But today the tracking down of early dumps provides great fun for many people. Careful digging (assuming you have permission) often unearths artefacts in surprisingly good condition, including pots, jars, buttons and badges. But it is the bottles which attract most people, a huge variety of mostly blue, green, red and brown containers for spirits, beer, ginger beer, lemonade, ink, medicine and so on. Cleaned up and suitably displayed, they can make the most colourful collections and ornaments. But I cannot imagine men of the twenty-first century going to the same trouble to retrieve the aerosols, beer cans or plastic squeegie bottles which we now dispose of. In any case, most of our rubbish is much more perishable.

Now cobalt-blue poisons, sheared-lip inks, embossed beers and picturesque pot lids vie with mineral water bottles such as the rugby-ball-shaped Hamiltons and globe-stoppered 'Codds' for pride of place on the shelves of collectors. Sadly, most of the latter were broken apart by boys in search of marbles. But apart from the enormous variety I love the imperfections of the old glass which turn each piece into a little ambassador from the age of craftsmanship.

It is along the river, especially after a stormy period such as we have just had, that many finds are to be made. A common practice in Victorian times was the building up of river banks to prevent flooding, to reclaim land and to increase the depth of water. Much of the material used contained large amounts of household rubbish. But as the banks have been eroded many of the items have found their way into the water and have often travelled surprisingly long distances.

One of the best hunting spots is around an ancient bridge. For example, I can just imagine an old countryman leaning over the edge to stare at a trout and puff contentedly on one clay pipe while throwing another, whose fragile clay stem had broken, into the water. The variety of clay pipes was remarkable, many of them commemorating famous men or events from military history.

I doubt if the Victorian rustic ever imagined that one day man would both collect his throw-aways and fly to the moon! His was undeniably a very hard life, but there were major compensations, then generally undervalued, such as working in everyday contact and harmony with nature. Too often nowadays we dwell on the efficiency of modern farming and rarely is a voice raised against the materialistic scheme of things. Too little do we hear of the real values, of the countryside's stability, peace and continuity; not justification of green acres as food-production zones or even habitat, for we all tire of the same old song, but simple concern for the quiet corners where we can walk with the sense of belonging known to our grandfathers. To enrich our lives the countryside need not always be spectacular or 'important', with wall-to-wall nature reserves or SSSIs. All we ask is a place to 'do our own thing' responsibly in an age when there are far too many of us to permit throwing bottles into the ditch.

1988


## Fantasy fields

One day recently, after three hours tramping, my game bag was empty save for a few bloodied old feathers, but my spirit was buoyant with the sights and sounds of a winter's morning. In the half-light at 7 a.m. my fingers stuck to the frosted metal gate which opened into West Wood Field, where the thin mist was utterly still above the hoary way. Not much chance of surprising a rabbit as the rimed grass, winter wheat, ploughland and woodland litter all crunched loudly beneath my wellies while the pre-sunrise sky was still kindling.

I rounded the copse, where a pheasant stirred in his black roost, and turned into Deer's Field – what a simple yet evocative place name, created by my children's world of fantasy along with many others such as Summer's Field, Oak Field, Stoneford, Pineford and Heron's Pond.

As I neared the undulating main road there was the intermittent drone of an engine as lights slowly approached, twinkling carefully down the icy highway. For a moment I thought it might be old Jack coming to surprise a few woodpigeon, but it was only a passing stranger. So I turned and continued alone as the eastern sky grew riotous, orange-chestnut like a stonechat's breast at the centre and

39

pinky-buff like the whinchat's further out where the thin veil of cloud was increasing.

1980

## Loss of Trees and Hedges

Many centuries ago, when wolves and bears roamed the English countryside, a tiny sapling struggled for space in the vast forests of Wessex. Against tremendous odds, in competing for light and avoiding the attention of animals, it weathered the ravages of man and elements, eventually enjoying the protection of the church built alongside. While woodlands perished all around, this monument to medieval England battled on into the twentieth century, a triumph of evolution needing only a prop or two for its ancient limbs – just like an old man with a walking stick. It even survived the Great Storm of October 1987. But on 25 January this year its incredible 1,500-year history came to an abrupt end. This fine old yew, which stood in Selborne churchyard, was toppled by a gale of horrendous ferocity.

This was no ordinary tree – in fact it was world famous because it grew within the parish of celebrated naturalist Gilbert White. Even in the eighteenth century he marvelled at it, measuring and recording its girth at 23ft. When White's book, *The Natural History of Selborne*, became one of the all-time most printed books in the English language, people flocked from all corners of the world to touch and wonder at the tree this great man had loved.

Some disciples were themselves famous, including traveller William Cobbett, who described the yew on a visit in 1823, but there have also been legions of other folk, such as myself, who have found simple enjoyment in the yew's shade.

But even in death the tree's intrigue remains, for beneath the roots a human skeleton has been discovered. Presumably older than the tree itself, the bones may have been part of a pagan sacrifice.

How tragic that such a tree should perish in this way, especially as so few are being planted now and hardly any are likely to survive for another 1,500 years, unless human attitudes change drastically. Maybe it was only one of three million or so lost in this latest series of major storms, but every time such a calamity strikes the longer are the odds against individual trees attaining great age.

Because most old trees are so big, any felled by storm or

40

man are very obvious and almost always attract widespread public comment, unless they are hidden away on some great estate. Hedges, however, are less fortunate. Despite antiquity sometimes exceeding that of our oldest trees, they are generally well-trimmed and much less conspicuous, so their removal, especially when piecemeal, is far less noticeable. Yet the disgraceful decline of the hedgerow continues. Therefore I was very pleased to learn that the Council for the Protection of Rural England has launched a new campaign to stop continuing hedge loss.

Anyone who doubts that this is still a major problem may be shocked to learn that in the period 1980–85, hedge loss was at its highest recorded level, averaging 6,400 kilometres (4,000 miles) a year in England and Wales. For the period 1969–80 the annual loss averaged 4,600km (2,900 miles) and for 1947–69 4,200km (2,600 miles). And it's not only direct physical removal that is to blame: straw and stubble burning, spray drift, neglect and indiscriminate trimming have been significant too.

It is thought that hedges became common during the Bronze Age (around 1,000 BC) as ancient forests were increasingly cleared for agriculture and later for the construction of buildings and ships. Networks of hedged fields older than the Roman roads which cut across them survived in East Anglia into the nineteenth century; fragments can still be traced.

During Saxon and Norman times, in some areas hedges were removed to create expanses of arable land for open-field strip farming. But during and after the Middle Ages many of the field strips were again enclosed by hedges. Areas which escaped the move to open-field farming have small, irregular fields enclosed by dense hedges; narrow, deeply hollowed, winding lanes; small woods and dispersed settlements.

A major boost for hedges came with the Parliamentary Enclosure Acts (chiefly affecting remaining open arable land and commons). Enclosure was at its peak between 1750 and 1850, when hedges were planted at an average rate of 2,000 miles a year. But the process probably covered only a fifth of the country and the hedges it brought were straight, following the planner's lines and less pleasing to the eye. Nonetheless, their conservation value is generally just as great as that of more natural hedges.

Relatively few hedges were planted after the Parliamentary Enclosures ended in 1914 and it is only very recently that conservation requirements have had any significant influence.

Whether it's trees or hedges, planting for future generations calls for considerable unselfishness and capital commitment. But without concerted action now there will be few specimens such as the Selborne yew to marvel at in the next millenium. This year the Tree Council is hoping to exceed the record 666,000 trees planted in National Tree Week 1989.

1990

## Village Sledging

'The essentials for coasting are in the first place a heavy fall of snow, the heavier the better; in the second, a moderately steep hillside, with a surface that is fairly smooth. If you live near hills, or where the country undulates, this will be very easily found, but it is wise not to try a mound that is very steep till you have gained confidence and experience.' These apparently obvious and simple words are as true today as they were when written by P. Anderson Graham for his entertaining book *Country Pastimes for Boys*, published in 1895. I found his latter remark especially telling last week when I took to the local slopes for a spot of sledging after a snowstorm.

Anderson wrote only for boys, but in my experience just as many 'grown-ups' take to the slopes. And not all, by any means, venture forth only under the pretext of having to be there 'for the children', as I generally do. With me were ladies and gents, boys and girls of every shape, size and background, and even a great-grandfather leaning on his stick with an envious, glazed expression recalling the days when his bones too were strong enough for such dashing escapades.

'Vehicles' ranged from the conventional sledge to a tiny tin tray marked Guinness, and their riders from a babe in arms to a red-faced lady with a turned-up nose, who queued for best spot with great seriousness and competitive edge. One intrepid group of twelve teenagers rocketted down as one body, in three rows on one very large plastic sack!

We had a conventional toboggan of wood with metal runners, which ran very well, and a plastic fertiliser sack which ran even better but did tend to get out of control more easily. Furthermore, the sack gave no protection from any hard bits and each time I risked taking off over the ridge halfway down the slope I ended up

42

facing the wrong way on landing and had to continue the descent backwards.

All good, clean fun and one of those rare things which unite a community in exhilaration, even people who rarely venture beyond the 'nest'. Yet it must be said that many children now seem to lack the spirit even of my youth, and their general inability to amuse themselves and find entertainment in cheap and simple things may have led to much of the aggression now vented on society.

Country boys have always been luckier in their variety of opportunity, but even they have suffered through increasingly restrictive legislation. This is easy to see in looking at Anderson Graham's book. To begin with, the first 100 pages are devoted to bird's-nesting, giving great details of how to discover the breeding haunts of rarities as well as common species. Of course, it was not thought that such activity, which remained widespread into the 1950s and my childhood, would ever have a depressive effect on bird populations. And generally it never did. It was only a tiny hard-core of 'professional' adult egg collectors, who sadly continue today, whose selfish pursuit of the rare posed a great threat.

The book's next eighty-four pages are concerned with bird pets and 'familiar birds for taming', another interest which was knocked on the head by inevitable legislation. Again, it was never the *volume* of such interest that mattered, for in most cases these were passing phases of youth and a largely unspoilt countryside rich in wildlife was not unduly troubled. It was subsequent universal destruction and despoliation of habitat, largely brought about by human population increase, which decimated our wildlife and increased pressure on what had been insignificant and relatively harmless pastimes.

Indeed, youthful participation in country pursuits subsequently outlawed often led to lifelong interest in natural history and even the development of leading biologists. Of course I am not advocating that bird's-nesting or wild-bird keeping should return, as they would be quite out of place today, but I am warning that more outdoor pastimes and sports may be picked off by legislative snipers as pressure on countryside and habitat increases.

Failure to maintain and improve the widest variety of habitat, so that we have enough wildlife to satisfy all interests, might put us on the slippery slope leading to cessation of all country sports and a welter of ridiculous licences in a fossilised countryside. We might even need a permit to 'coast' for fear of bruising the grass with our toboggans!

1986

## Eerie Screams

Now nature is recovering from the silence of midwinter. Many of the spring's fox cub litters are being conceived as the dog fox's peak of fecundal activity continues into February. January saw the dispersal of juveniles but still we hear many of Reynard's twenty-eight different recorded calls beneath the rising moon. Especially between one and three hours after sunset, we hear the intermittent, high-pitched barks, mostly in groups of three or four, as well as a hoarse, wailing bark. Both sexes bark and chill the investigator of moonlit woods with their eerie screams, punctuated with chattering somewhat like the jay's alarm call.

1981

## 'Greenhouse' Problems

The season of mud is over. Gatherings of gumboots about the yard have ended and Guns have marched off to slip on the softer footwear of spring. Britain's first 'greenhouse winter' is almost at an end and in some ways we feel cheated. Not only children have been denied the iron hand of frost, to marvel at and permit skating on pond and mere. Men, too, have missed its firmness and stamp of authority on the landscape, so clearly dictating the seasons of rest and regeneration in an order which man has been able to count on for millenia.

In this winter of turmoil, north-western Britain has been as exceptionally wet as the south-east has been dry, but now, if anything like the old order is to return, we can all look forward to a shift of wind to blow away the moisture underfoot. For even in dry winters there is a clinging dampness which no breeze can shift. Only when the sun arcs by at greater height will the vapours of decay leave the woods, making our passage more pleasurable.

With spring on the horizon, it is among the stirring copses and forests that I love to wander and sport. There the great pigeon roosts throw down the gauntlet, birds flighting to and from their feeding grounds with new-found vigour.

Now, we are told, is the time of year when pigeon control is most effective for the population is at its lowest and those birds which remain are the greatest survivors. But this year is different and the flocks are large. Even inexperienced birds have found no difficulty in getting through the lean times. The mild winter has provided much more food than usual, and with unusually high air temperatures the birds have not needed to use much of their energy reserves in keeping warm. In better condition the pigeon will be stronger and faster and more difficult to shoot.

For a roost shoot I prefer a strong wind, for then the pigeon flight over a longer period and move about more. Shots are muffled by the gale and the birds are more testing, coming in at a wide variety of heights and angles, with wildness and spirit hard to match. Strategic placing of several companions should cover all approaches.

There is no doubt that the woodpigeon flies faster than most birds but its speed has often been exaggerated and the species finds difficulty in reaching 40mph in steady, level flight. Trained and specially bred racing pigeons can do much better. The highest race speed recorded averaged over 110mph when birds were backed by a powerful wind. But in level, calm conditions it is doubtful if even a champion racing pigeon can exceed 60mph. Thus there is no doubt that you will enjoy better sport when flighting pigeon on a windy day.

The woodpigeon beats its wings about four times a second, compared with the slow herring gull's 2.8, the slower rook's 2.4 and the very slow vulture's single beat per second. At the other extreme, a hummingbird called the amethyst woodstar powers away at an amazing ninety wingbeats per second!

Not only the woodpigeon will have been affected by the mild winter. Many other species throughout the animal and plant kingdoms will have been thrown into confusion, their biological clocks gone haywire in unprecedented conditions.

Many people have found birds nesting exceptionally early and we can only hope that those which fledge successfully are not killed by a likely return to cold or wet conditions. We must also pray that the many garden plants which have been drawn into premature flowering will not be lost to returning frost.

With so much natural bounty lingering on – even houseflies have been a-wing in February – the bird table has been little patronised this winter. But the provision of water – something often overlooked in an average year – has been especially important.

Perhaps best of all has been the opportunity to hear birdsong on days which are normally associated with brooding melancholy and avian silence. On many evenings the pigeon shooter waiting in the wings of the wood has been beguiled by the robin. And the gardener, who has been busy on more winter days than he can ever remember, has enjoyed the constant musical accompaniment of blackbird and song thrush.

In recent years a small but increasing number of summer visitors, such as blackcaps, have taken to overwintering in Britain, making good use of the insect life and shelter afforded by modern glasshouses. But now it seems as if they could endure our climate the year round without such artificial environments, for the entire land is living in a 'greenhouse' without windows. In looking too closely at the crops man has lost control of the garden.

1989

## Balmy Breezes

After the dark, damp days a mild south-wester crept up over much of England, bringing a premature spring, and suddenly everyone was out and about. All that postponed garden tidying was at last seen to and both country and suburb smoked like indian reservations (my bonfire still had the Christmas tree on it!). In rare sunshine dogs were walked till weary while heaths and commons were full of birdwatchers with their swinging binoculars and beaming 'good mornings'. Suddenly lay-bys were crammed with cars and down at the Dog and Pheasant lunchtime pints were supped outside for the first time this year. Housewives smiled as washing billowed in balmy breezes and even the skylark delivered his joyous cadence. This morning I even awoke to the sound of the thrush singing 'each song twice over lest he never could recapture that first fine careless rapture'.

1980

## Close Encounters

When I was walking the hedgerows the other day I was struck by the tameness of a goldcrest. I puzzled why this highly vulnerable, diminutive species inevitably allows close approach when, for example, finches generally become agitated 100 yards away. How is it that some species are particularly wild or tame, and why do individuals vary?

This is certainly a subject of great interest to gameshooters because, as the movement towards quality rather than quantity gathers momentum, many Guns have come to appreciate the extra wildness of hopper-fed rather than hand-fed pheasants. Proper wild-bird shoots, where the reliance is on vermin control and habitat management alone, are the luckiest of all, with quarry as elusive as a country fox.

Edward Grey (1927) pointed out that individuals become tame in relation to places rather than persons. One has only to look at the woodpigeon: in London parks they will share your sandwich, but out in the sticks they certainly know a gun from a gamp and keep their distance accordingly.

Perhaps the best place to study this subject is in the back garden – or at least looking out of the window. Most of us feed wild birds and we are sometimes surprised by the habits of individuals. Most outstanding is that great gardener's friend, the robin, which hops about the turned earth picking up exposed morsels, occasionally resting on the fork handle while we empty the barrow. Yet on much of the Continent, where it is more often migratory, the robin remains a shy woodland species, even in areas where it is not persecuted. Perhaps there is some correlation between wildness and increased migration in colder climes.

Another common bird which is noticeably timid in some areas but tame in others is the moorhen. We often see it feeding alongside ducks on town lakes, or even along those rivers which run through populated areas. But try approaching one in the countryside with a gun under your arm.

Some birds become noticeably tamer at certain times of the year, as if possessed of some special intelligence. But whether tameness is acquired by individuals or communities, or whether it is a characteristic of a species, there is always a genetic element in that some species are tamed more easily than others. In the old days country folk were commonly aware of such tendencies in their selection of pets. But why magpies were so popular I'm not sure, because even slitting their tongues did not really change their inherent wildness.

Sadly, many species appear to become used to captivity and seem tame, when the truth is they have been forced by hunger and weakness into accepting human presence. They become mere creatures of habit and their true, natural wildness is suppressed.

Isolated communities of wild animals may show extraordinary tameness, including colonies of seals and seabirds on remote islands. Unfortunately, this makes them especially vulnerable to exploitation (by skin traders, for example) and predation by carelessly introduced predators, such as rats and dogs.

Apparent tameness may also be caused by poor condition. For example, when migrant wildfowl and woodcock arrive on our shores after long sea crossings they are frequently emaciated by the effort and exposure to severe weather. In such circumstances they may simply flop into the nearest ditch to recover and are easily approached and shot. Then no sportsman worth his powder would take advantage of them.

Other, usually wild, species show a marked tolerance of man and his environs in the search for food. Perhaps the kestrel hovering over the motorway verge is the most striking modern example. But an avian habit with far greater ancestry is that of rooks following the plough. And in more recent decades gulls have followed suit, especially as they have moved inland in substantial numbers, having learnt to exploit food sources such as refuse tips.

For me at least, birds wheeling behind the plough provide one of the great delights of early spring. It has a freshness and timelessness which I find especially invigorating, but now, alas, it is a much rarer sight with the trend towards autumn sowings.

Now, as we enter the early breeding season, we may easily confuse boldness with tameness, especially where adults continue sitting on eggs or defend their young in the face of man or predators. Some species may display extraordinary seasonal changes in behaviour. For example, in winter the wild grey partridge is always secretive and bent on escape, yet on the nest it may sit so tight as to permit being stroked by the observer!

Such boldness may lead to a bird's downfall through predation, but poachers, too, may benefit from a wild creature's bravado. In particular, many villains take advantage of the willingness of both birds and mammals to accept the presence of vehicles. For some odd reason, a car or van, though much bigger than a man on foot, does not evoke much alarm and allows the hunter – as well as the nature watcher or photographer – to get within range more easily.

Most of us have special stories to tell about exceptionally tame birds or mammals, such as the badger which feeds by the open door or the blue tit which hops about the kitchen. And thank heavens for such variety, for it would be a dull world if the activities of every species were entirely predictable.

1992

# Song of Hope

Now February is setting records for cold and it is hard to believe that within a few weeks the first few brimstone and tortoiseshell butterflies should be about the garden. The land is iron-clad and the wagtail in my yard is glad of the little water cupped in the manhole cover: the liquid is as scarce now as in high summer.

While temperature change plays a part in stimulating wild birds to commence courtship and breeding, other factors such as increasing daylight hours are probably more important. Why else should the male great-spotted woodpecker have commenced his courtship drumming as usual, in my garden on 17 February, when the ground was snow-covered and an exceptionally cold spell had persisted for two weeks and shown no sign of relenting?

And it's not just woodpeckers which have this instinct lost to man. In these days of deep-freeze when spring is but a myth there is already something in the voice of the thrush, dunnock and robin which suggests that regeneration is well underway. Theirs is a true song of hope.

1986

# March

## Fickle Month

March started oddly with an exceptionally early cuckoo calling four times in my garden, at 8 a.m. on the 1st. The weather was suddenly mild, and despite big, drenching drops of continuous rain, most creatures clearly had the message that days of sparkling renewal were not far off.

Frogs had been active for several days and moles threw up a range of hills in the soft earth around the pond's edge. Garden handouts of nuts and crumbs still attracted some birds, such as the smart, spear-headed nuthatch, but others found sufficient sustenance among the drowsy, overwintered insect life.

Windows were opened to the softening air and at some unspoken command dull-witted flies crept out of the pelmets and curtain folds onto the dazzling glass. Yet just two days later those which hadn't been swatted had to creep back in again at the return of ice and snow. Oh fickle March.

1987

## Politics of Apathy

Despite some encouraging noises, I fear that neither Mrs Thatcher nor any of her chief ministers fully appreciates public passion for environmental issues. Recent commitments to healthier living and a cleaner countryside appear to be no more than enough to pacify pressure groups and the Government does not seem to have its heart in a green and pleasant land.

Last week neither the Prime Minister nor any of her henchmen attended the environmental crisis conference at The Hague, where leaders of twenty-four countries affirmed their intent to clean up the world and make it safe. Maggie had been invited, but refused, saying that we did not need any new initiatives as experts were already working on relevant problems. I believe that her insular attitude was very wrong because – apart from maintenance of peace – nothing else in the world demands closer international co-operation than conservation and management of the environment. The international ozone conference which Britain hosted in the previous week was but one of the bottom rungs on a very long ladder, and to think that holding this exempted this country from attendance in Holland was the height of arrogance.

Not that Britain's other major political parties are any less pig-headed. Indeed, their interest in the environment is even more slight and I do not believe that either of them is consumed by a burning desire to make green the password. Their pathetic squabbling is enough to make any self-respecting 'green' go yellow at the gills. If only they would realise that conservation is no longer only for those a colleague irreverently calls 'lentil heads', but also a major concern for almost anyone above the 'breadline'. Like Comic Relief, conservation transcends politics and I am sure that many millions of people around the world will rally round to sponsor it with equal generosity once the stark facts are made plain to one and all. Addressing the world's major environmental problems will simultaneously remove the need for so much overseas aid.

Thus it is pleasing to note new initiatives among Western nations whereby Third World countries are shown the folly of habitat destruction and come to appreciate the importance of sustainable resources; for example, in the rain forest. Now few people are unaware of the stupidity of a smash-and-grab economy. No responsible forester will ever fell more than he plants, any more than the sane hunter is ever going to wipe out next year's breeding stock.

As well as trying to influence others without first-hand knowledge of the natural world, we can also reassess our own commitment to local conservation. But this should never mean stagnation and total opposition to all change, for everything is relative to that we have known. We have to believe that things can be made better and not allow our vision to be clouded by nostalgia.

For my own part, I derive constant comfort in reading about the countryside of past decades, to discover what was important to the visionaries of yesteryear. And again and again, when it comes to basic motivation, I find little new under the sun, for man has long been both conservative and unwitting conservationist. The difference now is the great urgency which attends every matter as the simple fact is that in most countries there are just too many of us humans.

But let's not get too maudlin. After all, from this week spring is officially with us, so we can look forward to some snow! And as I watch the daffodils bludgeoned by hail (record size of course) I can savour the prospect of waterlogged Wimbledon, ice in August, drought in the South and floods in the North – all courtesy of environmental abuse, of course!

Diverting from global issues, to matters microcosmic, I have been lamenting the change of landlord down at the local, for there is no doubt that mine host can bring great heart to a small community. But then, in casual reading, I discovered that even in such relatively paltry parochial concerns there is little new pottering about beneath the firmament.

The Victorian writer of an entertaining little work on rambles about this neck of the woods made some remark on the hostelries of Haslemere, just a couple of gunshots away from my present abode. 'It is a rambling place with several inns, in not one of which you can depend upon getting a good clean bed for the night. The White Horse is not what it used to be, the ostler told me, and for the sake of those who have lodged there, I hope he is right, for the bed on which I passed an uneasy night was neither dry nor clean, and the taproom just below was filled with noisy drovers who had come to the market that day, and who were now quarrelling, swearing, and getting drunk over a game of dominoes.'

In many ways I envy those drovers. What splendidly simple and rumbustious lives they appear to have led. They had no notion of anything so heady as the ozone layer, and even that itinerant author who begrudged their merrymaking had no concept of planetary environment. But what is clear from further remarks is that they all shared a love of outdoor life and expressed great delight in the green lanes – over 100 years ago. Even when unspoilt England still stretched for mile upon mile, they had a clear view of natural wealth, and I am sure that if they were alive today they would be the first to give Maggie a roasting over her environmental apathy.

1989

## *March of Progress?*

March comes in like a lion and goes out like a lamb, according to weather lore. But, so far as the Meteorological Office is concerned, the saying holds no water because the month is just as likely to start quietly and go out with a bang. One study found the old saying worked in only twenty-two out of 100 years. Despite this, there are many people who still have faith in countless country sayings, and the reasons for this are not hard to understand.

It is not so long ago that most country communities were fairly isolated; without TV, radio and telephone, and perhaps only the occasional letter, they had nothing but word of mouth to rely on. The rural labourer had no science to guide him, only the word of his father, his own limited experience and the observations of friends and neighbours. Without education to refute the law, the man on the land was always open to exaggeration.

I envy the simplicity of earlier country life – not the undoubted poverty and privation suffered by so many, but the greater sense of place, community spirit, self-sufficiency and closeness to nature.

Now that mechanisation rules, one man can control a vast acreage, but having dumped most of his companions, both human and animal, he is an unfortunate loner. No wonder the suicide rate among farmers has increased dramatically. The air-conditioned tractor cab with its personal stereo is no substitute for conversation. As folk have said so often, a trouble shared is a trouble halved. The man behind the wheel might be richer materially but his spirit is often flagging.

There was a time when early March heralded a reassuring burst of activity in the fields and woods, the passage of man and horse being as natural a part of the landscape as the rooks returning to their tree-top nests. Now most of the trees have gone, the rooks are homeless and the plough teams are but memories on picture postcards. Now, if you see a man about the hedgerows he is more likely to be a poacher, someone dumping litter or a rambler rather than a farm worker.

Drums of chemicals stand in the yard where farm workers used to sit on upturned buckets dressing mangolds, their red faces the picture of rustic health. Now, too, garish, blue fertiliser sacks weigh heavily on the silence of the old dairy, where Mavis and Bella once churned butter and ladled cream, their gossip drifting across to where Harry and Fred carted manure into the potato rows. And where the Shires and Clydesdales once waited patiently for their daily round, the horsepower is now turbocharged and without character. Neddy has become Nippon and much of the countryside has lost its heart.

Of course it was hard work in the old days. No one is denying that. Working all hours in all weathers for 30 shillings (£1.50) a week left little room for leisure activities; but, from what I'm told, a game of darts and 'a good ol' sing-song' down at the Dog and Duck brought more laughs than a modern-day mini-bus trip to some bowling alley in the nearest town.

Perhaps the saddest thing of all is the way in which the general public has grown away from wildlife. Now some folk wouldn't know a cuckoo from a cormorant. So you can understand why some schools feel the need to bus town kids into the sticks to learn how to identify cows!

Before the war, any old rustic Tom, Dick or Harry knew a golden from a green plover because they were all around them in their daily toil and the workers were true guardians of the countryside. Thus, when the ploughman spotted a peewit's nest he moved the eggs, marked the spot with a stick and returned the eggs after he'd been about his business. Now there are few nests to watch for because the tractor has squashed them out of existence. I shudder to think of the number of birds and mammals which are killed in the corn by insatiable, unseeing machinery.

However, while the March landscape has become a lonely place, our birdlife is on the move, and with Britain at a great international crossroads, there are many migrants to watch for. The grey geese gather for their long flight north as the first summer songsters flight in from the south. Any time now there will be a welcome day of bright, spring sunshine when the chiffchaff will call its name from a nearby birch and the sulphurous brimstone will bring a welcome splash of colour.

We can also watch for bats, hedgehogs, snakes and all those other creatures which have spent the chill winter in a state of torpor. How they will fare depends on the caprice of our climate. In no other country does the saying 'make hay while the sun shines' have more relevance.

The word is that our weather is changing, that winter is later, spring is colder, and so on. Ern says we are heading for another ice age and Charlie that his grass is 'pegged back 'cos the wind's shifted'.

But whether or not March is ever like a lamb, we can be sure that the month will bring us lambs, though some are born much earlier. To many folk, a sheep is a sheep, but to the farmer the choice of breed is crucial.

This century, specialisation in sheep farming has seen the decline and even disappearance of many breeds which were selectively nurtured since Roman times. But now, as in so many other walks of life, there is renewed interest in old ways and old breeds. Mountain sheep in particular have retained their hold in traditional areas.

There is no doubt that we have been too hasty in sweeping away the old countryside for the sake of supposed efficiency and productivity. We now regret so much, yet there is still a wealth of tradition to save, and in so doing we should have as much respect for the men on the land as the wildlife around them. The countryside should not be a place devoid of workers and their heritage, but stuffed full of visitors looking for rarities. First and foremost it must be home for the shepherd, his sheep and his sayings.

1992

## Parrot Pests

When King John signed the Magna Carta at Runnymede in 1215 I don't think he saw any wild parrots. But I did recently, when I passed the famous site on my way into the office just as the snow began to fade after February's rigorous reign.

Actually the exotic was a rose-ringed parakeet and, although I was delighted fortuitously to 'twitch' a first, I did not then realise the significance of the sighting. Feral parakeets have been reported regularly in south-east England since 1969 and their spread has been steady, but experts said that the acid test would come with the first really severe winter. Well, now we have had that mega-freeze and the adaptable rose-ringed parakeet, a native of India, has shown that it can withstand such a testing time.

It is certainly worth watching the progress of this bird very closely for there is a distinct possibility that it could become a significant pest. In India the species causes enormous losses in taking ripening grain and orchard fruits, frequently destroying much more than it can eat. Furthermore, at rail sidings they are commonly seen clinging to sacks of grain, which they bite into and help themselves from.

This parakeet has frequently escaped from captivity in England since about 1855, and in the 1930s a number apparently frequented the gardens around Epping Forest, where they remained for a few years. The major spread from the 1970s has been in Kent, Surrey, the London suburbs, East Sussex and Essex. Odd individuals have been seen in Berkshire, West Sussex, Buckinghamshire and other counties. Although many escapes have added to the number, it has been suggested that deliberate liberation has almost certainly been the main cause of establishment in the wild.

What these birds live on in England I do not know but they are common visitors to bird tables and the safety of suburban parks and large gardens is a great attraction.

Nobody knows what effect they will have on our native birds, but their spread could be much more serious than that of the much-publicised collared dove. That species appears to have filled a vacant niche, but the rose-ringed parakeet could well displace some birds through competition, especially over nest-sites.

To generalise, the parakeet's main foods are grain, seeds, berries, fruit, blossom and nectar, so the threat to agriculture and fruit growers is obvious, especially as this normally sedentary bird will flock to food sources. Thus, over food the main competitor should be man rather than other birds.

But when it comes to nest-sites there is conflict with endemic bird species as the parakeet favours tree holes. Our native hole-nesters have a hard enough time as it is with increasingly tidy forestry removing all but the healthiest trees. Decaying trees, with all those intriguing holes which small boys love to thrust their hands into, are now generally only found where woodland is on a reserve or has amenity value. Little wonder that parkland suburbia is favoured by parakeets.

In this context our larger hole-nesting birds are threatened, especially the owls, which are already under pressure and need all the help they can get. Barn owls are especially vulnerable. Even though they may resort more commonly to buildings for nesting, they undoubtedly still rely on the original, natural tree sites in many areas, and anything which threatens a species in major decline must be viewed seriously. The Hawk Trust has already shown that there is a probable direct link between barn owl decline and tawny owl ascendancy, and obviously we don't want to complicate the position further with aliens!

1986

## Diary of Sadness

Looking back through my childhood diaries, which I kept from the age of eight to sixteen, was, of course, very nostalgic for me. But it was also the cause of great sadness because I logged in detail all the suburban infilling and so-called development which robbed my patch of a character acquired over centuries. As everywhere, pockets of wildness hung on, sandwiched between supposed advancement, chiefly because their mostly aged owners knew better days and saw no reason to change what had given them enormous pleasure. These were great haunts for us lads, but their owners were regarded as eccentrics by incomers who would in no way tolerate things such as 'dirty' piggeries, overgrown orchards and crumbling barns around their 'luxury' bungalows.

Yet change there must be. All we can do is try to ensure that it really is for the better. For anyone who doubts the continuing pace of change I thoroughly recommend keeping a detailed diary. A surprising amount of local history and wildlife observation is preserved in this way. Furthermore, diary notes are much more 'alive' than generally bland published reports because the writer can record all the gossip and libel which local newspapers may not.

1986

## The Very English Elm

Every time a great wind gets up and moans about the eaves I remember the early hours of 16 October 1987, when some 15 million trees were blown down by what has come to be known

58

as The Great Storm. Those trees represented a volume of almost four million cubic metres of timber. Three-quarters of the damage occurred in privately owned woodlands and the volume of timber toppled was far greater than that felled by any other recorded storm this century.

By the end of March 1988, nearly six months after the storm, it was estimated that 16 per cent of the volume of fallen timber had been cleared from both private woodlands and Forestry Commission forests. But since then foresters and nature reserve wardens in many areas have had to continue with the endless monotony and back-breaking task of track clearance, diverting precious skills from long-term improvement programmes. Day after day they have set forth with their chainsaws and winches, toiling from dawn to dusk to reinstate the order which mankind craves.

In many woods without paid custodians the devastation will remain for decades and is especially easy to see at this time of year, when winter has bared the landscape and spring is still very much in the bud.

In the aftermath of The Great Storm we have heard comparatively little of Dutch elm disease, yet the number of trees affected by this scourge has continued to increase despite rigorous control measures.

For me, the tragic loss of our elms is particularly apparent at this time of year, when we look to the rookeries for a sign of spring. So many trees have been lost that a huge number of birds have had to find other quarters and often be satisfied with shorter specimens of other tree species. But nothing can ever replace the noble silhouette of the elm, once bestowing such majesty to every vale and anointing every skyline with such 'Englishness'. As Howitt said in his *Book of the Seasons*, every month, like a good servant, brings its own character with it, but March will never be the same without the peaceful elm.

Elm disease (*Ceratostomella ulmi*) was first noted in Holland in 1924, but its origin is unknown. Since then it has progressively attacked the elms of that country, which are nearly all of a single strain, until today only a small fraction remains. Nobody knows how the disease reached England, probably in 1927, but it is likely that it came on nursery stock as there were no quarantine measures affecting elm at the time. Fortunately, diversification of the elm strain in Britain has proved a useful means of defence.

It is thought that the elm does not figure more largely in English woodlands because, by the time the great plantations were laid out, enough was already growing along the hedgerows for all foreseeable local demands, and landowners saw no reason to increase an already abundant tree. Yet the elm has a curiously uneven distribution, being absent from some districts where conditions seem well suited to its growth. Perhaps in such places it was wiped out by the open-field and common grazing systems before hedgerows were planted so extensively.

On good land, the quick-growing lowland elm may reach a height of 150ft, probably greater than any other British broadleaved tree, which is especially remarkable in that most tall elms are open-grown, enjoying no shelter from other trees. Such giants carry a great deal of timber – 100–200 hoppus (cubic) feet apiece.

Lowland elm is especially important for the craftsman in that it is our only native wood that shows a uniformly high resistance to splitting. Thus it was commonly used for the seats of chairs, especially Windsors, into which both legs and uprights have to be driven firmly to achieve a tight fit. Under such pressure the interlocked grain of elm holds firm whereas any other common timber would break.

Water pipes, too, were once made of elm, the heart of the wood being hollowed out with an auger. And village water pumps were originally tubes of elm trunks instead of metal. Even the pump bucket would be carved out of elm.

Beautiful as they are, elms are not entirely satisfactory as landscape features. Large, old specimens are often unsound at the heart and cannot even be saved by major surgery. They are also very susceptible to windblow, the roots tending to give way when a gale follows heavy rain that has softened the earth. There is also the tendency for large, apparently healthy elms to shed big, heavy boughs.

But for all their faults, elms remain firmly implanted in my nostalgia banks. Dreams of walking-up hedgerows are always punctuated by their comforting presence, and no summer picnic is so sweet as one within their shade.

1989

## Sea Fever

There was an air of excitement about the Hampshire coast last week, with restless skeins of brent geese arrowing endlessly up and down the shoreline, the call of the north filling their bottle-shaped bodies with new life. Most would be gone by the end of March, though some might linger into May. Mankind too was moved by the change of air: beach huts were being painted and the ever-increasing swarms of sail-boarders cut the white horses with admirable ease. With black wetsuits, ruddy cheeks and all the gear like men from a James Bond movie, the prospect of spring had roused them from their wintry lethargy.

Less seasonally inspired were the hardy saltwater anglers, whose great, green brollies brave this windy quarter the year round. Munching doorstep sandwiches and sucking gingerly at cups of scalding soup from Thermos flasks, they huddled in twos and threes, weather eyes alert to the twitch of a rod tip, citizens of unsurpassed patience. Quite rightly they viewed passers-by suspiciously, fearing that their unleashed dogs would snarl the casts or irksome children would toss stones into the critical zone. I knew how they felt, for sea-fishing has always been a great love of mine.

Beneath one enormous umbrella an old salt entertained his grand-daughter, but sadly their bucket of water contained no fish. Only a fund of yarns from generations of Solent days relieved the relentless moan of the westerly. But a half-mile on, where even full tide failed to claim the shingle promontory, a young blood with a woolly hat and a cod-sized grin fared better.

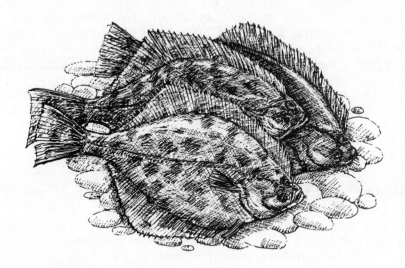

As we passed, the lucky Rod's mighty beachcaster trembled and after a few minutes' steady retrieve there was a splendid flounder of some 2lb, flashing white as it spun around at the end of the line in sparkling sunshine. This exceptional fish was consigned to a bucket of sea-water containing three other similar-sized flounders and the lad quickly threaded another ragworm onto his hook –

one of three spaced at intervals of about eighteen inches up from an end weight of 2oz.

As the noonday high tide sucked at the headland we noted the fishing spot for future visits and crunched on along the shingle. Clouds threatened a soaking as three turnstones tripped along the waterline ahead of us and a meadow pipit foraged among the harsh tussocks at the base of the cliff. Halfway across to the misty Isle of Wight, sunlight burst through the cloud bed, spotlighting a glimmering, silver stage on which dozens of small yachts jockeyed for position at the start of a race. White sails tilted haphazardly in little clusters, feeling the wind for every advantage as eager helmsmen licked salt from their lips.

In complete contrast, just a few yards inland from the cliff, a tractor chugged on with the spring ploughing, the head-phoned driver oblivious to the cheery cries of blackheaded gulls which danced on his tail after worms and insects. Strange to think how this species and some other gulls were rare in the last century, before open rubbish tips came along to boost their food supply and playing fields multiplied to provide safe roosts, enabling the birds to remain within 'striking' distance of the new food sources.

How I wished I could stay there, soaking up that odd mixture of maritime wilderness and vigorous human activity, marred only by the ever-increasing, plasticated flotsam and jetsam cast overboard by the world's sailors. But all too soon it was up and away to Ruraltania, before the Sunday rush choked the A3 in the drift back to town.

1987

## Lark's Lament

At this time of year the sighting of an early brimstone butterfly on a day of bright sunshine will always lift the spirit. Pure yellow wings and endless blue sky offer such vivid contrast to the months of grey just ending. Yet even this sulphurous messenger does not carry the tidings of spring as clearly as the skylark. The only trouble is, this superior songster is suddenly in retreat due to man's spread and activities. Today Vaughan Williams' celebrated music would be better re-named 'The Lark Descending'.

My perfect picture of March is one of the South Downs where stiff sea breezes ripple across the grasslands, but never so strongly that the lark is unable to climb his invisible string up into the wide blue yonder. There, among cloudlets that drift like mirror images of the sheep below, he seems to hold station through sheer *joie de vivre* rather than the need to procreate. It seems hard to believe that man has abused this species so.

In olden times the skylark was taken in large numbers because it was, apparently, very good to eat, and in great demand as a caged songster. Fortunately, it existed in numbers great enough to survive such interests. But now the insidious attack on its habitat is causing serious concern throughout Europe.

For centuries the lark was the ploughman's constant companion and even now, when so few men still work the land, the phrase 'up with the lark' remains in constant use. Not only has the rural labourer loved the lark for the quality of its song but also because it will sing continuously for up to half an hour or more. Furthermore, it will sing regularly during some eight months of the year. I have even listened to one on Christmas Day and at other times in midwinter when the weather was sufficiently stimulating.

When I walk the downs the skylark is a welcome companion. When he tires of his song and sinks back down into the all-concealing grass the ensuing silence is all the more noticeable because there are few other great songsters to take up the challenge on those wide, open lands.

Many of us have a false impression of the skylark's abundance because, although it is the most widely distributed of British birds, it is only the twelfth most numerous. The latest estimate of Britain's breeding population is around two million pairs, only about half the stock of both blackbirds and wrens.

The species did enjoy a long period of stability through much of this century, but since 1981 there has been a marked decline. Loss of habitat and changes in agriculture are to blame. Let us hope that new awareness of man's impact on the environment will ensure that this bird of the poets will continue to delight us throughout the next millenium and beyond.

1993

## Satisfying Self-Sufficiency

In my garden a few leeks remain, though the purple sprouting broccoli holds little promise after constant attention by woodpigeons. There is a pleasing continuity as we collect the last of the old year's harvest and prepare the rested earth to nurture the new. October's apples have stored well in the cold attic and, although the remaining Cox's are wrinkled and golden and really only fit for cooking, the hard, green Bramleys are superficially unchanged.

If allowance is made for one's time, there seems to be little financial gain in growing your own on a small scale nowadays, when specialists continue to sell most vegetables in season at a reasonable price. But the true reward is in the satisfaction and unending fascination of producing a crop. There is also that extra flavour and succulence through freshness, and the delight of always having your favourite produce to hand. Add to that the sportsman's ability to bring home the meat and many of us certainly have the potential to enjoy the occasional totally 'home-produced' meal.

1984

## Ways of Old

As the days lengthen and winter dries out we have more opportunity to stride out into the countryside. Now it is more comfortable to spy for spring migrants and discover how woods and fields have fared through storm and tempest. Also, apart from the intrigues of nature, there are the many marks of man's earlier existence which I like to look for in the clean, open landscape of March, before dense foliage masks the view.

In my corner of the kingdom, where Surrey, Sussex and Hampshire weave a complicated, highly wooded boundary, there is an abundance of roads and trackways worn down by constant use to a level well below the surrounding land. To me they are places of great mystery, where exposed, hanging tree roots provide homes for wren, wagtail and robin as well as free rein for the imagination. In olden times some were widely avoided as 'places so grotesque of aspect that ladies commonly take afright'. And for centuries, for carriage and motor car alike, they have been renowned snow traps where blizzards can ensnare the unwary traveller.

The deepest hollow ways are not necessarily the oldest. It all depends on how hard the underlying rock is. For example, one in the hard limestone at Willersley Hill, in Gloucestershire, has worn down at about two inches a century and is thought to be about 6,000 years old. There are many others crossing hill ridges which have been trading routes and livestock tracks since the new Stone Age, some 4,000 years ago. But those in the sand and clay of my patch, and others in Devon and the Weald of Kent, are thought to be much more recent, especially in areas of high rainfall, where erosion is greater.

To me, footpaths and bridleways lost much of their mystery in 1968, when Parliament required county councils to signpost them where they leave the metalled road. The result is all very well for hikers with targets to make, but it's a bit clinical and does away with any sense of discovery – not that I would ever sanction wandering where one should not. On the contrary, I am a firm believer in controlled access to the countryside. We all know what happens when countless feet trample willy-nilly over our precious acres; erosion creeps in and the wildlife (including game) creeps out!

Public paths are not all clearly marked, so anyone armed with great patience and an Ordnance Survey map may still enjoy tracing our history. Along the way I like to imagine the wayfarers of long ago who walked these paths into existence on their way to market, farm, church and pub. Others were trodden by packhorses carrying salt (so vital to preserve meat during winter in the days before refrigeration), or miners with their tin, lead and slate. Where Rusticus now roams with his Barbour and binoculars, some other rustic once strode with his staff and cloak.

Even main roads have been built over ancient footpaths. It's odd to think that the motorway may once have been nothing more than a track traced on the landscape by warring armies, or that the site of the crossroads service station was the haunt of highwaymen.

Along the modern way we encounter many fences, which are now likely to be of unscalable height or viciously barbed, if not electrified. In some parts, pleasantly rustic fences of chestnut or other 'sympathetic' materials are almost impossible to find. But then, should we expect more when the word fence derives from 'defence', from the days when land was first enclosed and intruders had to be barred?

How refreshing to roam parts of our landscape where wire does not rule, where those more natural and traditional forms of 'fence' – the hedgerow and the drystone wall – still keep close stock control.

Fence sites mostly relate to the boundaries of fields, which also mostly stem from the enclosures of land during the late eighteenth and early nineteenth centuries, but on Dartmoor there are traces of Stone-Age fields of more than 3,500 years ago. Unlike the strips and squares of later periods, these were small, circular clearances of about an acre, which were stripped of scrub and stones and then hoed with sticks or antlers to plant primitive cereals.

Some of the old granaries that still exist are among my favourite buildings. Nowadays most grain is stored in huge bins in multi-purpose drying, cleaning and storage units, but before this century grain stores were buildings of many shapes and sizes and with all types of roof, from stone to thatch. The only essentials were dryness and resistance to vermin. Many were square, wooden buildings set on pillars capped with mushroom-shaped stones. Although many people now think these quaint old stones were purely decorative, they were very practical in that their shape prevented rats and mice from entering the store. At the same time, the air circulating beneath the buildings helped to keep the grain dry. Today the 'mushrooms', known as staddles, are collectors' items.

During the late eighteenth century, granaries and cart sheds were often combined in one building. On the ground floor the carts and farm machinery were protected from bad weather, while the top floor – where there was less chance of rats entering – was used to store the threshed grain. This arrangement also made it easier to fill the carts with grain.

Other old buildings which have survived to delight the wayfarer include dovecotes. Despite the fact that many are decorative and sometimes of sufficient architectural and historical merit to warrant safeguarding as scheduled buildings, most were primarily meat factories. Some dovecotes had as many as 1,200 nestboxes. The doves and pigeons which they housed were not pets, but important sources of fresh meat before the days of deep-freezes.

1993

## Knock Knock . . .

Dutch elm disease has been aggravating a problem for electricity board workers in rural areas. In the short term dead trees harbour considerable food for birds, but as diseased trees are felled quickly and their numbers decrease woodpeckers have been turning their attention to electricity poles. Engineers have been forced to fit metal plates to prevent power lines being pecked. Yet woodpeckers have always done this to some extent, especially when courting males try to drum up interest.

Every year we have a whole family of great-spotted woodpeckers hammering on an electricity pole near the house, but the birds appear to do little damage. Perhaps they are holding pecking lessons?

Anyway, if the pole plates are successful the birds may turn to doors. Many years ago a friend of mine had a persistent caller at his front door, but when he answered there was never anyone there. Then one day I happened to arrive when the knocker was present. When John answered the summons he found only me there, but I was able to tell him that a great-spotted woodpecker had kindly tapped on the door for me! Unfortunately, he would not stay for tea.

1982

## *Joy in Simple Things*

The countryside and wildlife have an unfailing ability to lift the human spirit through every mood and in every season. A country walk, preferably alone, is always worthwhile no matter how busy one is, and for me at least is usually so restorative as to make me work harder on returning home. However, when completely absorbed in a very long project such as writing a book, which demands so much time, it is quite easy to go out one day and discover that one has missed much of the year's passage. Whenever this happens I feel cheated, for no two years are the same, though each nurtures that basic joy in simple things.

After the game and wildfowling seasons ended I did not get out much at all and I cannot remember even walking around the garden in February. But within four days of the ice sheet lifting spring got underway with a vengeance and the shallowest and warmest side of the garden pond rapidly became a heaving mass of frogs and spawn.

A wren built in one of my junipers at the end of January and was only preceded by the magpies high in a neighbouring cedar of Lebanon. I debated removal of these pied marauders in view of their depredations among garden birds, but then February's chill set in and I thought that this would put them off. It did, but only temporarily for they resumed activity in March and by mid-month were sitting tight.

On several mornings I have been showered by clumps of moss falling from the roof where a cock chaffinch has copied the example of starlings and tits in picking about for insects. This chaffinch has claimed a garden territory but does not yet appear to have started building. He has a very strong competitor.

Each morning, when my younger son (actually it is usually his mother, for the novelty soon wore off) feeds his white rabbit at the end of the garden a robin comes to take his share. Progressively bolder, the robin now perches on top of the hutch within a foot of the 'zookeeper', often trembling with song and with his full black eyes ever alert to danger. Peaceful he may appear, but he is 100 per cent robin in his unrelenting aggression towards other small birds.

Further afield, on the surrounding farm my first walk for some time came in mid-March in very kind weather. At Heron's Pond the usual Jack heron sprang up on lanky legs to drift away on shadowy wings over the crops where he would pretend to fly right off but would really trace a large circle and return as soon as I was gone. Pale green tips of iris leaves pierced the surface like sword blades, rising on cue from the brown beds of rootstock and matted vegetation near which the angling club, come June, will sit and watch their bright floats in a spellbound dream. By then the yellow flags will mark each station.

Again on the sunny side, in shallows among rocks, were swollen masses of black-dotted spawn, like a mysterious hoard of human brains. And, as in our 'grey matter', a miracle of evolution is encapsulated there within each seed.

The stark, sombre architecture of winter was already softening with a yellow-pink flush of catkins and silver studs of 'pussy willow' set upon the trees like Christmas decorations. February's grey sky had given way to white, fast-moving clouds and a true blue that reflected a new intensity of colour in the stirring water.

Slowly but steadily skylarks wound themselves up on clock-work motors in the gusty air before falling to release the rising exuberance of the season. Everywhere magpies chattered excitedly as I approached each cradle of thorns so obvious in the still-bare hedgerows. All simple, everyday sights which stimulate most of us.

1983

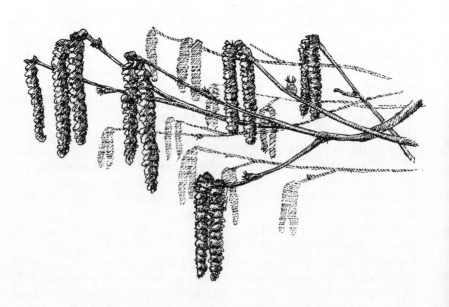

# *April*

## *Cuckoo Days*

Even in a forward year such as this, March shows mere promise whereas April always produces the goods. That great factory of the outdoors now has sufficient solar energy to set every production line in motion and steadily lengthening days provide a much wider canvas on which to paint the country scene.

There is always something very special about the year's first clutch of wild bird eggs. Whether it's the blackbird's in the laurel, the song thrush's in the bramble or, more likely, the mistle thrush's in the high crook of the old cherry, the sudden discovery of freshness and colour is indeed a tonic.

The first butterflies, too, come as bold splashes of colour in a relatively dull countryside whose intensity is still leached by cold, driving rains. Brimstones, orange tips, small tortoiseshells and speckled woods turn dim glades into treasure chests and gardens into glory.

And then there are those other reliable heralds of better days – the frogs whose periscope eyes now line the pond edge; the willow warbler whose cascading, silver song drifts across the common on every day of bright sunshine; and the first real dawn chorus. It seems as if every bird is a-wing and every voice determined to make its mark.

But perhaps above all others, there is one spirit of spring awaited in north-west Europe with unrivalled interest. In Britain at least, the cuckoo is *the* voice of hope and renewal.

Long ago, when it was thought that swallows spent the cold months in the mud of ponds, it was suggested that cuckoos turned into sparrowhawks for the winter. Thus it is not surprising that the dates of the first cuckoo arrivals are noted with care in many diaries.

In fact cuckoos have been recorded in Britain in all months, but the small number of winter sightings is open to suspicion. Cuckoos are commonly confused with collared doves and male sparrowhawks, especially on the wing. The earliest thought to have been a genuine spring migrant was the bird seen and heard singing in Surrey on 20 February 1953.

The main arrival dates ('cuckoo days') vary by county and, not surprisingly, people in the south record the bulk of early sightings. For example, Sussex usually sees the first birds between the 12th and 23rd of April, but 21st to 30th of April is more likely in Yorkshire and 1st to 7th of May in the extreme North and Scottish islands. Males usually arrive at least a week before the females.

There is something magical about the cuckoo's call, and inevitably it is first heard at considerable distance, rising and falling on the breeze, the 'wandering voice' of the poets defying all attempts to track it down. It belongs to the male alone and there is a considerable number of variants uttered from any sort of perch or on the wing – even at night. The female has an entirely different, water-bubbling chuckle and other peculiar notes which I always seem to hear at very close range, frequently giving me a start when creeping about the woods just before dawn.

No less remarkable is the song of the common wren, probably the loudest of any British bird when size is taken into consideration. Parts are above the range of human hearing, but lower elements can be heard over 500 metres away. The rattling warble of clear, shrill notes is usually delivered from some low perch, but not infrequently on the wing and occasionally at night.

How fortunate we are that this most common of British birds has such a stimulating song. If ever a wild voice said 'get up and go', then surely this is it.

Another great delight at this time of year is the dreamy cooing of the woodpigeon, and its nuptial flight is sufficient to stir the most winter-jaded heart. Sometimes its airshow seems to be put on entirely for our benefit as the ring-dove inevitably chooses a glade or open space above field corner or garden in which to perform. There it floats out from its favourite budding tree at little more than stalling speed; takes three beats up to its aerial pinnacle, to poise for a mini-second, then glide so gracefully down on level wings, repeating the joyride over and over again. At the same time the bird's wings make a resounding crack which breaks the woodland silence and draws the eye up into the sprouting canopy.

But just when we have become accustomed to April's newfound softness there is a turnabout. On a night of stars the silhouetted weathercock suddenly swivels. Several degrees of frost distil from the heavens and when morning comes we discover that all the magnolia blooms have been spoiled.

1988

## County Set

Sir Arthur Bryant once wrote: 'England has 39 lovely counties and I do not know which is the loveliest.' Many of us will have very firm opinions about this and I am sure most will have an irresistible affection for the county in which they were born. Others identify more strongly with counties where they settled in later life.

Today England has forty-six counties and not all of Bryant's survive, though many people still think of the 'extinct' ones as home. The casualties include Rutland, Huntingdonshire and Middlesex. And while Herefordshire and Worcestershire have been officially joined, they will always remain separate in the minds of many people who live there. As James Bishop said, the subject is 'determined by the logic of loyalties rather than the preference of planners'. Not surprisingly, some of the new official counties, such as Cleveland, Avon and Humberside, have yet to establish themselves as anything more than administrative units.

1985

## Village Earth

April is so called from the Latin *Aprilis*, which is derived from *Aperire* – to open, and in the old days this really meant something.

Indeed, up to the 1960s the climate seemed pretty reliable and we could all look forward to a great burgeoning of plant life in this scintillating month. But now, as you read this, there is as much chance that you will be huddled before your fire, the door stoppered against icy blasts, as there is of you reclining on the lawn with a Pimm's or pint at your elbow. And don't go putting all the blame on all those peasant farmers hacking away at the rainforest. Ozone destruction, the greenhouse effect and acid rain begin at home. They are the legacy of the industrial revolution that began in western Europe and North America and is now being copied by Third World countries justifiably wanting their fair share of the cake. Indeed, Britain started it all, primarily in the nineteenth century, so now we must lead the way in putting things right.

Sadly, when it comes to environmental issues and the survival of life on earth, most people find the enormity and apparent hopelessness of it all so daunting they feel powerless to act. Like the farmer, they want rapid returns and few are generous enough to invest in future generations.

Yet there is much to be done, not least through a regeneration of village life. Without the feeling of belonging to a community many people simply have little or no regard for their environment. They like the idea of living in the countryside but treat it like a dormitory and contribute nothing to its upkeep, bumbling around at weekends as if living in a museum.

The trouble with many so-called villages is that they lack heart, consisting of mere extensions of suburbia or straggling assemblages of relatively isolated houses, often over very large areas. Further disadvantaged through not having suitable centres, such as village hall or pub, where people can meet to discuss topics of common interest, they are little more than hermit communities. Then, when the sole surviving shop draws its blinds for the last time, the bell no longer rings at the village school and the bus company diverts to more lucrative routes, is it any wonder that people drift away to find companionship in towns?

Shooting, fishing and hunting are among the very best ways to hold rural communities together, especially because they attract followers from all walks of life. In autumn and winter they stir folk from their hearths and in the close season they are the focus of pleasant work parties and social gatherings.

Equally important are sports and games such as cricket and darts, both engendering fierce village pride through regular competition. Once a sense of identity is established through sport, it is but a short step to development of other interests such as history and natural history societies, horticultural and flower-arranging groups, birdwatching clubs, tug o' war teams and even entry into the 'best kept village' competition.

Once the custodial attitude is established at local level, especially where whole families are involved, people will acquire concern for the nation and eventually for the planet itself. Simple, unselfish acts such as plucking someone else's litter from the village green or bothering to use the bottle bank can inspire others in so many ways, leading to great community spirit and pride of place.

1990

## Who Killed Cock Robin?

Many people assume that the easily tamed robin which comes to the bird table, or even to hand to feed, is the same individual year after year. But this is most unlikely as the sad fact is that the robin is one of the shortest-lived wild birds, with an average life expectancy of only five to six months, well below the average of nine months for small songbirds. Probably 60 per cent of all adult robins die each year, though the known record is for an individual of 12.9 years. Yet the robin is not so very different from other species in that it is estimated that up to 75 per cent of all wild birds die through starvation, disease, accidents and bad weather before they are even six months old!

1987

## Busy Doing Nothing

Often I wonder how those great Victorian naturalists and country commentators found so much time to ramble and observe at leisure. Presumably most of these gentlemen (and there seem to have been few ladies of such a disposition) were of independent means and knew little or nothing of a nine to five routine. Yet, in a way, their good fortune is ours too in that we now enjoy their record of a wilder countryside lost forever.

Whether rich, poor or middling, most people today are obsessed with commitment, competition and ambition and have lost the childhood art of idling or musing in the countryside. The tycoon might collapse into his weekend, rustic deckchair, but he is contemplating the board report on the morrow rather than the blackbird building its nest right in front of him. The executive has the barbecue going in a leafy glade, but he 'must be back by three for an important phone call'. And although the craftsman left his tools on the bench when Friday's whistle shrieked halt, he 'simply must mow the lawn, fix the leaking roof and paint the window while the weather holds'. We are all uneasy in our relaxation, riddled with a sense of guilt in the accursed competition of 1980s society. Even a simple stroll has to be excused as 'taking the dog for a walk'.

When we do manage to 'get away from it all' temporarily we tend to cluster around 'honey pot' sites for convenience, to make best use of limited time. Although we are supposed to be enjoying ourselves and releasing all our tensions and frustrations we feel that we have to do or see something worthy – an ancient monument, birthplace of some notable, renowned view or plant collection perhaps. But immediately the competition returns as everyone else has the same idea. Competition for road space, competition for entrance, access and picnic sites. You name it, somebody else wants it!

Why is it that so few people seem able to idle away a few hours alone? Today the chances of encountering a kindred spirit sitting on a fence merely chewing a straw or dozing beneath the cool hedgerow are slim indeed. Some activities, such as angling and roughshooting, do move us in the right direction, but even these comparatively slow and ostensibly peaceful pastimes fill our befuddled brains with tactics. No, even these are not ways to do nothing.

Country rambling is a good way to free the mind, but only when there is no really planned route and little commitment to time. We don't have to follow the neatly signposted tracks (assuming there is no trespass), the red or blue arrows and the glaring sign indicating that a particular corner of a field is a picnic site whereas a much better adjacent one is not. Who wants to be an automaton?

Louis Jennings had the right idea when he wrote *Field Paths and Green Lanes* in 1878, though he still felt the need to have some 'point' to his book, in subtitling it 'Country Walks, chiefly in Surrey and Sussex'. He was 'not without hope that this little book will prove interesting, and in some degree useful, to those who find an unfailing source of pleasure in wandering over England, deeming nothing unworthy of notice, whether it be an ancient church or homestead, a grand old tree, a wild flower under a hedge, or a stray rustic by the roadside'. Oh, how I would like to be that stray rustic, without the encumbrance of ambition: yet I am one of the greatest hypocrites of all. Occasionally, when I wander from the earmarked way my heart sings 'tally ho!', but dreaded 'plans' soon return to clutter the brain.

I thoroughly agree with Mr Jennings in suggesting that you should 'take care to go with no other companions ... for then you can cry halt whenever you please and have no one's whims or oddities to perplex and harass you'. This would, 'by proper management', put you in a better position to 'get the country folks whom you meet to talk to you, and from them pick up many a quaint saying or odd scrap of information; but they are as shy of the tourists who hunt in couples as they are of the wild man who flies past them on a bicycle'.

One of the best ways to get a good helping of rustic lore and observation is to sit quietly supping your ale outside a backwaters pub just after opening time on a pleasant summer's evening. Avoid the trendy hostelries with easy access to main roads or towns, but choose an unpretentious 'spit and sawdust', stone-flag establishment where a penny on beer brings a month-long inquest.

Don't go on a Sunday lunchtime when the lanes burr with motorised exploration, but on a weekday as soon as the doors open to admit the parched farmhand from his dusty tractor. And there's none like a rustic's curiosity. Just as you long to get closer to his world so too is he fascinated by the glitter of 'foreigners'.

As I sat in such a situation last year, three Gloucestershire locals discussed the unprecedented wheeling and assembly of house martins relative to the prospect of rain. The more they drank the more definite were their views, till at last I was invited to give mine and a pleasurable exchange of ideas ensued. Yet had I arrived in a glossy charabanc with a group of companions I doubt whether my thoughts would have been welcome.

Frequently in such restful situations I try to picture the scene a hundred years ago, when the old brick-and-thatch building would have been much the same but the 'made-up' road merely a gravel track or deeply rutted wagoners' way; when, instead of a few old 'bangers' steaming in the forecourt, horses champed at the bit, and the countrymen wore simple cotton smocks rather than gaudy 'man-mades'.

Miraculously, you don't have to traipse up to Northumberland to find such centres of physical and spiritual refreshment today. Here and there some remain in pockets of southern England not yet strangled to death by the ever-changing entanglement of roads. For example, in this south-west corner of Surrey, and in nearby Hampshire and Sussex, are densely wooded hills which stoutly resist the spread of tarmac.

We still have the deep, hollow lanes of which Rusticus I wrote so affectionately in 1849. Here, too, are the 'steep banks and great thick hedges on each side a-top; hedges run to seed as it were, and here and there grown into trees – gnarled oak, bushy rough-coated maples and so forth – trees, in fact, that, stretching their arms from both sides of the way, shake hands over your head and form a kind of canopy of boughs'. In particular I love the riotous entanglement of roots where centuries of rain have eroded the sandy soil to leave a profusion of hollows for the robin to nest in, the wren to feed in and me to peer in. I don't really know what I'm looking for but I can't stop peeking and hope I never will.

Now with Easter behind us we can tramp these lanes with special pleasure. The blackcap's silver songburst is back in the early-morning coppice, and at noon the sun gets high enough to pierce the budding labyrinth and colour the mossy banks of primroses. The afternoon is soft with the scents of overdue spring and the prospect of 'a long hot summer' puts spring in our shoes. It's good to be out and about, 'letting the spirit move you', but beware of too much subconscious planning. Live for today and fasten your seatbelts for a journey back into olde England. There's nothing wrong with doing nothing, for tomorrow we could all be 'nuked'.

1987

## Selling 'Weeds'

One thing the ploughman does not see so much of now is wild flowers, as the unrelenting chemical storm weeds them out. Is organic farming the answer? Would there be enough bread to go round if we farmed to allow the flowers to multiply? Now someone is even cashing in on this dilemma. I have just been given two packets of wild flower seeds – Scotch thistle at 35p and poppy at 29p. What a fascinating shift in the attitude of society has made it possible to market profitably these wild plants which our forefathers regarded as weeds. I must say it seems rather funny to read about sowing 'wild' Scotch thistles *indoors* in March and hardening them off before planting out in April/May.

1980

## Snake in the Grass

My sympathies went out to a correspondent when I read that his young labrador had suffered an adder bite while being trained on heathland. I think he was right in suggesting that recent warm weather had encouraged adders to come out of hibernation early.

It is the adult male adders which emerge first from hibernation, over about a week, followed by the adult females over about a month, and finally the immatures. The males will have spent about 150 days in the torpid state, but the females hibernate for about a month longer.

In most years the males become especially active and bad-tempered during the first half of April, when they shed their skins and assume brilliant coloration. They dart about and hunt for the females which pass through their territories on their way to sloughing (skin-shedding) sites. The general excitement is made all the more intense when they scent the pheromones released from the open vents of females moving about.

Dogs and cats are often bitten about the head when they try to seize the adder. Cats especially will play with snakes, patting their tails to make them angry. Cows, goats and horses are sometimes bitten on the legs or about the head while grazing. Humans, of course, tend to get bitten on the leg or hand, but fortunately fatalities are rare. Up to 1945 only seven deaths were known in England and Wales, plus two in Scotland. There have been a few others since, but those of two boys were due to sensitivity to the antiserum and not to the venom. In fact, statistics show that the adder bite is a less likely cause of death than a wasp or bee sting, or even the mosquito bite.

1990

## Wolves in Sheep's Clothing

Most of us are aware that all creatures on earth occupy what ecologists call niches – vacancies within the web of life to which they have become adapted. Together they form food chains in which the general rule is that the smaller and weaker fall prey to the larger and stronger. But it would be wrong to assume that every individual animal knows its place. Just as the human underdog may unexpectedly turn to black the oppressor's eye, so weaklings or generally placid individuals within the animal kingdom may suddenly act right out of character. In extreme cases the predator may suddenly become prey.

More commonly, the underdogs rise up in numbers to overcome greater 'firepower', such as when songbirds mob an owl. Even tiny tots such as goldcrests and robins acquire surprising bravado when gathered in superior numbers. The odd thing is the way in which powerful killers allow themselves to be bullied.

One of the most surprising accounts of 'turning the tables', which I heard of recently, involved a magpie killing a sparrowhawk. A birdwatcher in Kent was watching a flock of house martins feeding over a reservoir when a male sparrowhawk suddenly flew through the birds, apparently having captured prey. But the hawk was pursued by two magpies.

As the pied marauders closed, the hawk was bundled to the ground, a house martin flew out of the mêlée and some starlings joined the attack, which continued in the corner of a meadow.

After a while the starlings and one magpie moved back a couple of metres, leaving the hawk locked in combat with the other magpie. The observer mistakenly believed that the struggle was over the hawk's prey. Anyway, it soon became obvious that the most aggressive magpie was attacking and dominating the hawk, eventually pinning it to the ground by standing on it and stabbing at the hawk's head with its bill. The hawk fanned its tail and desperately tried to break free, but the magpie remained in control and started to pull small feathers from the raptor's head and neck.

When the watcher's friend arrived they decided to try to rescue the hawk, and as they approached the magpie flew off. The hawk looked moribund, apparently having lost an eye and some blood. However, the victim still had a strong heartbeat so the rescuers wrapped it in a blanket with the intention of seeking the help of a local bird-care specialist. But within a few minutes the hawk was dead.

Domesticated animals, too, can behave in surprising ways, such

*April*

as the time when, as a lad, I used my air rifle to bag a sparrow in the garden. The bird tumbled out of an apple tree to fall wounded in the chicken run, where it hopped about.

Before I could get to the bird, the chickens tore the sparrow to pieces, swallowing the last morsels as I arrived. Yet only minutes before several sparrows had been pecking among the feet of the hens without so much as a wing raised in anger. What caused the Rhode Island Reds' sudden change of temper?

I suppose the obvious answer is that the hens saw a weakness and took advantage of it, but the injured sparrow was quite calm and not clearly disadvantaged. It stood upright and did not flutter unduly before the frenzied attack. The chickens, however, had other ideas and clearly spotted something vulnerable about that sparrow.

Even ducks can be surprisingly bloodthirsty things. A mallard, for example, will suddenly look up from its gentle dabbling to drown a passing water vole. The reason for this is unknown.

Sometimes the inter-relationship between major predators is equally puzzling. For example, tawny owls sometimes prey on goshawks, but there are plenty of records of goshawks taking tawny owls – and these involve adults as well as immatures.

Because we are more familiar with their sleepy, daytime image, we tend to think of owls as rather passive creatures, merely mustering enough energy to take a rodent or two each night. The truth is that they are powerful and voracious hunters, sometimes preying on each other.

The tawny owl is a particularly strong and aggressive bird. Among other raptors, it sometimes takes the barn owl, little owl, long-eared owl, sparrowhawk and even its own kind.

Even the little owl is not so friendly as it appears, winking at you from a fence post before flying off with a worm by daylight. It is a powerful and formidable predator, frequently taking prey larger than itself, including the magpie.

Mammals, too, are often far less cuddly and predictable than they appear. A grey squirrel may look pretty while gnawing at nuts, but some stalk and eat small birds such as house sparrows, and they are known to attack and kill red squirrels.

Neither is Mr Hedgehog merely a rooter and grubber of low life and plants, the friendly character of children's books. He, too, has a 'sweet tooth' for flesh and happily kills and tucks into birds, small mammals and reptiles.

79

So you see, there are plenty of individuals in the animal kingdom. It is wrong to slot any species firmly into a rigid niche because there will be many times when it surprises us. All are constantly varying their diets and behaviour in that evolutionary spiral we call survival of the fittest.

1991


## Game out of Season

When we were visiting friends in darkest Northants on Good Friday a hen pheasant burst up from the hedgerow to commit suicide against my car. As I prepared this free meal back at home a brace of young Rustici peered inquisitively over my shoulder for another object lesson in avian anatomy. With a mixture of disgust and fascination, they were magnetised by my crude surgery, which allowed curiosity free rein among the twining entrails. But here was a 'first' for them as – remarkably still intact – there was a fully formed egg about to be laid. Further in among the nameless organs were yolk sacs at different stages of development.

I did not eat that particular egg, for the boys wished it to be blown for their 'museum', but I have eaten pheasant eggs before: they are delicious. Once I thought it was probably my imagination that pheasant and duck eggs had an unusually high yolk content, but subsequently I learned that this is normal. This is because the amount of yolk in an egg varies from about 20 per cent in species which are blind, helpless and naked on hatching, such as blackbirds, to about 35 per cent for those ground-nesters which hatch with a downy birthday suit and must be strong enough to run about almost immediately.

1981


## Country Blues

With the first real spring warmth many people are lured into the countryside. But along with their picnic baskets and cameras they bring many problems, some borne of ignorance, others through sheer weight of numbers. Never before have so many people been encouraged to visit the land their forebears forsook and never has there been such a need to protect against the patter of eager feet.

Recently I happened to meet a council worker picking up litter along the roadside by my house, and I stopped awhile to sympathise with his unpleasant task. Yet he had a cheery disposition, perhaps through the ironic situation that man's thoughtlessness had saved him from the dole queue.

'How disgusting,' I said as the man paused to pick up a Coke can and a sandwich wrapper that some selfish traveller had lobbed out his car window. And, as he neatly tackled some paper, cigarette packets and unmentionable human cast-offs with his seizing device, I added: 'Surely the people who do this don't live locally!'

The man paused for a second or two and in an instant seemed to reflect on both his situation and the whole of humanity. He uttered a few words of sympathy and was outraged that an area of outstanding natural beauty could be treated in this way.

But the real answer was in his eyes: he did not have to say what I was thinking, that those of us who care so much for the countryside are wrong in assuming that most others share the same views. They do not. Not only are there legions of folk who regard country roads as no more than ways to get from one town to another, but many others who would always choose the bowling alley before birdwatching when it comes to entertainment. It was ever thus.

Nonetheless, we must never abandon any sector of the community as a hopeless case and can only hope that the promising way in which environmental issues have come into our education system will eventually produce an entire generation who really care. In the meantime, some people may have been lured into a false sense of security by recent developments on the 'green' front. With all the hullabaloo over wildlife and countryside matters assailing us through every media outlet, we could easily assume that the green watchdog is winning. As the following facts show, he is definitely not.

In each of the last five years an average of nearly 14,000 acres of countryside has been developed. During the period 1984–90 more than 64,000 miles of hedgerow were lost in England and Wales, often simply through poor long-term management. The loss equalled 25 miles a day and totalled nearly a quarter of the national stock. More alarmingly, in my own patch of south-east England the rate of hedgerow removal has doubled since 1980. On top of that, dozens of nationally important sites, such as the nearby Hindhead Common and Devil's Punch Bowl National

Nature Reserve, are threatened by road development. Of course we should ease congestion and minimise fuel consumption, but not at the expense of our national heritage.

In 1990 three-quarters of the population of England visited the countryside at least once, together notching up a staggering 1,640 million trips and goodness knows how many footsteps. Significantly, many of these visits were to a small number of the most beautiful and sensitive areas.

Such an exodus can cause much damage and may destroy the very things which the people have come to admire. Footpath erosion and gradual change of route are the most obvious, but there is also damage to surrounding areas and disturbance of wildlife, especially where people wander off suggested routes. Gates, fences, signs and even farm buildings are frequently damaged, and the cost of repairs to something like a drystone wall can be considerable.

Yet at the same time farmers are expected to put up with and pay for this invasion, even though their incomes fell by an average 15 per cent in 1990 alone. Upland farmers have been particularly badly hit, with the price of wool falling and that of lamb plumetting by 50 per cent from 1989 to 1990, during which time their average income fell from £9,000 to just £3,000! At that rate they might do better recycling all that rubbish left behind by visitors!

There is no doubt that as the workforce has drifted away from the countryside, the woods, fields and moors have become much harder to police and care for. In the past the average estate had many workers such as ploughmen and gamekeepers to act as custodians, but now all we have is little groups of residents who mostly confine their interest to village centres. So I find the Rural Development Commission's prediction of up to 125,000 job losses in the countryside over the next five years quite alarming.

Workers who cling to traditional country life, following in father's footsteps, are often disadvantaged. A man on agricultural wages has little hope of competing with a town-rich incomer when buying a house. The RDC estimates that some 25,000 rural families need re-housing each year.

For many years now we have seen the gradual disappearance of the village shop, which leaves rural workers stranded unless they have a car, and even those with transport have to absorb extra petrol costs. But now we have the frequent disappearance of the village pub, too, as breweries sell off less profitable places during recessionary times. Most of the buildings make very attractive residences and are soon snapped up by relatively wealthy incomers. Sadly, the new boy may then find he has nowhere nearby where he can take a jar, and without the pub the village loses its heart.

Some people might argue that we already have enough reserved areas, what with the extensive acreages owned by bodies such as the Royal Society for the Protection of Birds and English Nature. But obviously the general public as a whole is not yet capable of caring for the countryside without their guidance. Furthermore, nationally important sites are no longer regarded as mere museums in which rare species are preserved.

There is a concerted effort to reinstate traditional country life in many of these precious places, as the old ways once worked well in harmony with nature. Therefore, although a body such as the National Trust may already own 570,000 acres plus one sixth of the coastline of England, Wales and Northern Ireland, I say dig deep into your pockets to help them. Through their lead our children may one day see the countryside restored to its former glory, and that litter-picker I met may find himself more usefully employed elsewhere.

1992

## Unlucky Swallow

The most surprising shot I ever saw while clay pigeon shooting was at a national championship, at a point of high tension in a shoot-off for one of the top prizes. The Gun killed stone-dead a swallow which rocketed across the path of a clay just as it was being broken. In no way could the Gun be blamed as the insect-chaser appeared in an instant and in my opinion was actually overtaking the clay. It could hardly have been called 'no bird'!

1986

## The Green Dream

Now the damp is out of the grass the drone of lawnmowers temporarily masks the equally urgent hum of bees. Both gardeners and insects weave industriously around the herbaceous borders, fuelled by the spring sun's gathering strength.

The smell of new-mown grass sweetens the breeze and the powerful scents of fresh flowers are as aphrodisiacs for low-spirited souls. Only on rare nights does frost hinder the advancement of the season, and by day we are assured that winter is finally vanquished.

The swallow is back on the television aerial and the skylark is suspended by chains of music above the thrusting barley. Sam the cat slumps on the red-brick path, the blackbird warbles contentment and the idyll of English spring is writ large on every aspect. Every corner is painted in bright colours and every way busy with townsfolk in search of refreshment.

It is a familiar scene and, of course, there is little new beneath the sun. No sudden appearance of new species to surprise the observer, no catastrophic reversal of seasons and no major overnight shift of society to devastate our beloved land. Only the slow demise or ascendancy of familiar birds and animals according to habitat or climatic change, mere hiccups in weather patterns and the insidious movement of man in response to varying prosperity. Yet our fascination with detail remains, and in this, as in every century, we scribes do our best to record the complexity of it all.

For some the attraction of the countryside is centred on an unending search for the truth, through a meticulous study of sciences such as botany and ornithology. For others the irresistible magnet is amenity and sport – shooting, fishing, hunting, rambling, birdwatching, orienteering, canoeing and much, much more.

But there is an equally important group who seek no more than good, old-fashioned peace, a place in which to avoid an often humdrum destiny, and the chance to let the poet loose.

I think it is fair to say that no subject has been more important to the English bard than nature in its teeming variety, and none so vital in the civilization of man as the poetry of countryside. From unproclaimed medieval monks to swinging Sixties songsters, from supreme Shakespeare to experimental Spender, again and again the pen dips into the inexhaustible well of outdoor life and the country scene.

Fortuitously, our romance with nature is instinctive and largely irrepressible, for if ever we should lose our love of the land and give way totally to the advance of sterility and uniformity then England would cease to be a green and pleasant land and life on earth would perish out of time.

Yet as I write, reclining in full April sunshine in my garden chair, the green dream remains. A humble robin – national symbol of serenity – trebles peacefully while his more energetic mate constantly darts back and forth to her nest in a tall, thin juniper. She alone builds the cup of dead leaves and moss, lined with hair and a feather or two, but at least he will share the feeding of the young.

Their juniper is one of a pair which guards the steps to the lower garden, and sadly, since October's hurricane half tore it from the earth, clings to life only with the aid of a support. Whether or not it will recover fully to stand sentry in the 1990s I do not know, but now I am pleased that I gave it a chance as its dense cone continues to offer refuge to birdlife. One more family of robins to extend the dream, to fill the garden with music when autumn broods in the shrubbery, and to charm the grimness from the gardener's face when snow shrouds his passion. A succession of redbreasts to inspire new poetry and prose just as their ancestors did so successfully for Shakespeare and Keats.

1988

## Death in the Garden

One sad evening in late April I looked up from my desk in the bay window to see my neighbour's cat at the robin's nest in the juniper. Cursing and cussing we rushed to the rescue, but to no avail. There was no sense in recrimination as the maligned moggie might well have been ours.

The mossy nest which had taken so long to create was pulled asunder and just one chick remained alive. One naked nestling panted feebly on the grass, rocking from side to side in black confusion, its eyes still unopen. An ugly, pathetic offspring which bore no resemblance to its bold, bright parents.

Feeding the bird presented no problem, for it responded readily to our scratching approach, thrusting its gaping, yellow gullet upwards to accept worms and insects. But, despite every care, it died the next day through, I believe, our inability to maintain its body temperature at a constant, high level. Of course, it could have sustained internal injuries, but whatever the cause of death the poor bird departed this life without so much as a glimpse of it.

In the meantime, another robin brood successfully fledged from an identical juniper just 40ft away – surprisingly close for these pugnacious, highly territorial birds. Fortunately, the second pair nested several feet up, whereas the unlucky ones were right at the base of their tree.

1988

## Kamikaze Beetles

While we watched the softly croaking chorus of frogs at the pond edge a hitherto unobserved monster of the deep surfaced for air. It was the great silver water beetle. This, the largest of all British coleoptera except the stag, was so named because of the bubble of air which covers its underside as it swims down after poking its head out of the water. Although its larva is carnivorous, the adult is vegetarian, unlike the slightly smaller and much commoner great diving beetle, which is very fierce and will even eat small fish, newts and tadpoles, not to mention its own kind at a pinch. We were especially pleased to see this beetle because its numbers have diminished catastrophically during this century.

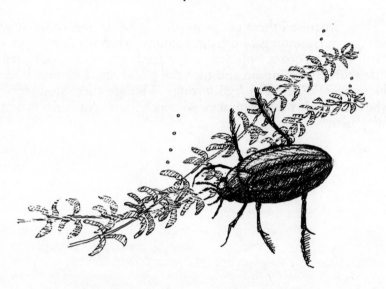

One fascinating phenomenon concerning water beetles involves their night flighting to colonise new ponds. Apparently these kamikaze creatures achieve a considerable height but when over suitable water simply fall out of the sky. I was intrigued to learn that many have been baffled by moonlight gleaming on glasshouses and have dropped onto these by mistake.

1981

## Ulterior Motives

This year's first cricket match, a day-long affair on 28 April, was held amid gargantuan, swirling snowflakes! But my boys were pleased at the sport's return, for these very young colts in this most English of games are more than happy to flip over the scores all day long knowing full well that such 'helpfulness' will bring lashings of cream cakes and rolls come teatime. And, unless the 'visitors' are unusually ravenous, six eclairs and a dozen sandwiches might well be considered just the average young scorer's portion! If such untroubled days of youth bring envy to me now, in my 'mid-term', how precious will they seem through the rushing spectre of my dotage.

How organised these chaps in pristine white are: sport in such pleasant surroundings, fresh air, suntans (when it's not snowing!), lunch in the boozer opposite, more fresh air, scrumptious tea, a little more limbering up and then the grand finale inquest back in the boozer. Where did *I* go wrong? Who are these stout fellows whose correct routine makes so much time available for pure enjoyment?

1985

# *May*

## Ups and Downs

Very recently we found a delightful place to picnic, high on the South Downs near Storrington, where we happily parked on the edge of a fairly empty 'official' spot. There the tiny bright-blue speedwell and the yellow coltsfoot quivered in the fresh breeze while rushing windscreens glinted across the great, flat weald below. All was tranquil as we ate our sandwiches and the peewit passed with his throwing up and down of black and white.

After eating, we took a path at random and walked within the limits of the children's legs. The grass was thick with meadow pipits, the turbulent air resonant with the spring-filled song of the newly arrived willow warbler in the gorse and the raucous calling of the corn bunting on a fence post. We marvelled at how flimsy butterflies mastered the strong air currents and how the very thin, flint-filled chalk soil could grow any crops at all. The unending struggle of farming there was epitomised by a huge lorry that repeatedly strained up the hill with ton after ton of manure to add to the mountain already there.

Soon we were on the South Downs way itself, only to have the idyll torn asunder by three buzzing motorbike scramblers. We jumped aside as passing ramblers' lips quivered on the brink of shouting abuse. But that was not all. The three easy riders dismounted, took their whirring hornets through a gate and went up onto the fragile turf of a high, hidden farm field, to engage in what my younger son described as a series of 'wheelies'. By their guilty manner it was obvious that they did not have permission to be there. Farming is difficult enough up there without that unnecessary erosion.

1980

## Bird Casualties

Amid all the wild energy at nest time there are many minor tragedies. One blackbird was so proud of his nest he pinched the tag from one of our roses and named his home Super Star. Two weeks later a cat killed his entire brood.

A local thrush did not even get that far. Sadly, I found him dead at the roadside with tiny strips of paper he had torn up for his nest still held tightly in his bill.

1980

## Spell of the Rook

For many decades early May has been the traditional time for gathering the 'harvest' of rooks. Mostly using .22 or specialist 'rook' rifles (including airguns), countrymen have sallied forth to bag the 'branchers' – the tender, young birds about to fledge from the rookery – before the foliage is too dense to see them. But today only a few gastronomic adventurers bother to cull rooks for a pie.

Certainly I would not now kill any rook for, on balance, it is highly beneficial to agriculture and, more importantly, for me at least it epitomises the timelessness of unspoilt, rural England. Although I am opposed to a close season for the woodpigeon and magpie, if threatened European legislation brings protection for the rook then I shall not be sorry. It is a magical bird, a species of great resilience, whose communal life marks the passage of seasons in a swirling cloud of animated punctuation marks.

Whenever I see rooks on their daily round I am immediately filled with deep calm; all the turmoil of twentieth-century life drifts away and I am transported back to medieval times. Watching the black sorcerers flap and tumble in unhurried, homeward flight – especially into a winter sunset – I am transfixed; all the vulgar trappings of today dissipate before my eyes and I am drawn into another, magical world.

But sadly, so-called Merrie Englande knew little science and our superstitious ancestors gave little quarter to all 'black-hearted' crows. The rook appears in British literature from the eighth century onwards, and study of the records reveals that the relationship between rooks and man has always been uneasy. As Britain's blanket of woodland was cleared to make way for the rook's favoured farmland habitat, and the bird's population subsequently increased, then persecution began in earnest.

Rooks have always been regarded as pests on newly sown or ripening corn, but without guns there was little man could do to thin the rookeries. However, after James I of Scotland introduced his 1424 Act for the destruction of the rook there was a more concerted effort, and later villagers began to set nets to trap the birds coming down to corn. In addition, boys were commonly employed to scare all crows from the fields. Indeed, it is not so long since this practice died out as I still know one or two retired gamekeepers who started their working lives bird-scaring in the early years of this century.

But the rook really is a charismatic bird. Why, even in the dark days before the Industrial Revolution there was something about it that touched the hearts of many men. And its readiness to live in man's company always helped to give it the benefit of the doubt when it came to an assessment of the bird's diet.

Thomas Bewick summed it up in 1797: 'We have always had occasion to observe that they are useful in preventing a too great increase of that destructive insect the chafer or dor beetle, and in this very special way make large recompense for the depredations they may occasionally commit on the cornfields.'

Charles Dixon was another rook enthusiast. In 1880, he wrote: 'To visit a rookery in the building time is a real pleasure . . . There we see them perched on the topmost branches of trees, seated in their nests, or winging their way through the trackless air. What an animated scene!'

Dixon also noted how disputes over nests often gave rise to 'combats of such a severe nature as to leave one of the birds bleeding and dying at the foot of the tree, and throwing the entire community into a fever of excitement and disorder'. Reading this passage reminded me of the first time I witnessed such a scene, though at the time I did not really appreciate what was going on.

I suppose I was about seven years old and, on one of many egging expeditions, I ventured into a strange wood with great oaks, elms and beeches which seemed to stretch on forever. For all I knew no one had been there for centuries. It was just the sort of place to fire a lad's imagination.

Anyway, after about half an hour I came across a huge rookery, and the deafening caws drew me ever on until I was right beneath the centre of activities. My little heart pounded with excitement as there was no rook egg in my collection, but I quickly realised that even my dogged determination would not take me up to those tree-top fortresses.

But as I rooted around in the undergrowth I came across a rook egg which had obviously fallen from the heights and miraculously remained unbroken. So I smartly popped it into my binocular case (to avoid suspicion) filled with cotton wool and triumphantly marched off home. I also carried off the corpse of a rook which would be boiled in a tin can in the garden, the meat picked off and the skull added to my collection.

In those days I would also bury bird and mammal heads to let the ants clean the skulls, but at the time of my visit to the rookery the ants were not very active. In any case, there was always the risk that a cat would dig up the body, and the rook's great dagger of a bill was a superb prize from which I would not be parted.

When I returned to that rookery the young birds were sitting outside the nests and on the branches, where they would remain until able to fly. The leaves were expanding, partly hiding the young from view, and one or two of these 'branchers' made tentative first flights from tree to tree. Meanwhile, the noisy adults dived about, trying in vain to get their innocent offspring to fly to safety.

Suddenly the wood fell quiet and I hid in the bushes in anticipation of some dire consequence. Immediately there were several shots and past my refuge in the bramble strode a mean-looking man with a string of dead rooks about his waist.

Later there were more shots, and as soon as I was sure the men were far enough away I raced from that ancient, haunted wood, never to return.

1989

## Life from Death

When I visited a famous gamebird shoot on the southern downlands last year I was shown the grave of a local poet, who had chosen to be buried in one of the most glorious spots imaginable. Not for him the higgledy-piggledy hotchpotch of memorial stones beneath the great yew in the parish churchyard, nor the stark regimentation of the city cemetery. No, our man of inspiration had chosen to be as near God as possible, in one of his favourite haunts, where the wind speaks the language of the seasons in no uncertain terms – soft and soothing in summer but penetrating and moaning in winter.

Another favourite burial place of mine lies in a dense, mixed wood on the Solent coast, adjacent to my old school. There, in Stanley Park, I used to creep, crawl and climb in search of finch, warbler and woodpecker nests, and it was on such an expedition that I found the little cluster of graves, mossy and half-hidden by riotous rhododendrons. It was (and still is) the very private resting place of beloved pets, remembered in stone from the more tranquil decades of the early twentieth century. Of course, I liked to pretend that I alone knew this place and that it was the subject of some deep, dark mystery, but over the years, as the park was tidied up and attracted more visitors, the burial ground became obvious to every passer-by and I was sad that its privacy had been invaded.

Graveyards have always fascinated me, both for their crumbling history and their largely unappreciated role as mini nature reserves in a country where all space is at a premium. The churchyard is one of the most reassuring and enduring features of our landscape and there are some 20,000 of them in England and Wales. They are found in almost every habitat, wherever man has settled, from wild and rugged coast or island to mountain, moorland and woodland. Within them lives a huge and diverse community of birds, mammals and flowering plants, not to mention less popular but equally important life forms such as fungi, lichens, ferns, mosses, amphibians and insects. In many areas the churchyard is the only place where you are likely to encounter a whole host of wildlife, from the butterflies and anthills which were once so common about the fields to grasshoppers and 'bugs' such as beetles.

Flowers, of course, thrive in churchyards for, although more recent graves are generally surrounded by well-kept areas of grass, there are also less disturbed areas where longer growth may flourish and only occasional cutting is a positive benefit. Furthermore, the absence of chemicals in the form of weedkillers and fertilisers gives all a great boost, providing almost ideal conditions for colonists from the preserved meadowlands commonly adjacent. Some rural parishes even dispense with much of the grass cutting and let sheep in to graze; and there are few domesticated animals better for plantlife than the sheep.

Should churchyards ever be decreed a waste of space, Britain will be greatly impoverished, both scenically and spiritually, not to mention environmentally. Churchyards are not often the haunts of rare species, but they are almost always havens for a host of what were once 'everyday' plants and animals, in a land where anything wild has to be justified to the unseeing.

1987

## By the Woodman's Hut

Seven months after The Great Storm, vast tracts of forest remain devastated, many foresters having had time only to clear the main tracks. Many minor trails and deep recesses may wait for years for the tidying teams. Now coded paint marks on trees mean little as the work programme has been thrown into confusion.

Recently, on the year's first day of high humidity and thunder, I set out to explore one of the great woods close to my home. Along the way I paused to admire an old woodman's hut, suddenly visible from the path after cloaking trees had been felled by the scything wind. The rough-hewn planks were barely tight enough to support the rusty, corrugated iron roof, yet sufficient shelter remained to protect me from a sudden downpour.

Here was but an echo of those long, hot days when bronzed men paused in their tree planting to take a well-earned sandwich within cool walls or stash their sturdy tools at day's end. I could imagine them arching their strong backs here during one of those golden autumn days which were so common earlier this century. Would the gangs ever return to make order out of this unprecedented destruction? For now their plantation is entirely in the care of wild creatures. The smothered ride where their hut moulders away is the haunt of deer, fox and rabbit, and the trees about pulsate with birdlife.

The songburst of morning was scarcely diminished by the great raindrops which sliced the still air, bombing the spiders' webs strung precariously around me. But as soon as the sunshine returned there was newfound vigour and insects clustered in shafts of light.

From some unseen, lofty pinnacle a blackbird scattered his music in all directions above the canopy, while in the deepest shade, where layers of dead branches marked the passing years, a wren erupted in a song of unbelievable power. Between these two, the great tits, blue tits, willow warblers, chiffchaffs, robins and chaffinches bubbled over in proclamation of summer, all the while their vibrant leads accompanied by a hidden chorus of woodpigeons and turtle doves. And that touch of mystery was added by the cuckoo which encircled me with his plaintive call, never revealing his exact position.

Half hidden by younger trees, lay the mossy stump of a massive beech. What tales of the wild that old gentleman of the woods could have told. But now his head was barely raised above the soil, overrun by ants and suffering the indignity of being anointed with rabbit droppings.

Then came the full power of the sun and the brimstones took wing, tracing paths of sulphur along the fresh, green rides. First three singletons and then a pair, the bright yellow male wobbling slowly along in courtship flight, just an inch or two below the near-white female. Apparently oblivious to me and every other creature which stirred in their path, they floated along through the trees with deceptive agility, their frail wings not once brushing the foliage through which they passed.

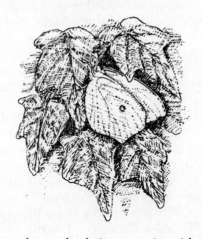

By virtue of its colour, the brimstone is said to have been the original 'butter'-fly, the term eventually being used to describe other insects in the order Lepidoptera.

Last year all this natural wealth was threatened by the greed of a big oil company, but now the men in hard hats have gone away to try their luck in more profitable areas. Their intrusive signs and prefabricated buildings are falling into disrepair, gently being swallowed up by the forest, just like the woodman's hut has been. I hope that the advance of technology or the impoverishment of man never brings the mineral moguls back. Theirs is a fleeting, alien world, far removed from the gentle regeneration which has sympathetically shaped these Surrey hills over many centuries.

1988

## Video Man

Deep down I knew that no good would come of my rebellion against rusticity. It was bad enough being ribbed about allowing a microwave into my rural seat, but surely not a video! Surely quiet rustication required – nay, demanded – baking by Aga and making one's own entertainment when day was done.

But I would have none of it – the time had come to enter the twentieth century. So the said machine – apparently state of the art – was duly installed and sat quietly in the corner, viewing me sceptically through its cold, blue electronic eye.

Next day came the first opportunity to engage the new toy. A favourite TV programme coincided with dinner, so Video Man to the rescue. We could chomp away and linger over the last mouthful of Claret with smug satisfaction, knowing that *The Darling Buds of May* was being recorded for subsequent viewing at our leisure.

Scarcely had dinner – and taping – begun when the power failed and it was time to light the candles. Fortunately, there was still just enough light in the dusk to facilitate groping for matches. But – wait a minute – why should the juice go off on a fine, still evening? In this area, with a whole labyrinth of overhead wires overshadowed by trees, we rustics are used to frequent power cuts, but only during gales and blizzards.

It was not until the next day that I discovered what had happened: a hot-air balloon carrying four people had hit an 11,000-volt cable and interrupted the power supply to about 1,000 scattered homes and farms. Not only that – sparks from the shorting cable had set fire to nearby Thursley Common. Luckily none of the balloon passengers was hurt.

1991

## Ghostly Impressions

When we visited my brother for dinner, I was shown a remarkable photograph taken by a friend. It clearly showed the impression of an owl on her bedroom window, but the photographer had not found any bird nearby. Surely the confused night pilot had wobbled off with at least an awful headache.

On investigation, I discovered that this is by no means a very rare occurrence, but a 'picture' as clear as this one is truly exceptional. Nonetheless, the precise reason for such 'imaging' remains baffling.

The Royal Society for the Protection of Birds told me that general opinion puts the phenomenon down to 'feather dust', and two leading bird photographers I spoke to offered the same explanation. But surely this requires further investigation because it would need a very dusty bird to leave something like the imprint I saw. Perhaps we should not rule out the part played by dust already on the window.

Other examples quoted to me involved tawny owl, kestrel, sparrowhawk, heron and pigeon. Now all these birds have something in common – their plumage contains a high proportion of powder-down feathers, whose precise function is not fully understood.

Powder-down feathers produce a fine powder, and in some species – such as pigeons – the powder grains come from cells surrounding the future barbules on developing feathers. In other species – such as the heron – parts of the actual feathers disintegrate to produce the powder. The most specialised powder feathers consist of little more than barbules attached by strips to the calamus, and are clogged with powder. It is assumed that species such as birds of prey and fish-eating herons need a liberal supply of powder to soak up the blood and slime which come with their everyday diet and could affect flight performance as well as temperature control.

However, even assuming that there is sufficient powder present, how on earth can it be distributed evenly enough to form such a perfect picture on impact? And what makes it stick to smooth surfaces so well? Oil on the plumage perhaps? Or could it be static electricity or grease on the glass?

Another point may be worth considering. History is laced with stories of 'ghost' owls – phosphorescent birds whose existence science is prepared to support. Apparently these birds occasionally roost in hollow trees where luminous bacteria or the common honey fungus, which is also sometimes luminous, live on the rotten wood inside. When particles of the decaying wood covered with luminous bacteria or fungus stick to the plumage the ghost owl becomes reality. Perhaps, when such luminous specks are mixed with a generous sprinkling of powder-down, a 'ghost' owl becomes a prime subject for window-printing.

1991

## In Touch with Badgers

Late in the evening I was at Heron's Pond, where the air was heavy with the scent of blossoms and the grand smell of cows in hot pasture. The air swarmed with insects while gossamer and dandelion seeds passed miraculously where not the slightest breath of wind was apparent. Midges seemed content to circle in rhythmic cliques heedless of me, yet a general itchiness indicated that some six-legged suckers had sampled my sweetness.

As I returned home along a woodland bridleway a grey-black shape 'flowed' across the path some ten feet ahead. That shape was rapidly pursued by another and I hurried quietly on until I could see what had run into the undergrowth. Suddenly, about 35 feet away, two well-grown badger cubs shuffled back onto the path. One raised his head, sniffed and ambled off. But the other just buried his snout in the herbage and foraged towards me. I could hardly be upwind of him for there was no detectable wind. He came so close I could hear him chewing and chomping. He seemed to be eating plant roots and insects, and perhaps a snail.

I know badgers are very short-sighted but this was indeed a surprise: it seemed as if he was going to bumble right past me. On he came till, just two feet away, he stopped and concentrated on some subterranean morsel his snout had detected. I felt an impulse to bend down and stroke him but remembered how powerful badger jaws are. Then he raised his head, puzzled over my leg, moved forward and actually poked my shoe with his snout. Immediately he retreated, but it was a controlled exit, and when he was about twelve feet away he stopped and looked back, as if to say: 'I've never sniffed one of those before'.

1980

## Dawn Chorus

Even on cloudy days there is no denying May's great natural stimulus – the marked increase in day length. Leave the bedroom curtains open and you will be amazed at how much earlier the light awakens you. Leave the window open, too; not only for that magical aroma of a May morning, but also the dawn chorus, which is at its peak.

Well into May there begins that all too short period when there is such a hustle and bustle about the land that even the short night seems vibrant with the energy of wildlife. Owls, of course, bring the darkness alive, but even some of the daybirds may sing to the stars. And then there is the nightingale, who always deems his song so precious as to be worthy of the ears of both night and day.

As dawn approaches, increasing intensity of light stimulates the main chorus, though the birds are known to have a circadian rhythm which generates a state of readiness. There is a critical light level at which each species begins morning song, though this is tempered by other factors such as the precise period in the breeding season. Thus all species start up in a clearly defined daily order, but all singing is delayed on dull, rainy mornings. Generally it is the insect eaters which start first and the seed eaters follow.

The best place to study this is not from the bedroom window

but actually out in the bluebell woods, where the sweet-scented flowers and good earth will make your nerve ends tingle. But do get out very early, while the eye of the poacher still gleams in the black woods. As you wait on the tail of night, a burst of nightingale song may startle you, but generally only a whispering breeze stirs the bushes.

Perhaps one-and-a-half hours before sunrise, the restless peewit may call his name from across the water meadow, and about an hour before dawn the cock pheasant will crow, for he is astir long before most people imagine. Slowly he abandons his tree roost, a student of robotics pausing here and there to pick unsuspecting spiders from the dew-laden cover. He is in no hurry, for there is now such a long day in which he will work his way over to some favourite sunspot.

When the skylark's trilling fills the air – often before there is any trace of light in the sky – we know that dawn is definitely on the way. Next comes the cuckoo, who wanders about the glades alerting the woodpigeons. They, too, have a very leisurely approach to daybreak and it is some time before their half-hearted, isolated coos develop full-throated ardour and amount to anything like a chorus.

Then comes the mainstay of the choir – the blackbirds, thrushes and warblers – and when the wren's incredible vivacity bursts upon the scene at, say, 4.15am, the tumult is approaching its peak.

Careful observation can detect the great wave of song beginning in the east and burgeoning west for about an hour of sheer exuberance, after which the countryside suddenly seems quite empty. And although we like to think that the avian chorale is a marvellous expression of joy, its prime function is no more than the marking and confirmation of territory after a period of inactivity and silence.

The dusk chorus, with its reversal of 'batting order', is far less intense, though its purpose is similar and undoubtedly it casts a spell of its own. Blackbirds often open with their dreamy melodies, and never will I tire of their warbling from my chimney pot just at the hour the sun goes down. But, when the 'day boys' have finished, the nightingale will always have the last word.

1985

# The Bee and the Blackbird

Blackbirds are transporting great beakfuls of food to their noisy young in the top of a cypress at intervals of no more than thirty seconds. But another pair, on the other side of the house, have had mixed fortunes. They chose to nest in the honeysuckle which is very close to my neighbour's bird table and also very close to where we put our scraps. Unfortunately for the mother of the honeysuckle brood we had an indoor chrysanth infested with greenfly. We put the plant outside to dust it with a suitable insect killer and avoid inhaling the poison. Unknown to us there was a bee in the plant. It crawled out covered in dust and, as my wife watched out of the kitchen window just yards away, the female blackbird flew down. Before we could do anything the bird tweeked the poor bee twice with its beak then swallowed it whole. The wretched insect would, according to the puffer pack label, die anyway. But what of the blackbird? Well, a week later she appears to be all right.

1982

# Dusk Excitement

Deep in the woods I sat within the still grandeur of four ancient beeches, at one of my favourite pondering places. There the changing bark still revealed that CED was in love with PM in 1953, but older testimonials were grown out of recognition. All around me woodpigeons pulsed and glided between the long buds, down to their ivied roosts while silent squirrels floated from bough to bough, suddenly to appear statuesque at my side. Now the blood-sap flowed again, through veined, creaking branches which drooped over the field edge where a thousand creatures would forage before the bronze leaves fell again. High above, an unsuspecting crow treated me with the lesser range of his throaty vocabulary while his awkward feet showered me with twigs.

As dusk slipped among the trees and I left it to the very last minute to creep back to *my* roost, a strange tension crept over me and I became acutely aware of every sound and movement. It was as if I were a prey, yet I relished the excitement.

Back in the fields I wondered at my earlier presumption of impending darkness. The cold north wind had parted the cloud long enough for the sun to cap the grey of High Button with the same magic tints which had often held me spellbound in childhood. As I approached the pond a teal swept in on the last traces of daylight. Fish broke the surface where bats traced a repetitive line, and the rustle of night silenced the last thrush.

Back indoors, a moth fluttered out of the darkness to the magnet of my reading lamp, only to patter vainly on the glass; an emissary of nature sent to remind me of the unseen but unending vitality of night.

1980

## After the Deluge

Despite its dull, wet masquerade, May has delivered summer to our door. A very slight rise in temperature made me suspicious, but then a little bird told me so. But my first cuckoo of the year is only used to April showers and May flowers. It didn't fly all the way from Africa to miss the cricket and sit on soggy nests.

Irresistibly, Earth's recycled goodness erupts in a cascade of blossom and men revisit neglected garden corners. This third week of May is crucial for pollination. If the blossom is not pollinated within the next few days it will not be viable. But bees are most reluctant to leave their hives to provide pollen when it is so wet and cold, and there are already genuine fears for the English apple crop.

Our herds have had a tough time too, with many fields just too wet to turn the cattle onto. However, winter feed has been exhausted in some areas and cows have had to be put out to grass. The result is thousands of acres of pasture turned into quagmires and the poor grass destroyed. Feed is at a premium and animals bellow their unease around the countryside.

Tractors have been unable to get onto fields, sowings have been well behind and goodness only knows what vegetable prices will be by the end of the year. One colleague blames it all on the comet!

Despite the persistent, cold north-wester, butterflies have occasionally taken to the sparkling air between thundery showers over my garden. Orange tips continue their apparent population ascendancy, wandering past as shuddering petals; brimstones dazzle like sunlight through the yellow leaves of early autumn, and the exciting glimpse of my first blue of the year confirms that at long, long last we are out of the darkness.

The wheelbarrow remains on the lawn, half full of weeds and dead vegetation and awash with the monsoon since I broke the garden fork back in the early dry spell. As the sun beams again the old cherry's tired and cracked limbs are cast in grey shadow across the wet grass where the blackbird runs in a worm bonanza. At the beginning of May the blackcap returned to warble from the riot of bramble which protects us from the main road and a week later the spotted flycatchers took up their traditional hawking stations. Above them the swallows and martins are back feasting on Surrey flies, but they certainly need to put in a long day to get sufficient sustenance at the moment.

1983

## Road Priorities

One of the more unpleasant aspects of May in the 1980s is the vast amount of wildlife which is killed on our roads. And, in this backward year, for many a rushing commuter the pathetic sight of a hedgehog ball or young badger lifeless in the gutter must have been the first indication that the seasons really were changing. Only this week I had to brake hard to let a rather moth-eaten old fox slip through the beam of my headlights. It is not that I specially like foxes, but one slams the foot down automatically when anything hits the tarmac hell-for-leather. But there is no doubt that I would try *not* to brake for or swerve around any wild creature if I thought that collision with another vehicle or risk to human life might occur.

1985

## Harvest of Hope

While the woodpigeon sits tightly on eggs halfway up a nearby ivied oak, once again I sow the vegetable plot with packets of enthusiasm rarely equalled by the harvest. But now at least all is tidy and, with luck, once this second drought has ended, straight rows of seedlings should soon fill the spaces between markers. Naked bean sticks await their creeping canopy and, as I hoe the finishing touches to my Garden of Eden, wobbling cabbage white butterflies spiral upwards together in crazy flight, probably hoping that my 'Greyhound' cabbages live up to their name.

1982

## 'Cloth of Gold'

Everyone has noticed the addition of bright-yellow fields to much of our countryside in recent decades. These brimstone seas of oilseed rape constitute a valuable crop qualifying for EEC subsidy. Originally the crushed seeds were wanted to yield lamp oil, which burnt with little or no smoke, but now the main interest is in producing oil for margarine so that there is less European dependence on American soya, a crop our climate will not support. Crushed rape seeds are also used in animal feed.

Fortunately for pigeon shooters, but unfortunately for farmers, the rape fields have boosted the woodpigeon population. But now comes the possible introduction of another EEC-promoted crop, and immediately one wonders what the effect on our birdlife will be – either as a food source or in replacing other crops.

The present 'cloth of gold' could soon be broken by patches of white – lupins, which the EEC will subsidise from July. They are grown for their protein-rich seeds, and might well be an attraction for farmers seeking an alternative crop now that the Brussels Commission is preparing to crack down on cereal surpluses, after their success in limiting dairy gluts. Lupin seeds will be used in animal feed, the protein content of the latest varieties grown in British conditions being up to 10 per cent higher than that of peas or beans.

Any variety among crop monocultures is welcome but the effects on our wildlife must be closely monitored.

1984

# Bagging the Green Vote

Sadly, in the run-up to the General Election, I feel that none of the major political parties really has the welfare of the countryside and traditional country pursuits at heart. What attention there is to matters rural and animal is basically cosmetic and remedial, revolving around expediency rather than a deep desire to carry out effective, long-term 'green' policies.

Yes, we have continuing 'official' interest in the shape of the Nature Conservancy Council and specialist conservation officers within organisations such as the Forestry Commission, but their budgets are abysmal and we rely very much on the enthusiasm of individuals. Even more we rely on the very important work of the voluntary conservation movement and the huge sums of money they raise through public donations. Isn't it about time that the *whole* of the population contributed substantially to maintaining our wonderful countryside and wildlife through the direct taxation system?

Almost everyone enjoys the occasional ramble through the fields and green lanes, yet the chances are that they will 'use' land now owned by bodies such as the National Trust or county naturalists' trusts, to which they have contributed nothing. Many will abuse the privilege by letting their dogs harass farm stock or wild animals such as deer, and the only reminders of their presence will be cigarette packets, plastic cups and sweet wrappers discarded along the way. And in my experience the overall blame cannot be apportioned to any particular age group.

There is no doubt that, as the total amount of wealth and leisure time in the country increases, interest in wildlife conservation and amenity landscape will grow; but, with further pollution and an increasingly mobile population to contend with, this alone will not be enough to preserve the green belt. There must be a much greater and wider appreciation of the environment as a resource, both spiritually and economically. Only a minister of conservation can handle such an onerous task and he must be a senior politician with substantial legislation and finance at his disposal, not merely a junior duper who fields the brickbats.

The Department of the Environment has not been a great success in dealing specifically with the conservation of animals, plants and habitat because, ultimately, it looks at everything from the purely selfish viewpoint of man. Thus we have this highly confusing situation where PR men commonly talk about conservation of nebulous things such as historic areas of towns. Laudable as this is, it is born of nostalgia rather than true conservation, and the sooner we have a minister concerned wholly with 'green' affairs the better. True conservation is about living, *changing* things, not preservation of museum pieces.

Despite all this tub-thumping I am optimistic for the future of both wildlife and fieldsports, just so long as public pressure maintains its present momentum. We should soon see if we are to be thrown a couple of 'green peanuts' in the manifesto promises, but no matter how good they might purport to be they should be viewed with caution.

In recent years this country has fallen behind in its fervour for the outdoors when compared with some other countries. Take West Germany, for example, where the 'green' vote has increased dramatically, yet that country has not only managed to retain its strong sporting tradition but also cope well with increased demand for 'live' shooting. Where countries such as the USA and West Germany score above us is in perpetuating a good public image of the hunter. Fortunately, we appear to be catching up and all the hard work put in by British sporting organisations and individuals in recent years has brought us improved standing in the eyes of purely conservation organisations.

One thing bothers me in all this. I have assumed that the great majority of the British public are interested in at least some form of nature, even if it's only the blue tits which drop in to feed on the garden coconut. In watching the plethora of TV wildlife spots and reading all about the fantastic growth in membership of worthy organisations such as the RSPB, World Wildlife Fund, county naturalists' trusts, etc, I have assumed that the vast unseen audience must all be active enthusiasts. Could I be wrong? Are there whole legions of immobile people whose 'green' interest is confined to those precious moments filmed for channelling through the 'goggle-box'? Could these same sedentary beings be the ones who irrationally toss their toffee papers or fish-and-chip leftovers out of the car in front of me when I'm stuck in one of those fair-weather traffic jams?

One thing I am sure of is that the more people there are interested in shooting and fishing in this country the greater are the chances of a 'balanced' countryside in the future. The hunter is the original conservationist. He knows all about leaving seed for the future and creating suitable, if not ideal, habitat. It is something which politicians long divorced from the land and its wildlife know nothing about and now is the time to re-educate them. There are exceptions, of course, and some have 'done us proud', but I guess there are far more who wouldn't know a haggis from a cow's tit.

Given all this superficial interest in the great outdoors, I wonder why so few of us vote for the 'greens'. Is it because, in the final analysis, we prefer our own creature comforts to an extra cuckoo or two? Could it be that only when the 'greens' become more realistic and, like all the other parties, start tempting us with peanuts, will they make the major breakthrough for which they hope, and largely deserve? Yes, effective conservation does cost money – a lot of it, and at the moment, given continuing government apathy, it seems that the major source of 'green' funds will be the very materialistic excess which purists are so quick to condemn.

For politicians June is a great election month. Modern man goes about his daily round with hope in his heart. The sun is on his back again after a diabolically long winter, flowers adorn his garden, days are 'long' and the annual holiday is beckoning. He is temporarily at peace with the world and is deluded into believing that the heart of the countryside is pumping strongly. But now, when we are off guard and vote for stability, let us beware of false promises from politicians who are jacks of all trades and masters of none. They are all professional empire builders who, given half a chance, will erect their monuments to bureaucracy in blue, red and neutral all over our cherished greenery.

1987

# *June*

## *Swift Summer*

Now young robins call from the bank which was buried in a four-foot January snowdrift. Swallows swoop about the cowshed eaves where a frieze of icicles hung in February. Ducklings dabble on water which was white with March ice. Grass is lush in fields which barely stirred in April and the dance of insects is unending about a riot of flowers fresh sprung in May. The business of reproduction is at a peak within both plant and animal kingdoms and already the year is half over.

With but two months before the departure of swifts and the first grouse over the butts, we rush and crush in a bid to get our money's-worth from summer's spiral. Yet how futile our grounded efforts are compared with that sickle of the skies, the swift, whose jet-set use of summer's short-lived resources approaches perfection.

1987

## *The Importance of Rivers*

You don't need to be an angler to appreciate a river. For many centuries civilized men of all persuasions have been moved by the waters, in their literature and art as well as work and sport.

Before the explosion of road and rail, rivers were important 'highways' on which man could move both himself and his products easily and economically. They powered his mills and often acted as foci for the establishment of centres of commerce around which communities grew up, such as Newcastle upon Tyne and even London itself.

Long before the development of rivers as workplaces, man the hunter took his toll of their fish and fowl. Even today, with the need for pot-hunting all but ended, we crop the 'ceaseless waters' with rod and gun in pursuit of sport.

Early bards inevitably found inspiration along the riverbank, where their ink flowed as freely as the Spey in spate, chronicling the colour of every season. But such men of letters were marooned out of time in what was still largely a rural economy with poor communications. It was not till Constable painted his hay wain that the river became symbolic of the English idyll.

Since the eighteenth century, Everyman has sought to dangle his toes in the waters inspired by unending portrayal of river scenes. Some favourite views have been consigned to canvas more times than magpies have crossed my path. But, like the pied birds, they don't always bring joy.

They say that all life began in the sea, so it is little wonder that all men regularly feel the need to dally next to the waters, whether they be fresh or salt. Water on tap is not enough. Something in our souls demands spiritual refreshment by $H_2O$ beneath the open sky.

Even in our island of highly crinkled coastline, the sea is too distant for many of us. Why even today I hear of folk who have never even seen the briny. Some, of course, are still young and will eventually make the pilgrimage, but others have grown too old to travel, and now have no wish to in an age when every mode of transport is regarded as fraught with danger and inconvenience. For such recluses local rivers and streams have taken on special importance.

Having been born in a coastal town and schooled on the shores of the Solent, the sea still surges in my blood. But, being a native of Hampshire, I am also mightily moved by rivers as that splendid county is the home of kings such as Avon, Test and Itchen – known worldwide to brothers of the angle.

But hardly surprisingly, my favourite remains that which was most local, and even now – at great distance – remains meandering around in my memory of childhood. Fortuitously, the valley of the Meon remains much as it was then, partly because the A32, which accompanies the river for much of the way down to the sea, has been 'saved' somewhat by upgrading stretches of the nearby A3 to motorway status. This is a much quicker route to carry the ever-increasing procession of surfboarders, scuba divers and yachties down from Smoke for their shot of saline.

So the Meon continues to wend its gentle way down through a very English landscape largely spared the demons of development. It idles past sleepy villages such as Droxford, where anyone prepared to walk can still enjoy the delights known to Izaak Walton, the 'Father of Fishing', when he stayed there in the seventeenth century. There is also simple refreshment to be had in a wealth of Olde English riverside pubs such as The Shoe at Exton.

The Meon remains a real fisherman's river – not the source of giants, but the breeding ground of brown trout to satisfy all. There

is pace and variety in the water and a rich procession of wildlife
to entertain those for whom the fish won't rise.

In early June such rivers really come into their own, still charged
with the run off of winter but also sparkling with the colour of
early summer and vibrant with regeneration of life. All around are
flowers to match most colours in the fly-fisher's box, and when,
like a heron, he stalks the banks and shallows, our piscator thrives
in the company of swallows.

Nearby, local lads dangle their illegal worms from the roadbridge,
ears and eyes alert to officialdom, both frustrated and excited by
the shapes which hang in the shadowy waters.

In the old days many of our southern rivers regularly burst their
banks to bring duck and snipe by the thousand to winter meadows.
Today most of the marshes have been wrung dry by expertly
controlled, but insensitive drainage programmes. Many rivers have
become little more than natural drains, largely devoid of all cover
and so polluted they cannot sustain the traditional web of life.

Now we must fight for every reed-bed and runnel. Admittedly
there has been some success, though mostly with compromise,
but I fear we will never return to the great ducking days of
Colonel Hawker. Old Izaak must be turning in his grave. Rivers
are not there only for the convenience of agriculture and industry.
Neither are they only indispensable elements of ecosystems. They
have become ingrained in our culture – important features of art,
literature and sport – and their further degradation will be a giant
step backwards in the civilization of man.

1988

## Rusticus Reincarnated

Coincidence has figured prominently in my life and, occasionally,
to such a degree that the words fate and reincarnation have been

mentioned. But even the photograph of myself at twelve years old reading the magazine I would work on from age twenty-nine, pales into ordinariness compared with this latest episode.

When I started writing the 'Country Scene' column in *Shooting Times & Country Magazine* I came across the word rusticus in my Latin dictionary and it was eventually selected as my pseudonym. At that time I was not aware of any other writer having ever used that *nom de plume*. Therefore I was flabbergasted when my wife, recently browsing in a local antiquarian bookshop, discovered a work not only written by one Rusticus but also concerned with natural history, the country scene and the same part of Surrey about which I now write. In 1849 John Van Voorst published *The Letters of Rusticus on the Natural History of Godalming*. Today this is a rare and expensive collectors' item, but I had to have it! Now, after reading and relishing every word, I still find it hard to believe that 163 years ago Rusticus I came to work only two to three miles from where I now live.

Rusticus I was Edward Newman. Born in 1801 of Quaker parents at Hampstead, he was sent to school at Painswick in Gloucestershire, and from 1817 to 1826 he was taken into his father's business of woolstapler in Godalming. From 1826 to 1837 he owned a rope-walk at Deptford, and in 1840 he entered into partnership as a printer. He was primarily an entomologist and in 1826 was one of the founders of the Entomological Club and wrote notes on insect and bird life. In 1833 he joined the Linnaean Society and in turn published an *Introduction to the History of Insects, Notes on Irish Natural History, History of British Ferns, The Zoologist* journal from 1843 to 1863, the *Illustrated History of British Moths*, 1869, and a companion volume on butterflies in 1870–71. He was also natural history editor of *The Field*, from 1858 until his death in 1876.

The Godalming book was based on letters by Rusticus sent to the *Magazine of Natural History*, the *Entomologist* and the *Entomological Magazine* in the 1830s and 1840s, and provides a fascinating insight into a Surrey countryside far removed from that of today.

When reading earlier writers such as Rusticus I it is often apparent how the whole community not only accepted fieldsports as a traditional, rational and integral part of life but also encouraged natural historians to use them as adjuncts to their studies. Even the church, through envoys such as Gilbert White of Selborne, condoned the shooting of rare wild creatures to be stuffed as specimens to satisfy the new 'curious interest'. Many of the old ways were hardly compatible with modern conservation methods and only tolerable in an age when a reasonable human population level brought few pressures serious enough to start a trend.

With universal acceptance of fieldsports in Victorian times, the gun was virtually a naturalist's everyday tool. Describing one of many trips to secure specimens, Rusticus I wrote: 'On a fine morning, towards the end of May, three of us mounted the Rocket Portsmouth coach; double-barrelled patent percussions having been previously duly prepared, and a suitable supply of copper caps, powder and shot, and the etceteras of bird-stuffing laid in; and the close of day found us at Newport, in the centre of the Isle of Wight.' In Surrey, water rails were 'not uncommon' and Rusticus I had 'often killed them while snipe shooting; three or four of a morning', while at Old Pond (Broadwater) 'has been killed the Hooper or wild swan, whose grand trumpeting note I have heard while skaiting here by moonlight . . .'

Some birds, though, were shot in excess of the demand for specimens, even those without culinary value. For example, Rusticus I wrote of the fern owl's (nightjar's) incredible 'song': 'I have almost been induced to think this noise serves as a decoy to the male mole cricket, this being occasionally found in the craw of these birds when shot. The bird is very plentiful on every heathy district in the neighbourhood. On Highdown Heath Mr Stafford shot forty-seven in a very short space of time.' But this slaughter also yielded new information about the species: 'I have no hesitation in saying that moths constitute its usual food, and these it swallows entire and alive. I have known instances of their ascending the throat, crawling out the mouth and escaping, after one of these birds has been shot by moonlight.'

Rusticus I's account of the 'furze wren' (today's very rare

Dartford warbler, virtually confined to Dorset and Hampshire) is interesting: 'We have a bird common here, which, I fancy, is almost unknown in other districts. I have seen them by dozens skipping about the furze. Perched on the back of a good, tall nag, and riding quietly along the pathside, while the foxhounds have been drawing the furze-fields, I have often seen these birds come to the tops of the furze. They are, however, very hard to shoot; darting down directly they see the flash or hear the cap crack, I don't know which. I have seen excellent Shots miss them while rabbit shooting with beagles.'

Of more interest to today's sportsman is the black grouse, a species formerly much more widespread, with a range that included Dorset, Hampshire and Surrey. Sadly, they disappeared from most English counties in the late nineteenth and early twentieth centuries. But Rusticus I knew them well: 'From time immemorial black grouse have inhabited Hindhead. This noble bird usually prefers wet swampy places; I have known a pointer, when up to his knees in water, stand at a black cock, but occasionally, especially towards August, the black grouse get upon the brows of the hills, and then is the time when they are principally sought after by sportsmen. It has always been a riddle to me that Gilbert White should speak of the black cock as extinct. I can truly say with him: "When I was a boy a black cock used to come now and then to my father's table". But this is not all. The sportsmen here kill them every year. I believe Mr Wheeler and some of the Paynes go out regularly on the 12th of August, and always bag some grouse – from two to four brace; their beat is about Churt, a district well known to sportsmen. But the great destruction of the black game and its consequent scarcity is attributable to the unceasing persecution of the broom squarers (they cut the common ling for the purpose of making brooms), most of whom have rusty old muskets that once belonged to the volunteers. Armed with these they follow the birds day and night, especially in deep snow, when it is easy to track them.'

The blackgame may have gone from Surrey but the magpie and little owl are certainly no longer 'uncommon' and, like Rusticus I, I can still enjoy many of the simple pleasures; for only 'Yesterday (15 February 1835) I had the good luck to meet with a companion as idle as myself, and as fond of the smell of the fresh air; and, without horse, dog, or gun we wandered up the sandy lane ...' where 'Nature has so long had her way'; and 'there is not a foot of surface but has its peculiar charms'.

1980

113

## The Umbrella Effect

It is surprisingly easy to become attached to an umbrella – or gamp as I have always preferred to call it. (Mrs Gamp was in Dickens's *Martin Chuzzlewit*.) Admittedly it is the cause of colourful expletives when a squall turns it inside out, or when it has been forgotten on the very day Met man Michael Fish got his sums wrong. But in the main it is a faithful friend, a protector through thick and thin, storm and tempest. I even took mine trekking around the foothills of the Himalayas, our very British party being so sun-shy.

That well-travelled brolly had been a present from my wife-to-be some twenty-five years ago and I loved its hand-stitched grip. Occasionally it was to be brandished in high and mightily smart places, or those where footpads might lurk. But it was very much a real campaigner, sporting bloodstained leather from shooting jaunts and a friendly pinpoint of light which sparkled through the black shield ever after the day I trapped it in a cab door.

I lost the dear old thing several times – at least twice on the London train, including the occasion when I went up the 'Smoke' for the launch of a distinguished book, drank far too much of an equally distinguished champagne, fell asleep on the return chuffer, missed my station, woke up in a panic and dashed off leaving poor brolly on the rack. Fortunately, BR's lost luggage office served me well.

Finally, along came the gales of early 1990, which blew my battered brolly into oblivion, the mangled spokes and shredded covering too much for even the most expert gampinologist. Alas, it was a dustbin job, and in the future I would step out with my swish, new, ash-handled model, another gift from my long-suffering wife, and one decidedly more in tune with my rustic image.

Unfortunately, I'm still awaiting the opportunity to put my new rig to the test because, ever since it was first unsheathed, the clouds (what few there have been) have refused to part. I have had to content myself with a little posing on mildly threatening days. Something to do with the Greenhouse Effect, I believe.

It seems to me that future brolly merchants are in for a tough time – in Britain at least. In the old days we could rely on steady winter downpours – and autumn downpours – and spring downpours – and summer downpours. And gamps ain't much good in a gale of wind, are they? It seems that too much tinkering with the environment has got us into a brolly fine mess and the weather has become about as predictable as the English soccer team's performance in this month's endlessly publicised World Cup. (I'll still be watching.)

Against this background of gloom and doom, I was mightily relieved to listen to Prince Charles's from-the-heart commentary on his splendid, recent TV film *The Earth in Balance*. Here at last was a kindred spirit with a clear understanding of the enormity and complexity of the world's ecological problems, including Operation Clean-Up. But, more importantly, his message was underlined by compassion and common sense rather than the greed and dogma rammed down our gullible gullets by politicians.

One has only to remember Mrs Thatcher's recent pathetic reaction to pollution control to want to retch. Perhaps Prince Charles should tell her bluntly – there's no point in increasing disposable income when the entire population is choking to death. And there's little sense in this country refusing to lead simply because other nations lag behind.

When it comes to noxious, toxic and nasty emissions, Britain has an appalling record, yet still we dilly-dally beneath the smutty wings of the American Eagle, rather than follow the new, relatively clean, ozone-friendly path of Europe. Come on you dirty British coasters – don't always put guineas first and Greens last.

Mind you, there's an awful lot we can do without headmistress Thatcher who, incidentally, despite her lack of greenery, need do relatively little to get votes given the present opposition. For a start, we can all take simple steps to reduce the fug we puff out of our cars every working day.

The fug reduction is achieved firstly by minimising journeys – through sharing cars, hopping on the bike, taking the bus, and all that sort of thing – and reaching destinations with minimum delays (personally I believe that improvement of the road network is essential to get rid of jams). Secondly, we can ensure that our mean machines are fitted with as much environmentally friendly gadgetry as we can afford – catalytic converters, etc – and are well maintained. But thirdly, we must look to the man behind the wheel.

There is no doubt about it: the amount of fuel we consume is significantly and directly related to our driving skills and common sense. Of course we all know that elbowing up the M1, as if on the starting grid at Brand's Hatch, is going to burn the high octanes in a mega way. But how many realise that sweet Miss Millie from Number 2 Acacia Avenue is also grossly inefficient when pootling down to Bournemouth at 25mph – in third gear all the way! The answer is to find out at what speed (generally about 56mph) your car is most fuel-conservative and stick to it as much as possible. Also, build up to this speed steadily rather than roar away, and think well ahead to avoid braking.

Not only will these simple expedients help save the world, but also your precious pennies – through fuel economy and reduced garage bills. And I don't suppose Mr Roadhog Medallion Man will get to the party much ahead of you. I always seem to renew his oily acquaintance at the very next set of traffic lights.

1990

## Green England

On Midsummer Day England should be nestling in its greenest mantle, an infinite blending of emerald and sage, lime and jade, Lincoln and olive, all concealing with deceptive peace the high-octane life of our late-nesting birds. But within a few weeks this lush palette will fade and dry up beneath the drowsy dust of July. And now, on 11 June, we have already enjoyed a hearty helping of early-summer sun.

Sadly, I have not been able to enjoy these orchid days as I had planned, for a slipped disc has lain me low for almost two weeks. Now all I can do is look upon the garden where most of the nests are already empty, magpies teach their young to steal my cherries, and roses blaze where the azalea has fallen.

1982

## Making Hay

Whereas May often bowls a googly, such as the heavy snow which this year carpeted much of northern Britain, June's deliveries can generally be relied upon. Now both cricketers and breeding birds can expect a good, solid innings without the constant cry of 'rain stopped play'.

But whereas the covers are now off the hallowed turf, the woods are fully cloaked in summer green, so much of the business of procreation goes undetected. Songbirds brood or gather beakfuls of caterpillars unseen within oak or ash, so for the naturalist this is a time for great patience and keen observation.

With midsummer approaching, the farmer considers his hay-making. But whereas grandfather simply looked to the ripe seeds of the yellow rattle or other natural harbingers to proclaim that cutting time was nigh, the modern approach is considerably more scientific. Our young graduate of the agricultural college is a

116

hard-nosed businessman who knows that, in order to maintain the nutritive content of the hay for use as fodder, the moisture content must be reduced from about 80 per cent, when freshly cut, to below 20 per cent, to prevent rotting, moulding, heating and possible combustion.

Haymaking usually starts with natural drying in swaths in the field. For me and many other folk, this is a magical time, not only for the sweet smell of the new-mown grass, but also because many birds, such as buntings and partridges, are then especially active and noticeable about the fields.

Nowadays, frequent turning by a tedder helps release moisture from the hay's under-surface. The tractor-drawn tedder has tines which rotate horizontally or vertically and throw the hay backwards onto the ground. These machines may be designed to ted a single row or combine two swaths into a windrow. Modern tedders have adjustable spring tines to vary the throw of the crop.

Hay drying may be accelerated by conditioning with a crimper – a machine with ribbed rollers between which the grass is crushed, speeding removal of sap by sun and air. Moisture loss is also promoted by chopping with a flail mower. And if rain or heavy dew is expected, swaths are sometimes windrowed at night.

Despite technical back-up, it is usually the experienced eye which judges when to collect the hay, generally with a pick-up baler when the moisture is about 25 per cent or below. Further drying takes place in temporary field stacks or in a large stack within the protection of a Dutch barn. Adding chemicals to the hay during baling has become a popular way to prevent mould growth. Those huge, round bales are virtually weatherproof and are usually allowed to dry slowly in the fields over several weeks. But to many eyes they are intrusive to the traditional landscape.

Many people prefer to leave the hay in the swath for a shorter period, bale it at 35–50 per cent moisture content and dry it by various methods in the barn. However, power costs add considerably to the expense, so making hay while the sun shines is, indeed, best.

On some remote islands, smallholdings and hill farms, where the use of balers and other machines is impractical, hay is still cut by scythes, dried in haycocks and stored in haystacks. Fortuitously, this provides visitors with a nostalgic trip into yesteryear, a fact not missed by cunning tourist authorities.

This clinging to ancient practices also provides a bonus for beleaguered wildlife. Whereas powered machines without recently introduced flushing bars devour young mammals, close-sitting adult birds, chicks and eggs, the slowly approaching scythe provides ample opportunity for escape. Furthermore, old Ned's gentle pass disturbs little nearby wildlife, unlike the roaring, rattling hardware which causes widespread desertion of clutches as well as abandonment of young.

Mechanisation of haymaking is one reason why the corncrake has declined so alarmingly in Britain. But it is not the only reason. The agricultural improvements which go hand-in-hand with mechanisation have severely reduced the diversity of plant species in grassland. And as the variety of plants declines, so, too, does the range of insects and other invertebrates which it supports; as a result the birds' food supply is greatly impoverished.

Furthermore, corncrakes require tall and rank vegetation when they arrive, but this has become very scarce, except in more remote areas where traditional farming methods persist. No one can reasonably expect a total return to the old ways because no amount of scything could feed Britain's current population.

But there must always be room for areas where traditional methods encourage corncrakes as well as corn. And we cannot expect farmers to foot the bill; we should all pay towards maintaining our heritage. Sadly, with conservation still in its infancy, the colour and diversity of June countryside and wildlife are still largely the result of fortuitous land management.

1993

## Oh! Deer

Well, it had to happen sooner or later. Last week a deer ran into the front of my car and, mercifully, was killed outright. It was a first-year roe – surprisingly forward – which, despite its small size, made a considerable dent in my vehicle. If I'd struck its mother, which only just missed me while running ahead of her offspring, the car – and me – might have been very seriously damaged indeed.

Before that I had a long series of near misses. South-west Surrey is one of the most densely wooded areas of the country and the increase in roe numbers has been considerable. Little wonder then that the number of road casualties has grown in proportion. In just one week recently I saw three dead roe on a nearby short stretch of road. And no doubt the number is far larger than we imagine as so many people, understandably, whisk the fatalities away for a freezer-full of venison.

But the problem is by no means a local one and acquaintances tell me that the situation is just as bad in many parts of Hampshire and Sussex, also densely wooded counties. I suspect that the main problem, apart from greatly increased numbers of both deer and cars, is lack of deer management. The animals are multiplying unchecked in many places where shooting is never permitted, from large nature reserves to relatively small gardens.

1989.

## A Lesson in Pigeon

Encouraging youngsters to participate in the sport of quarry shooting is more important now than at any time in our history. Undoubtedly this is the age of the endangered countryman, and with every season that passes the average schoolchild becomes more divorced from rural traditions. With mollycoddling door-to-door transport and a social system which worships the god Economics, he grows up thinking that success is all-powerful, and with scant regard for the quieter ways of nature. Our national shooting organisations certainly have their hands full in acting as surrogate fathers for tyros without paternal sporting guidance.

Now I did not have the benefit of an outdoors dad. But, what I did have in the late 1950s and early 1960s, when I was the Young Entry, was easy access to relatively wild places and an overwhelming passion for natural history. Now all the natural nooks have been squeezed out of many areas by so-called development and the microchip child can only tell if winter has arrived if snow happens to settle on his cap – and that is a rare enough occurrence nowadays.

Of necessity, an impecunious child must resort to forms of shooting which cost little more than a handful of cartridges – unless he has a rich uncle. Thus he would naturally gravitate to roughshooting, which provides the wonderful stimulus of variety, is the finest tutor in fieldcraft and does not rely on artificially maintained bag levels. At its heart are the rabbit and woodpigeon. Fortuitously, both are major agricultural pests and may be shot throughout the year.

During those long, long, lazy summer holidays, which legions of schoolkids will soon be enjoying, comes a wonderful opportunity for pigeon shooting, coinciding with at least part of the harvest in many areas of the country. It is up to us to accommodate their bursting wishes, to think back to the days when we were lucky enough to have the virtual run of the fields, and resist the temptation to shoo them away in selfish anger. Let them have a taste of the action and we will have converts for life.

The excitement on a lad's face as he squats in a pigeon hide for the first time in his life is a joy to behold. His mentor has placed the decoy pattern carefully on the laid corn or stubble, explained how to make a hedge or bale hide and now the two generations wait with shared anticipation. The boy is fired up by the release from interminable exams and the man flushed with pride as he relishes the opportunity to pass on the skills and lore which he, in turn, acquired from his father. It is a scene enacted nationwide, for the woodpigeon is very widespread in Britain.

As he peers through the hide wall, the boy begins to amass knowledge of wildlife which would never come through mere rambling. For a few hours he merges into the woods and fields, and the unsuspecting innocents abroad show him their many and varied secret lives. Leaf warblers creep through the canopy above, finch flocks surge about the field margins and a sparrowhawk pursues a songbird so closely the boy can hear the wind through its rushing wings.

His senses are assailed from all directions. Calls from the woods and crackling in the undergrowth cause endless speculation over the species which made them. Butterflies and flowers daub the landscape with every colour in his picture paintbox and the headiness of summer scents stimulates as never before.

In waiting he tries to remember everything he has been told, especially: 'Don't bob up and down like a Jack-in-the-box, don't wait with your finger on the trigger, don't release the safety catch until bringing the gun up to fire, do not point the gun like a rifle and do not switch from one bird to another if a flock comes over'.

Meanwhile the gun feels good in his hands and he cannot resist running his fingers along the cold, steel barrels and over the walnut stock, whose deep lustre is the product of many years' love and attention. He is almost addicted to the whiff of gunsmoke still lingering from the man's last shot, and the dog sits patiently between them, tongue drooling and panting vigorously after several retrieves, occasionally pausing to swallow or cock his head to listen to some interesting sound. He can feel the dog's tremendous heat even through his jeans.

Inevitably, the birds do not come so freely as they did when the man was holding the gun, and as soon as he loses his concentration to admire the handful of pigeon on the floor of the hide he misses a great opportunity. 'Didn't you see that one?' asks the man.

But eventually there is a good chance, the world explodes and the boy is delighted to have escaped relatively unscathed. He has taken his first shot! Fear and apprehension have been overcome and whether or not a pigeon lies dead on the ground is, for the moment, unimportant. Now that he knows the gun he can get to know the pigeon.

At the end of the day he will probably go home without a single bird to his credit, but he will delight in carrying those the man has killed; it is as if they were his own. And when he greets his chums who have been playing soccer or eyeing the girls in town he will appear to have been unsuccessful. But deep down he knows who the real winner is. He is the one whose mind has been stretched to new dimensions, his senses stimulated as never before. He is the one who has found richness and fulfilment and is already counting the days and hours till the next taste of the wild comes his way.

1990

## Eater of Larks and Squirrels

Our powerful cat is aptly named Samson, for his strength and appetite are prodigious. Even so, we were surprised last week when he added grey squirrel to his diet. The unfortunate rodent wandered too close to the bench on which Sam lay dozing in the sunshine, and after a merry caper about the garden was firmly seized by the shoulders.

Ironically, this should partly redress the ills of Sam's bird predation as grey squirrels have become a thorough nuisance in raiding the winter bird feeders. But it is as well that the garden birds need no summer feeding as Sam has now taken to sunbathing on one of their tables, effortlessly springing straight to the top.

Many of the smaller prey brought indoors are released for feline frolics about the furniture. Some evade capture and take up temporary residence. Thus we are no longer surprised to find, for example, field mice nesting in the oven gloves or robins flighting from room to room.

Most of Sam's victims are species which live in close association with man – robins, tits and so on, but occasionally a wilder creature is nabbed from surrounding farmland. One such was a skylark, which we managed to rescue, literally from the jaws of death. Not surprisingly, it was in deep shock, but after a night kept calm within the confines of a cardboard box, it flew off strongly, apparently unharmed.

Of course, June is a month when all predators, not just cats, find great bounty in the British countryside. Not only is there a peak population of naïve juveniles to feast upon, but also parents preoccupied with family feeding. The lush, full foliage and tall grasses also provide ample cover in which to stalk or ambush. How easily the cavalier sparrowhawk rounds the green copse to pluck the blackbird from the fence, and how simply the weasel snakes through the long grass to seize the vole. So different from stark midwinter, when the landscape is skeletal, no foliage obscures the hawk's dash and the rustle of dead leaves betrays the weasel's approach.

1988


## A Place for Insects

When gnats besiege my brow on a summer's evening I am the first to complain and reach for the Jungle Formula. And when caterpillars shred my cabbages I am not amused. But these minor nuisances certainly do not stop me lamenting the overall decline of Britain's insect population. Numerically at least, insects are the most important class of animals on earth and must be the concern of us all.

A relatively small number of insects aesthetically enrich our lives, notably the butterflies, whose bold colours brighten what is often a relatively dull and uniform environment. Yet, with only a little judicious planting, even townsfolk can attract some of Britain's sixty or so species to their gardens.

Then there are the crickets and grasshoppers which charm us with their chirruping about the hayfields, the lamps of glow-worms which still fire the night in favoured areas, and the dazzling damselflies which haunt the pondside.

Many others which are neither beautiful nor dashing still capture our imagination with their ingenuity and industry. For centuries the social life of ants has been held up as a model of economy, and the humble bee has been the inspiration of many lifetime studies. Such wondrous diversity and apparent intelligence have done much to redeem the legions of 'creepy-crawlies' which eat, wriggle, sting and bore their way through the very foundations of our existence.

Equally importantly, insects themselves are key foods for a whole host of creatures, especially birds, many of which are utterly dependent on this source of protein for at least part of their lives. One has only to look at the sad tale of the grey partridge in modern times. Its population has tumbled to about a fifth of its 1950 level largely through habitat destruction and degradation wiping out its insect food.

Yet there are still many thousands of gardeners who blithely spray and poison out of existence everything that moves, and innumerable farmers who continue to use fungicides, herbicides and pesticides in excessive quantities rather than small doses more effectively, at the right time.

There is progress, of course. Witness increasing public pressure on farmers to account for their actions, and the new fad for garden conservation, not the least being the amount of air time currently devoted to wildlife on BBC 2's excellent, long-running TV programme *Gardener's World*.

It is an uphill struggle, and with every day that passes the need becomes more apparent. Surely few people would wish to see a world entirely without insects, and surely even the most intransigent would put up with a little inconvenience and the odd sting if the interrelationships of all living things were clearly explained to them.

I was pondering the matter one evening last week, when I sat cooling off among the garden flowers, washing away the day's dust with a fizzling Martini and tonic. As the thrush fell silent and shadows grew dark and deep about the borders, an air of peace descended. Just one creature remained at its labours, a bee working the foxgloves.

All our foxgloves are self-sown, and one of our great joys is that we never know where these bell towers will appear. We always leave most of them, not only to admire the blooms, but also to help the insects.

In this particular case the bee plundered a plant just two feet from me. The air was so still I could hear the rustling of his delicate wings as he rang each bell, and the purple blooms were sufficiently transparent to enable me to see the shadow of the insect bumbling away inside.

As soon as that bee left another sped over the fence and went straight to the same flower, even to the same bell which initially attracted the first bee! Was this coincidence or did that particular bloom emit the right 'bee language'?

The bee, of course, is especially important to mankind, including both farmer and amateur gardener. Not only does it delight us with its presence, epitomising endless summer days, but also it acts as chief pollinator; and as a bonus it leaves a jar of honey for the many folk who care for it. Also, like the adder, it generally only attacks when provoked.

Many years ago, when I wore short trousers and a school cap, I was stung on the head by a bee when climbing an elm after mistle thrush eggs. The insect did not set out to ambush me but had been disturbed when languishing on a leaf as my head brushed past. In my excitement I half fell from my lofty perch, grazed my knee and broke the egg which was in my mouth – punishment enough for a nest-robber. But there was worse to come – a caning from father for being late home and a week of staying in for tearing my new uniform.

In those days there were fifty butterflies for every one today, and the fields truly were alive with insects of every description. This is not nostalgia, but fact. Yet, when I talk to old keepers and other countrymen, it is quite obvious that even the good times of the 1950s and 1960s were relatively sterile compared with pre-war days.

Yet we cannot heap all the blame on farmers – even though so much land is devoted to agriculture. There must also be a place for insect life in our gardens – among the prize veg and flowers. For a start, pest control can be biological rather than chemical. And those who feel they cannot get by without puffing, spraying or quirting some substance or other should always seek advice before purchase. Read labels carefully, choose products which are the least harmful to wildlife, use minimum quantities, select application times very carefully and conceal baits such as slug pellets from the eyes of birds and mammals. Better still, forget the chemical arsenal, set aside a little wild patch and acknowledge the fact that even the ugliest of bugs are worthy of study. Look after them and the butterflies will look after themselves. From our garden oases wildlife can then recolonise the farmland which, hopefully, should become increasingly less sterile as the conservation bandwagon rolls inexorably on.

1988

# *July*

## *Too Hot to Handle*

On a hot day I love to hear the broom pods crack, firing their seeds off to germinate. The noise seems symbolic of the whole parched earth of July, yielding to high temperatures, rent asunder through contraction. Now the heat and drought are with us and the invigorating smell of new-mown hay is everywhere. Tractors rumble up and down and back and forth with dusty monotony, turning the cut grasses so they may dry more quickly, spooking the pigeons and crows.

The same farm gate whose frosted metal gripped my hand in winter is too hot to touch now, in the glaring sun, and where the ants criss-cross the brick garden steps an egg could be fried. On such days of great stillness, when the heat is oppressive, the nearness of water is a great comfort. Perhaps just a lily pond, where the silence is broken only occasionally by the *ploop* of a rising carp, or the luxury of constant refreshment from a well-charged stream.

Yet the heat is to the liking of the yellowhammer, whose golden yellow reflects the ripening corn at the end of this month, for it frequently chooses to lay now. I love the mad eccentricity of the long, hairlike markings on its eggs, which characteristic has earned the bird the local name 'writing' or 'scribbling lark'.

In the garden July is a month of great activity, with a never-ending chorus of lawnmowers across the nation. Watering, weeding, hoeing, sowing, quartering, feeding, coming, going. Topping, cropping, trimming, thinning, starting, stopping, never winning.

Now is the time to take special care with bonfires as young frogs and toads creep out from ponds, ditches and damp dens. They get in everywhere and one of their favourite haunts is in the base of a pile of garden refuse. As is now my practice, before lighting up this week I moved my heap, and a good job I did as underneath were two glistening adult frogs and a pathetic young toad which would never have escaped the rampaging flames.

1986

126

## 37 Miles from Hyde Park Corner

At the end of my drive, on the crest of a hill, and almost lost in the summer herbage, is a worn, chipped milestone with the once valuable information that Hyde Park Corner is 37 miles away. Free-standing and re-erected after discovery by my children, the stone also declares: Haslemere 3 miles and Godalming 5 miles, but the distance to Midhurst has lost its first digit. Beside the stone, attached to a very stout wooden post, is a tiny old 'GR' letterbox. Together they create a little outpost of civilization which is known locally as one of those signless but generally accepted bus-hailing places.

I wonder how many snippets of country life were posted from this oasis, or how many weary travellers paused here over the years, to wipe the dust from their eyes or mud and snow from their boots.

This is where I bought a house, but human life is so short in the 'Grand Scheme' that to speak of ownership is almost ludicrous. Lease, rent and custody are certainly more applicable in connection with land and property. Apart from ownership of a freehold currently conferring the legal right to indefinite occupancy (excepting Government interference with a compulsory purchase order) and the chance to bestow financial privilege on one's heirs, there is little to recommend house ownership against renting. For some mysterious reason, property mortgages attract tax relief but rents do not (though with Council properties one might well argue that relief is effected at source); but, more importantly, within today's law security of tenure is almost as guaranteed to a renter as it is to a purchaser. Unfortunately, the countryside still has a goodly sprinkling of dwellings tied to particular jobs, and when father must find new employment the tearing up of roots, especially children's, can be very painful indeed. Several times I have seen country family spirit fade into the drudgery of town life when, for example, a father injured his back and had to relinquish his farm job and, consequently, his tied bungalow.

I may think I *own* my house and the postage stamp of land it sits on in the country album but the building is strong enough to outlive my grandson's grandson; and the land, given that we have no significant earthquake or subsidence and England continues to show no sign of volcanic activity, should go on supporting life till the sun is exhausted. Therefore I am only a *caretaker* and must take care not to detract from the aesthetic qualities of my charge or impinge adversely on its environs.

Sitting here comfortably at home, sipping an exceptional

elderberry wine produced during last September's glut, I feel reasonably secure, even though rain is cascading from the overflow above a leaf-blocked roof valley and a spot of damp has appeared in one of the bedrooms. Those recurring problems will have to wait, for today I am still recovering from two hectic days at the Northern Ireland Game and Country Fair.

This morning, as I walked by Heron's Pond, I flushed dozens of electric-blue damselflies from the sedges where they sit with wings upstretched and touching. There was also a chestnut-red one dancing weakly in the shade of a willow. Which of Britain's seventeen species these were I do not know.

Out over the open, rippling water, in the sparkling sunshine which has been rare of late, one of the larger, 'hawker' varieties of dragonfly, the blue-green emperor, patrolled a particular swim while a russet specimen of the 'darter' variety perched in ambush with wings outstretched. It was sad to think that this fine water emperor would live for only a month or so while its ugly aquatic nymph had taken at least a year to mature. Some of our twenty-seven species of dragonfly take as long as five years to reach the imago stage!

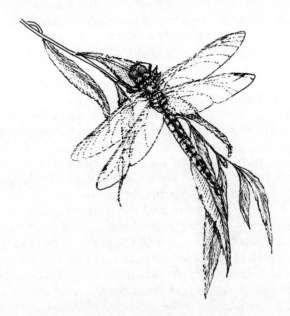

I sat for some time watching these magnificent insects, with their great, all-seeing compound eyes and thick bodies charged with aggression, quartering the waterways on flickering, transparent wings, deceptively delicate but developing proportionate thrust rarely equalled in the natural world.

Nearby, an olive-brown grass snake basked on a tree stump among the nettles and another just hung in the stingers till they sensed the vibrations from my approach and, defenceless, discreetly glided to safety. A few yards on, speckled wood butterflies danced in the shade near a bramble patch covered in winemaker's promise. Then I felt a wary moorhen eye upon me as she quietly kept me in sight, continually calling to her dispersed young which piped softly in the scattering breezes. They kept calling even after I left the pondside and made my way along the pond-feeding field drainage system, the excavation of which has stimulated growth of gigantic foxgloves and thistles on the earth mounds created. These, in turn, have attracted butterlies such as skippers and coppers.

Everywhere now young birds are clamouring for the natural food which usually peaks just at the right time for each species. Although most wild creatures and plants have life cycles running parallel with broad divisions of the year which, in human terms, might be described as the seasons of courtship, birth, growth, maturity, senility and death, there are exceptions. For example, the woodpigeon and house sparrow have occasionally bred in every month of the year, while with other species migration is by no means a certainty.

Exceptions aside, subconsciously we absorb all fleeting experiences of individual plants and animals *on any day*, add them to impressions of climate and perceive certain 'atmospheres' in the country scene which may be grouped into the four main seasons.

Every outdoor atmosphere is not only created by living things but also by inanimate static, motive and chemical factors such as rock, wind and scent. Unfortunately, sometimes there are such fine and subtle aspects of outdoor atmosphere, probably known to and appreciated by many, which are virtually impossible to record with the written word, even with the skilled use of language devices such as onomatopoeia. These would certainly elude the pictorial artist, and even musical genius such as that manifest in Holst's *Egdon Heath* can only work on some of the senses and must rely heavily on the listener's imagination to bridge the gap. Perhaps writing is the most 'five-dimensional' of all art forms, so I'll stick with it in trying to recreate many of the almost tangible atmospheres I experience and long to share with others.

1980

## Trapped Snakes

A friend has rung to say there is a snake in her swimming pool, but she wants to know what sort it is before attempting to get it out alive and safe. Snakes do have a great number of unfortunate accidents today, in an environment full of man-made traps. Drainage ditches are a special problem now, when they are bone dry, for there is rarely any escape. Fortunately, our grass snakes are wonderful swimmers, though polluted farm waters are a problem even for them.

1986

## The Jogging Mole-Finder

The main problem in jogging through Surrey's commuter country-side is having to suffer narrow roads without pavements while being subjected to the fire and brimstone of summer traffic. The customary, year-round procession of Volvo estates crammed with gesticulating schoolchildren is now supplemented by an unending convoy of trippers and yuppie BMWs who vie for every inch of tarmac, repeatedly forcing the hapless runner into the bush, where he is scratched, stung, tripped and left to weep in a pall of exhaust.

Yet all this would be braved for the sake of health. The scales confirmed what my increasingly unfamiliar silhouette had suggested – a pen-pusher's paunch. And endless hours spent watching the demigods of Wimbledon, with no exercise other than swatting vainly at passing flies, fixed my resolve.

'Beware the coronary!' they cried. 'You mustn't do too much at once, but build up slowly.' So, with embarrassingly fit son to heel (like a minder), I set off into the unknown, alternating periods of jogging and walking, calling in desperation on muscles which appeared to have atrophied. Yet my puff was good, after years of roughshooting and birdwatching.

Apart from that dastardly traffic, all went well along the roadside stretch, but on reaching the major and more pleasant part of the course, around Forestry Commission land, another problem arose – multiple distractions. A fungus here, a birdsong there, a flower by the way, an unusual smell, a fleeting glimpse of mammal or snake – all must be investigated. So much of the time was spent poring over natural objects, mostly rounded up or tracked down by my irrepressible thirteen-year-old, and the net result was minimal physical exertion for me.

Next day I slipped out alone and unnoticed and at least managed to work up a sweat, but my ego was entirely deflated when a bronzed athlete in proper running shoes and Union Jack shorts burst out from the cottage drive ahead and left me for dead, smouldering in dingy plimsoles. I'm sure he must have spied me the day before and decided to lay in wait, just to assert his 'first rights' over the training ground.

Anyway, I persisted, and on the fourth successive evening I managed to run virtually the whole course of several miles. On every occasion I flushed what I took to be the same pigeons from the same roosting trees and generally got to know the wild routine of what, for me, had been a little-known patch. But most pleasing of all was to find an area resonant with the purring of what must have been a very considerable number of turtle doves – a species which, in my experience, seems to have declined alarmingly since my childhood.

If there's one sound which encapsulates the drowse and drift of high summer inland then surely it's the call of the turtle dove, a delicate species which winters in tropical Africa. Around the farmyard summer is the twittering of swallows, in the old town the screech of swifts, and on the soothing coast the high-pitched, grating *keee-yaah* of the common tern as it hovers over the shallows in search of fish. But in the deep woods and whispering glades the turtle dove is the high priest of summer, an evocation of childhood spirits and a renewal of acquaintance with all those long, hot summers of cherished memory.

Other summer songs I dearly love are the scratch-warble of the dunnock – like an old 78 record on 45rpm – and the incessant, wheezing demands of soberly clad, young starlings, unseen by the sparrowhawk within the cloak of ash and hazel.

When sodden June relented and early July gave us those turtle-dove days once more, there was a very special tranquility about the evenings. The brash, rippling heat of Wimbledon Centre Court and a sky without cloud or ceiling yielded gently to the advance of day.

First came the long shafts of sunlight past peak of power, which sparkled among the intervening bushes and pierced surrounding trees to bathe the house in dazzling gold. Those of us who toiled the gardener's day mopped our brows, lit sweet-smelling bonfires and swallowed great draughts of cold beer on terrace or patio.

Thence to the glories and fragrance of a barbecue in the rose garden, pleasant conversation and cleansing glasses of chilled wine. Not even the biting insects can defeat us in these pleasant interludes, and long before we retire indoors the sun is but a memory and we are cast into the violet luminosity of a feeble, short-lived summer night.

After such an evening last week I went about the house to lock the doors, but all was not as normal. I'm sure you must agree that a mole in the kitchen is one of the more unusual episodes of country life. But sure enough, there it was, clad in black velvet, whiskered snout and spade-like forelimbs protruding from beneath the fridge!

Approaching it carefully provoked no movement so I bent down to touch it (ever mindful of the day another little 'gentleman' took a slice out of my finger), but a blob of fresh blood fixed to my thumb and it was apparent that the little digger had just died there. Quite obviously, the guilty party was our recently 'acquired', stray pedigree cat.

1987

## A Simply Pleasing Day

While spring was remarkable for its wet and cold, much of mid-summer has been memorable for its exceptionally high humidity. Lethargy is irresistible and there is a strong tendency to remain in the garden shade sipping iced elderflower cordial. Even better, every opportunity to take visitors to the cool inner sanctum of the Dog and Pheasant is seized with relish.

Despite this inactivity, I did dust the gun off recently, though perhaps the exercise was more of an excuse to go AWOL for a few hours. Yet it was a glorious way to do nothing and whet the appetite for resurgence of sporting activity in August and September.

On 10 July I awoke very early after yet another night in which even a cotton sheet was too much covering. The garden was ringing with the high-pitched revelry of finch families. Despite its inconsistencies, it seemed to me that the year's weather had been kind to small-bird production and average brood size had been good. I hope that gamebirds in the south have not been unduly affected by the remarkable thunderstorms.

Goldfinches, particularly, have been unusually abundant and frequently dance about the tops of my higher shrubs. One nest was right in the crown of an evergreen. Greenfinches seem to be making progress towards regaining their noticeable ascendancy of the 1960s. Bullfinches, too, despite their quiet ways, are much more evident and brightening more and more blackthorn thickets with their bold plumage.

Among these early-morning songsters a single woodpigeon crooned to lure me from tiredness and venture forth with the gun. Layers of thick mist hung here and there above the rapidly ripening wheat. Along the edge of Deer's Field an isolated clump of heavy-crowned oaks, beneath which the cattle love to cool, held a few pigeon. However there was little chance of stalking to within range.

Nonetheless, I tried creeping up with gun ready. But, almost immediately, clatter – clap – all gone! I reached the trees and paused, a little disappointed. Yet, as soon as my attention relaxed, out sped another pigeon – how typical! It's as if that odd bird which fails to register a Gun's approach deliberately waits for him to be offguard before slipping out the awkward side of a tree.

Beneath these oaks lay a great mound of farmyard manure still to be distributed about the fields. Surprisingly, hopping and feeding all over it was a kestrel within a few yards of a jay and two magpies. I imagine the raptor was after the worms and insects which figure significantly in its diet.

Despite wellies and dry weather, the heavy dew soon made my knees wet as I wandered along between corn and field edge. At Heron's Pond seven members of the angling club had already drawn pegs and were well into a four-hour 'friendly', mainly involving roach. Fish were coming in steadily to maggots at a few stations, and it was fascinating to equate the anglers' success with my own experience of the water. But for these fishers it was obvious that the real joy was in weekend release from industry.

I left the anglers in float-watching soliloquy to resume my ramble, with the half-hearted intention of investigating the railway rabbit colony. Pity the poor commuters speeding past in baking carriages day after day, jostling for seats or space at the over-priced bar, thundering ever onwards towards Town, hardly sparing a glance sideways from their crosswords to peek at the more natural way of life surrounding them.

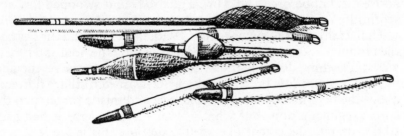

In the next field, where hay was cut some weeks back, a carrion crow tried probing the crusty soil. Almost immediately, it saw me, but before it was ten feet into the hot air my number 5 shot tumbled it back to earth.

An abundance of rabbits hotfooted it out of my way but no reasonable shot presented itself. (At least, that's what I told myself.) The heat rose quickly – too hot for prolonged tramping – so I set out a few 'shell' pigeon decoys near the embankment where rabbits had grazed a gradient into the barley. I sat among the bushes in the shade of an oak strip where there was a chance of both rabbit and pigeon. Flies were increasingly troublesome as perspiration flowed, so out came the Jungle Formula – and it really worked!

Even after two weeks of hot, mostly dry weather to hasten ripening, it would be another fortnight before harvesting the winter corn would commence. At least with both winter and spring sowings the harvest tends to be more protracted nowadays, and so too is stubble decoying, providing one gets in quickly, before burning commences. So far this year there has been little laid corn in my area.

Bother! Just as I was scribbling a few notes the first pigeon came in beautifully to my decoys, but before I could raise the gun the bird spooked and in the glint of an eye was away on a flicker of white wing-bars. The situation looked promising – best get a couple of hazel twigs ready to 'chin-up' some 'real' decoys.

Suddenly a turtle dove dived in and sat next to an old trunk, bobbing its head and flicking its tail, curiously peering down at me. Apart from that there was just the willow warbler's song drifting on the fresh-sprung breeze, and noisy troops of young, brown starlings in the shimmering canopy. I'd give it a while yet, though.

Flies clustered upon the dried crow's blood on the gun barrel. I admired the stock, the veins of walnut deep-toned with many seasons' use.

A pigeon cruised overhead, glimpsed fleetingly between branches, and two more moved inquisitively on the horizon, but all seemed bent on other tables. Suddenly another dropped from the very tree above me, but before I could bring gun to bear it swooped low and scornfully away over the decoys.

Thankfully, the hot sun was veiled with thin cloud and the sky had the bloom of a distant thunderstorm about it. One hour later there was still nothing doing so it was on to greener pastures. As the dew lifted, a few meadow browns and a silver-washed fritillary fluttered about the field margins, where foxglove and thistle threatened the corn's regimentation. But what a poor butterfly year it has been so far, despite the recent fine spell. I suppose this is the legacy of a miserable spring.

I set off to tramp the two miles or so to the other end of the farm. Dog roses starred the hedgerow and the long grasses shook their heads to coat my wet boots with seed. Two pigeon crossed the hedge but veered back in an instant. Their flash drew my eyes upwards to a white admiral hawking about a silver birch.

Back down near the pond, the plosh of tiny fish and swishing of rods drifted up through the clearing. Another white admiral, and then a ringlet fluttered past. The sun was hot on the back of my neck. I was glad to enter the cool wood again. A tree had fallen across my customary path. It was easy enough to go round it, so I did, and thus another bend in the track was established.

I did set up my decoys again, but little came along except another six white admirals, so I set off home to a barbecue lunch followed by an afternoon of Cub sports.

Dusk fell almost imperceptibly slowly, and as the mist reformed above the fields the cooling garden air distilled the unrivalled fragrance of honeysuckle and rose. I wondered why such simply pleasing days are so hard to arrange.

1983

## Pushing for Plants

At this time of year most of our grandparents would have enjoyed the spectacular, unbridled flowering of 'garden England' – in fields and woods as well as neatly contained within the borders. Wherever they went in July they would have admired the seasonal dominance of yellow and red blooms, reflecting the maturity of the summer and replacing the earlier preponderance of blue, white and purple varieties. But today there is little colour of any sort to relieve the often apparently endless, semi-sterilised acres. Green is all very well but it's not the only colour in nature's paintbox.

Our parents, too, knew far more colour about the land, for the sad fact is that 97 per cent of our wild-flower meadows have been destroyed since World War II. Twenty-two British species of flower – such as the once-common corncockle – have become extinct since records began, and a further 317, including the lady's slipper orchid and Snowdon lily, now stand on the brink. Urgent action is needed not only to arrest this awful decline but also restore much-needed brightness to the landscape.

Some folk are not too bothered about further colour in the countryside, finding sufficient variety in the varying seasonal shades of farm crops and trees. But just remember that plant variety is not only about painting pretty chocolate-box images of olde England; it is also central to the well-being of our wildlife, supporting the myriad of invertebrate species on which many of our birds and mammals depend for food. A bland countryside indicates an impoverished diet for wild creatures.

It's all very well having 'across the board' conservation bodies, such as the World Wide Fund for Nature and the Royal Society for Nature Conservation, but the battle for habitat and status has become so complex that each species group really does need its own special champion as well. No matter how good a job they do, the big, general conservation organisations cannot attune their ears every time the wind shifts but one degree. That is why we have seen the recent spawning of so many specialist groups concerned with species such as dragonflies, hedgehogs, bats and badgers.

Appropriately, with this great flowering of the conservation movement, plants too have mobilised their own 'green' army. Plantlife is Britain's only charity exclusively saving wild plants and their habitats, from seashore to mountain top. Through conservation and campaigning, Plantlife is aiming at and succeeding in stopping common plants becoming rare, and rare plants becoming extinct, and restoring lost species where they have disappeared. Its work includes buying flower-rich meadows to establish plant nature reserves, campaigning to stop peatlands being destroyed and establishing a 'great hedge' across Britain.

Plantlife has already had some notable successes. For example, through its care over 300 starfruit plants appeared in 1992, compared with just a handful three years before. Thanks also to them the mallow has made some progress. In Somerset, at one of only four British sites, scrub clearance has resulted in more than 100 of these beautiful plants growing where just four bloomed in 1989. Then there's the case of the ground pine, an inconspicuous little plant, looking and smelling like a pine tree, whose nine remaining sites are benefiting through Plantlife's close monitoring and protection.

In putting the colour back into Britain we must not forget our most widespread and obvious plant – the tree, defined by my dictionary as 'a perennial with a single woody, self-supporting stem or trunk, usually unbranched for some distance above ground'. In this context it is good to see that our largest tree grower, the Forestry Commission, is playing its part. With more than 50 million visitors spending at least some part of a day among their trees each year, the national body is increasingly concerned with amenity as well as efficient cropping.

Some folk visit forests for nature study, sport or to explore archaeological or heritage sites. Others just want to get away from it

136

all and take log-cabin or caravan holidays at special sites, or simply
go for a quiet walk and a picnic. All must be catered for without
detriment to the environment and wildlife, which is no easy task.
At the same time forest managers are conscious of the ecological
role of their trees, as purifiers of the earth's atmosphere.

We already have one generation who have never known flowering Britain at anything like its best. Let's act now to ensure that
their children are not similarly disadvantaged.

1993

## No More than Drinking Shops

Sometimes I think we would never get anywhere at all without
our wonderful English pubs. In town they stand magnificently
eternal at every street corner, sometimes providing landmarks for
the lost, but in the countryside they truly sparkle through the ages
as beacons in every route-giving.

Take my own situation, for instance. My guide for the first-time visitor always seems to end with the words: 'You can't miss it – no more than half a mile past the Dog and Pheasant.' And when it's coal-black and stormy in the sticks the stranger certainly needs the friendly lights of the local to find his way. With the windscreen wipers thrashing madly, and apparently nothing but miles of deep, dark woods and fields beyond your steamed-up car, the sudden twinkling lantern of the promised inn ahead is a real relief.

Whenever someone says to me: 'You can't miss us, we're the third turning on the left past the big farm gates', then I know I'm in trouble. Inevitably, there are thirty-three turnings on the left past those gates and my host has omitted to say that he talks only in terms of *main* roads. But when I hear those magic words: 'If you reach the Wheatsheaf you've gone too far', then I know all will be well. At the very worst I would be in for three wrong private drives, two backings into ditches and the occasional 'I told you so' from an eager spouse.

Yet, useful as they now are to the motorist as watering holes and period pieces for admiration, village inns reached their heyday in the stagecoach era. When the long, long trek north to grouseland was so very slow along the rutted and flooded way, the Royal Oak or Cat and Fiddle offered glorious relief. There was water for the team, restless in harness for many an hour; wholesome food, good wine and a feathered bed for the gentlemen of ease. Clients were generally men of means, with the wherewithal to pay for customary good service.

But when the railways supplanted stagecoaches the village inn was temporarily neglected. Even the commercial traveller ceased to be a frequent visitor. He whipped in with one train and whipped out with another, and the average landlord lost interest in sleeping guests. He laid himself out chiefly to cater for local customers – hence the term 'local' was entirely appropriate. The landlord was content to sell ale of muddy appearance and heady quality to the tippling rustic.

At the turn of this century the village landlord gazed with surprise at anyone who had the temerity to propose staying overnight at his hostelry. And he turned up his nose when asked for food, so to get even a mutton chop cooked was difficult for the wayfarer. The village inn became a drinking shop pure and simple, and the idea that favour would be bestowed on the traveller was entirely fallacious.

It was thought that the advent of the cyclist might have changed this, but it was not to be, for the pedal-pusher has never been a good patron of inns. He is keen on exercise and often not very well off.

Yes, some inns were transmogrified into hotels, but what unfriendly, characterless places they became. Tariffs were raised, meals were entirely regular and there was no accommodation for the traveller's on-the-spot requirements.

The beginnings of motor car popularity, in Edwardian England, brought the more leisured classes back through the countryside past village inns, but those who tried to cater for them were no more than second-class London eating houses. Imitation was not required. A hankering after the real flavour of country life remained then as it does today.

A 1900 inn would probably have a silly show of unnecessary trinkets yet completely lack essentials such as a basic toilet. Instead of simplicity and spotless linen in bedrooms there were dozens of objects to retain dust. An absurd idea prevailed, that genteel company required genteel meals, whereas what they really required was local fare.

Freshness and availability of food were very important before refrigeration, yet in the early 1900s very few landlords kept their own fowl to guarantee new-laid eggs for their guests. Also, fat chickens should have been on hand for the pot, but rarely were. Rashers of breakfast bacon rarely came from the innkeeper's own sties and few bothered to establish local contacts with butchers and farmers for reliable beef and mutton. Instead, it was French eggs for breakfast and foreign and colonial meat for other meals.

But change did come as motor cars proliferated, and after World War II landlords realised there was a considerable amount of tourist money to be had through providing some form of caring attention, as back in the old coaching days. After years of rationing, the countryside was seen as the store of good food, where merry England might be discovered once more.

I think it was from the early 1950s that food became a major requirement in most village pubs, and it was then that my father became the tenant of one for some ten years. Everywhere informal provision of bread and cheese with a pickled onion gradually drew the attention of strangers and the great British 'ploughman's lunch' was established. From then on it was a national race to provide the widest range of convenience foods, and standards soon slipped down through a series of microwave judders.

Today people on their holidays still go forth hopefully, searching for that elusive village inn where the flagstone floor beckons you into yesteryear. As you enter through the ever-open door momentarily you have a vision of Shakesperian England. Buxom wenches jostle past with three tankards of foaming ale in each hand, the room is bursting with merriment and pipe smoke, and at the long, oak table by a great log fire both locals and travellers consume roast meat by the pound and fine French wines bottle after bottle.

Suddenly the spell is broken. It is cool and dark. A young man with spiked orange hair plays space invaders in the corner and the landlord leans wistfully on the bar, talking about the old days with the only man who can still remember – the local gamekeeper. Above him are his old traps, now outlawed, and to the side his factory-made meat pie is warming up.

Your village might, as the estate agent said when you bought your house, 'have the benefit of two of the oldest inns in Barset', but their old atmosphere has gone for ever. How I wish to be back in the 1950s, when we had 160 hens in the pub garden, three pigs in the sty, and old Harry Ryves played dominoes with Bill Curby in the corner. Once, when I was seven, they let me play Newmarket. There was 'snow' (silver) in the kitty and I won 2s 8d on the King of Clubs, but I never did get to see the chamber pot full of old pennies which, rumour had it, was under Harry's bed.

When the builders brought our pub into the twentieth century and I scurried about between their legs gathering up the Victorian and Edwardian silver which lad lain hidden beneath the floorboards, it was the end of an era. The customers still came in droves but Harry was on his last legs.

1986

## Electrocuted Badgers

So far this year I have seen four dead badgers on the road in different parts of the country. But they have been a problem for British Rail too, hundreds having been killed since electrification. Now the Department of Transport is making more of an effort to save them. At points where badgers traditionally cross lines, something they do with surprising persistence, railway engineers are providing 'gaps' in the live conductor rail through the addition of insulated links. Of course, the badgers don't know the line is safe there; all they sense is the ancient badger ways which their ancestors have taken for many generations.

1986

## The Sound of Silence

For centuries the halloo and clapper of the bird boy was the hallmark of July, echoing among the fields of ripening corn. But now boys have other things to do and only the occasional dull thud of a gas gun or stuttering fire of a 12-bore stirs the pigeon, rook and sparrow in their harvest feast.

How gloriously refreshing those earlier farm fields must have been, with such sounds of wildness all around. When the labourers were at rest the boy guardian could settle down on some grassy bank, gaze out into the fullness of the year and let the sweet sounds of summer rinse away all earthly cares. Birdsong drifted around every corner and the intense hum of insects electrified the breeze. But now, in southern England at least, there is virtually no escape from the distant drone of traffic. Even those rare corners still shielded and cradled by wild hills constantly have their freedom and isolation despoiled by the overhead passage of jets.

Here we also have the fairly frequent passage of hot-air balloons, but I certainly have no objection to this form of transport, which is much more in keeping with quieter days. Indeed, were it not for the occasional sound of the gas burner being put on to maintain height, one might not be aware of their passing. However, balloonists must be very careful not to upset farm stock or grouse shoots and not to damage crops.

Even in the South, circumstances sometimes conspire to produce near silence, and when it comes it often strikes with spooky impact that sends a shiver up the spine. The roughshooter knows the feeling well. Lurking at the edge of a copse as the last few pigeon trickle into roost and rabbit tails flash white in the deepening dusk, he is suddenly aware that the birds have fallen silent. Then, in the few minutes before the first stars acquire real definition, there is a kind of lull in life, when the countryside belongs neither to the creatures of the day nor the denizens of night. And if that magic time coincides with complete calm, with not one black silhouette of a leaf stirring against heaven, then there really is a true sensation of silence and peace. Perhaps there is some meteorological reason why the wind seems so often to fall off sharply at dusk.

There is also a wonderfully invigorating silence after many a snowstorm, and it goes far beyond the fact that the way is barred to traffic, the progress of wheel and foot muffled by the crystal manna. It is as if the white carpet has magnetised and muted every soundwave which ripples overhead. The effect seems most intense at dawn and dusk.

Periods of intense frost also seem to attract deep silences, sometimes so great – especially in the night – that it seems almost as if you can hear the crystals of ice forming. Of course, it is all the more profound with the absence of traffic and the generally numbing effect on wildlife.

Back to summer, I was sitting in the garden enjoying the dusk the other day when one of those weird silences suddenly descended. One minute a thrush was singing the last post and a blackbird was chinking at Sam the cat, the next there was nothing. But then, as a kind of last gesture to the day's impetus, the papery wings of a late bee rustled up into the bell of yet one more foxglove.

As I write this, a couple of jackdaws are cackling away at the end of the garden and I am reminded of a most pleasant interlude spent looking around the delightfully remote Bepton Church in West Sussex. It was on an ordinary weekday and there was not one other soul about at this tuck in the side of the South Downs. The churchyard was alive with songbirds, including bullfinches, greenfinches and linnets, but also collared doves, which did not even exist in England when most of the graves beneath them were excavated.

However, it was those magical jackdaws which lodged that place so firmly in my memory – not for their friendly cackling, but the eerie scratching of their claws all over the roof as I sauntered around inside the twelfth-century building. I felt rather like the hero in Alfred Hitchcock's thrilling film, *The Birds*.

Deserted farm buildings, too, often enthral me. There is

something very mysterious about machines at rest, gathering dust peacefully. I cannot resist that loose sheet of corrugated iron banging in the breeze, beckoning me into the byre, or the half-open barn door leading to little enclaves of nostalgia. But what frights I have had when my passage through gloomy interiors has been arrested by the abrupt take-off of an owl.

On other occasions I have suddenly become aware of being watched, and turned slowly to see the bright eyes of a blackbird or pied wagtail peering at me, unmoved, just above the rim of a nest on some dusty ledge, sharp beak jutting out in stark contrast to the curved edges.

As a child I haunted such places in search of eggs. One of my favourite buildings was a huge, rickety, corrugated-iron shed which belonged to a rural woodyard. Swallows nested up in its almost inaccessible rafters and on the floor, around the circular saws, lay great mounds of sawdust just right for housing egg collections.

Despite all the dust and noise, that huge metal box was a regular wildlife dormitory, hosting families of robins, wagtails, wrens, blue tits, great tits and thrushes as well as those swallows. Outside there were always hordes of mice, voles, lizards and slow-worms, especially under sheets of corrugated iron and planks of wood scattered about the scrub.

Another building which fascinated me then was a tall, round, brick tower which could have been a folly but, given its location, probably had some early military use, perhaps as a lookout post. Anyway, whatever had been inside was long gone, so reaching the swallows' nests at some twelve feet up called for ingenuity. Indeed, it required circus tricks.

Fortunately, the tower was narrow enough for me to touch on both sides at the same time, so that I could ascend by pressing my feet and hands against the brick. Unfortunately, as I approached the precious eggs my chum squirted a water pistol up my short trousers and down I tumbled.

Now the days of nest robbing are rightly just a memory, sometimes stirred by the sight of an antique collection in local auctions, but the fascination with old or deserted buildings remains.

1990

# August

## When Twilight Thickens

One evening recently I sat in the garden savouring the rich scent which arises when dusk cools a hot summer day. Drought persisted, yet there was a mild threat of thundery rain, as there had been on many afternoons of late. Horizons darkened, contingency plans for withdrawal to the house were hastily made and temporary relief from the heat was welcome. Yet the rain would not come: it just refused to fall.

At long last the plumber had been summoned to fix the outside tap, whose pipe had parted during a savage December frost. So as I sat dreamily enjoying that evening air the hosepipe trickled relief down through the roses, past the herbaceous border and into the vegetable patch. I had no qualms about 'wasting' water for ours is a private water supply which appears to be inexhaustible, revealing not the slightest reduction in flow even during the great droughts of 1975 and 1976.

As I mused, the winter barley was pouring in, the great grain harvesters surging and rumbling towards owl-light. Nothing else stirred. It was otherwise totally quiet save for the occasional 'little bit of bread and no cheese' which a yellowhammer wheezed from a thornbush, while his mate sat snugly on a full clutch in the scrub-filled rife below. Buntings are probably our latest layers.

Drowsily I listened to the combine's relentless drone rising and falling as it topped the hill, turned, then sank from view time after time. Through a gap in the hedge I saw the monster appear on each run up the rise towards the house. First into view came the towering grain dispenser, like a huge praying mantis, then the glass-eyed workhouse on wheels with pilot cocooned by soundproofing and air conditioning. Alongside came the grain-receiving truck, wheeling about in a dust storm. How many creatures had perished in their path? How many wild homes had been bulldozed and how many eyes peered wildly through the dwindling acreage of stalks as the monster ate their domain?

As I witnessed the good harvest from just one field I found it hard to believe a recent report that if Britain had to feed itself entirely from its present food production we would be on a semi-starvation diet of only 1,600 calories a day! Apparently the average daily food requirement is 2,520 calories and, despite the great increase in agricultural productivity since World War II, the British shopping basket is filled, in cost terms, with 45 per cent foreign goods. The report by Population Concern also points out that Britain is 2½ times more densely populated than China and is one of the most densely populated countries in the world.

Eventually, as I sat reflecting that evening, the heavens did 'cackle with uncouth sounds', as described by D.H. Lawrence in his masterpiece poem *Storm in the Black Forest*, yet the rain which followed the thunder was hardly more than a dampening. However, it was enough to release that magic odour from parched soil which is suddenly wet, and sufficient to set the unwelcome slugs upon their slimy trails.

It was then that the combine ground to a halt for the day. The farmer slammed the cab door shut, secured the creaky metal gate to the field and crunched wearily up the drive to the farmhouse. Stars were mere pinpricks of light in a purple sky as silence momentarily returned to the half-cut cornfield. But then, as if by magic, the yellow moon swung into view from behind a black copse, a breeze moved among the bushes, a shrew rustled in the dry grass and a tawny owl declared that supper was about to be served. Temporarily, the field had been returned to nature.

1984

## Barbecued Fish

Sam the cat lay heavily in the shade of an azalea, snapping half-heartedly at passing insects. Flower heads bowed in the

afternoon heat and the curtain hem rolled slowly like an ocean
swell, fanned only by the cool draught created by open windows.
Yet even this sultry air supported the dreamy drift of minute
spiderlings on unseen lifelines of gossamer.

On the barbecue were fresh mackerel caught that same day on
a boat-fishing trip off the Needles. Stuffed with garlic cloves, bay
leaves and garden herbs they made one of the most delicious
alfresco meals I have ever had.

Almost as good was the barbecued sea bream, but less successful
were the 'wings' of a spotted ray. I believe that it must be the oily
nature of the mackerel which lends itself so well to this type of
cookery.

1987

## Down on the Farm

It is said that Britain has the best climate for growing crops but
the worst for harvesting them. Rarely has this been more apparent
than this year, when the continuing trend of topsy-turvy seasons has
threatened disaster for the specialist and brought mixed blessings
to mixed farms. The 'small' man is particularly at risk through
excessive diversification as he may create crop or stock units too
small to take advantage of the benefits of large-scale production,
such as in bulk buying. Add to this the increasing pressure on
farmers to be conservation-minded and tolerant of public access
and it is easy to see how they deserve our support.

Earlier I welcomed the return of a traditionally unsettled summer,
but there are limits and, even though the Asthma Research Council
has been able to report a very low pollen count for hay fever
sufferers, no one wants to see tons of hay rotting in the fields
with inevitable rocketing prices to come.

Not surprisingly, the usual mid-July start to the harvest was
delayed just about everywhere, but in the South-East winter
barley, traditionally the first, started to come in in the second
half of July and the yield looks quite good, ripening having been
almost amazing considering the conditions. Thankfully, lodging,
in which the wind and rain flatten the crops, is not such a problem
with sophisticated modern equipment. Generally the North and
West have been worst hit.

The winter wheat yield, too, looks quite good, although there
has been a considerable amount of rust and other fungus, especially

146

in the Midlands, but with the onset of fine weather towards the end of July things started to look up.

Although the first and main hay cut has been the farmer's black spot, producing a crop of poor quality, high in water/fibre content and low in sugar, further cuts look more promising, but timing them remains a great problem. Apart from hay, field strawberries have probably fared the worst, and at a particularly bad time, when overseas crops have been good and cheap enough to attract even the jam-makers. On the other hand, conditions have been excellent for raspberries and all the pick-your-own addicts, such as I, are having a ball.

Also pleased are the apple growers. The South-East especially should see a bumper crop as the early fine spell gave good pollination and setting while the ensuing monsoon brought excellent plumping. Potatoes and virtually all roots have come on splendidly in the wet, but let us hope for drier harvesting conditions. Perhaps the brightest spot of all has been for the livestock man, as the unseasonal rain gave an unusually late flush of grass to vastly improve the milk yield.

Despite the vagaries of our climate, the farmer and grower's lot is advancing technically at a great rate. One has only to look back. In 1849 'Rusticus I' wrote about various pests which today are easily controlled by the chemists. For example, concerning the gooseberry fly and gathering leaves with concentrations of the grub, he suggested: 'If you have no time to look for these leaves yourself, get some children to do it; surely you would not object to give a child a halfpenny a score for such leaves, and that price would be quite sufficient to clear the vision and sharpen the intellects of many a hungry boy'.

With little technical advance, economic survival was much tougher in the early nineteenth century. In one instance, Rusticus I rather uncharitably wrote concerning one of the 'blights': 'Others may contend that the evil done is accompanied by good; for example that the ravages of the hop-fly keep up the price of the hop, so as to afford a tolerable profit to the grower; whereas, were there to be no fly, the crop would be larger than the consumption, and the price consequently not a remunerating one. I well recollect, that after the immense crop of 1826 the price did not repay the grower his rent, taxes, and labour; and the farmers, a set of men, I am sorry to say, with less forethought generally than any other class of tradesmen, most improvidently went to work and were silly enough to grub up their hopyards and sow wheat. This took place in several instances between Farnham and Alton.'

Today, with a bureaucracy bonanza, crop selection is increasingly less a matter for personal choice. For example, this summer has seen the EEC banning the sale of seed from 500 species of lesser known vegetable species unpopular with commercial growers. Although it is still legal to sell the actual vegetables it is even illegal to *give* the seeds away – so how will the species survive? Will we see the founding of the Royal Society for the Protection of Vegetables? Luckily there appears to be a loophole in the law – it is OK to *lend* the seeds provided the same quantity is returned.

It is interesting to note that some seeds will germinate after up to 200 years in deep-freeze, so why not have a seed bank for posterity, to ensure that these 500 endangered veg, such as the custard marrow, are around to bring variety to a space-age diet.

Despite their growing problems (excuse the pun), quite a few farmers are striving to bridge the gap between town and country folk, which is now the widest it has ever been, as a result of the continuing population drift away from the land into industry and commerce. Some try to demonstrate, through open days, that the countryside is a place of work, that conservation can go hand in hand with efficient production, and that a responsible public is welcome. Regrettably, a minority sees only profit, even trying to fence off traditional footpaths. But sometimes necessity is the mother of invention and open days can provide more cash or educate schoolchildren from neighbouring population centres which bring a vandalism problem. Yet there are farmers who really have the nation's inheritance at heart and have successfully conducted long-term experiments to prove that even the most productive unit can boast a great variety of flora and fauna.

1980

## Toad in the Shoe

When I was busy about the garden plot recently, during the pro-longed, hot, dry spell, I got into the habit of leaving my gardening shoes outside the door, ready for the next session. However, I did turn them upside down in case of a rogue thunderstorm.

Unfortunately, on one day I overlooked one of my golden rules – always examine any item of apparel left outside *before* popping it on again. How many times has that old sweater, temporarily tossed on the ground, acquired a dozy wasp or platoon of red ants before it was needed again. And on how many occasions has that old wellie harboured a big, juicy spider, nipping earwig or belligerent beetle.

So when what I thought was the curling instep of my old gardening shoe just wouldn't flatten beneath my thrusting toes, I should not really have been surprised that a big old toad was in residence. The real wonder is that I didn't kill him, and I was mightily relieved to see him hop off – admittedly a little dazed – into the more hospitable shrubbery.

1989

## A Drink for the Birds

Many animals are scarcely affected by water shortage because they do not actually drink, gaining sufficient moisture through their food, while innumerable plants set deep roots to suck the subsoil dry, resisting all elemental extremes with baffling durability.

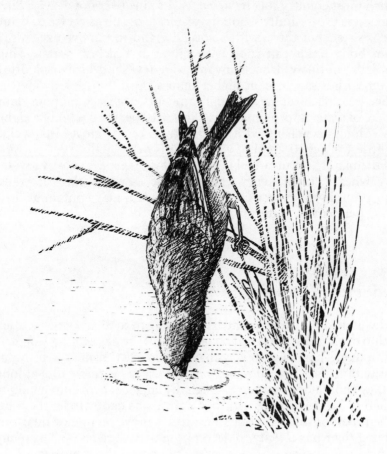

Birds need to drink only if their food does not provide enough water to compensate for that lost through excretion and pulmocutaneous evaporation (loss of water through the lungs and skin). Thus it is not surprising that birds with dry diets need to drink more often than those with succulent diets. For example, the seed-eating finches, which I have seen so often at the pond edge in recent hot weeks, have had far greater need than the blackbirds and thrushes which tuck into soft fruit, worms, slugs and snails.

That said, this year's conditions have been so extreme we have had an exceptional variety of species at the bird bath, which also serves to keep the plumage in order. Others get by on water taken from rivers, streams, lakes and the sea, or even condensed fog and dew. In more normal times there are puddles to sip from and tiny pools trapped by plant leaves. Blocked gutters and cattle troughs are other sources.

Some birds drink on the wing, including the swifts and swallows which most country folk have seen swooping over ponds with their beaks open to skilfully scoop up water. Most birds prefer to drink fresh water, but those with a special gland to remove excess salt from body fluids can cope with saline or brackish water. Thus seabirds routinely drink seawater, but few land birds can drink water with a salt content higher than a third that of seawater.

Seed-eating birds in arid environments need a minimum daily intake of water approximating to about 10 per cent of body weight, the volume increasing with temperature. But as most birds weigh so little the actual amount consumed is very small.

Fortunately, birds are able to minimise their evaporative water loss when pressed. They can also increase the rate of water resorption in the cloaca so that their excreta may contain as little as 50 per cent of water by weight.

1990

## Uninvited Guests

As I watched the wasps going back and forth to their nest concealed within my house I marvelled at the straightforward economy of their commune. There was no way that I could evict them as their home was within a sealed section of roof above a bay window. But as long as they chose not to invade through the adjacent bedroom window, which I like to keep open for fresh air, I was happy to let them be. When their business is done they always move on to new quarters, leaving their papery city to decompose over decades, just as many of man's settlements have disappeared down the centuries.

The house has been well used this year. Apart from the resident bats – mainly pipistrelles – we have had starlings down the chimney and blue tits raising a family successfully from a nest behind hanging tiles, despite the building of an extension within inches! While brickies, carpenters and roofers assembled their imitation of aged structure the blue tits doggedly stuck to their task and amassed their bundle of straw, moss, wool and feathers in a recess behind the tiles. Never before have I known birds to put up with such protracted disturbance.

As far as I know, only one blue tit chick failed to fledge successfully. Instead of flying forth to explore summer in Surrey, it managed to tumble down into the cobwebbed interior of the cavity wall and could not find the way back. The parents maintained contact with calls and on the following day I was amazed to find the chick still alive. Furthermore, the parents were still managing to feed the beleaguered offspring with green caterpillars which they passed through a little gap between an oak beam and the brickwork. This went on for two more days, but sadly there was nothing I could do to effect a rescue. Then, one morning, no more plaintive cries came from the imprisoning walls. Presumably the chick had died.

1984

## Memory Trails

Suddenly I realise that my favourite summer visitors, the swifts, will be gone with the whims of August. So, mindful of the endless hours spent watching them through a childhood idyll, I rush outside to gaze spellbound at their aerial mastery, in screaming arches, while there is yet time. When the first partridges fall to shot next month only the swift's vapour trail will remain – etched in my memory.

Now is the month when birdsong dies away and the near dumb robin only regains bravado with his new feathers. Location and identification of many wild creatures is particularly difficult now, even without the lush growth.

1980

## Rabbit Revival

It's often rather amusing and sometimes quite pathetic the way the media latches on to anything 'newsworthy' in the countryside.

151

Newshounds feed off each other like leeches and as a result often get their facts wrong or shift the emphasis to suit their biased stories.

A good example was the recent 'revelation' that rabbit numbers have made a strong recovery to approach pre-myxomatosis levels. Now I am fairly confident that it all started with a recent *Shooting Times* feature that discussed the matter very sensibly and advised readers on good shooting tactics. But before you could say Brer Rabbit up jumped a dollop of dailies and a rush of radio stations who blew the whole thing out of proportion, culminating in tales of 'super bunnies' and farmers 'going to the wall'. And I know, first hand, that it was the paper publicity that stirred the warrens of television centres. The lemmings were up and running in force.

Anyone who spends even a modicum of time in the sticks – or even leafy suburbs for that matter – will have *already* been aware of rabbit numbers creeping up in recent years. And now rabbit ascendancy has gathered pace aided by an unprecedented run of clement weather – warmest this, driest that, and so on. But this same climatic shift has also stimulated a whole host of other species, most of which are not usually deemed newsworthy by the general press because they do not, normally, threaten man's economic well-being as the rabbit does. Take away the human factor and the story stinks.

There is certainly no shortage of news concerning less dynamic or less familiar species. For example, this year is by far the best I have ever seen for poppies, and surely other people have noticed many more butterflies and the remarkable increase in songbirds generally, especially finches. Yet none of these has attracted significant media coverage.

As for rabbits, well, most farmers I know like to see a few about the place and anyone with real problems can rest assured that there is an army of volunteers out there only too willing to undertake control free of charge. Of course, any farmer shelling out big bucks for major rabbit clearance is not wasting his money if it increases his profits, but he certainly is making unnecessary expenditure.

It would, of course, be nice to see the rabbit properly regarded as a good crop, which provides superb meat and the bonus of fine sport, rather than as a disease-ridden pest. Surely there is much to be done to promote the sale of rabbit meat to the general public. Some people might be reassured to know that, apparently, anyone who unknowingly eats a rabbit which has contracted myxy but has not yet developed visual signs of the disease will come to no harm.

An increase in the number of rabbits is also helping populations of avian and mammalian predators, which take bunnies both live and as carrion. Perhaps the greatest of these rabbit hunters is the stoat. This fierce mammal kills a rabbit cleanly and neatly, and in the old days country people regarded the white flesh of a stoated rabbit as particularly good eating. Indeed, even in my youth the rumour was still rife and I made a point of trying one. However, as far as I can remember, there was little difference.

The recent rabbit 'plague' has been wreaking havoc at a local school playing field, to the extent that the field has been out of bounds for many weeks, and even sports day was cancelled! It was felt that the many holes excavated by the rabbits could be a hazard to children walking or running on the surface. The county council made valiant attempts to fill in the holes, but without success, so this month they have set about clearing the pesky burrowers.

Meanwhile, roadside verges seem to be alive with naïve young rabbits, many of which soon get squashed by passing traffic, providing yet more sustenance for unpopular magpies and carrion crows. But at least while these corvids are gorging on carrion they are not plundering the nests of other birds. And while they have plenty of live rabbits to prey on, foxes too will be less interested in birds, including game species.

More importantly, the rabbit revival should provide a much-needed spur to the recovery of our raptor population. When myxy ran riot through the warrens in the 1950s, birds of prey – already threatened by greatly increased use of chemicals in farming – were robbed of a major food source. Now several species are benefiting greatly through more rabbits, particularly the common buzzard, whose British population peaked along with rabbit numbers back in the early 1950s.

Now that we have rabbits back in the garden Sam the cat is even more scornful of his processed dinner, local boys are busy with their airguns about the hedgerows, and there is plenty of skinning to do.

1990

## Winged Shoplifters

For many decades now birds have shopped at our doorstep, tits sipping the cream from our milk and magpies filching the eggs. But, not content with this, some species have now learnt to get their provisions from the supermarket itself!

It was several years ago that I first noticed considerable numbers of birds, mostly sparrows, flying about the ceilings of large food stores, and I wondered how health authorities allowed this to continue over long periods. But now some have obviously clamped down, as illustrated by a recent court case.

A branch of Asda supermarkets in Rochdale was fined £100 for selling ham affected by bird droppings, and a further £100 for having a damaged door. In mitigation, a representative of the chain explained to the magistrates that this is a widespread problem which is certainly not restricted to one company as birds seek the comforts of these vast buildings. He said: 'Strong blasts of air at the doorways and ribbon curtains had been successful – until the birds rode in on the backs of forklift trucks! The sparrows and starlings find there is warmth, food, water, perches and no predators. No wonder they want to stay.'

Apparently, a sparrowhawk got into a store in Rotherham – no doubt in hot pursuit of a sparrow – and cleared the place of pests in half an hour. But when a model hawk was brought in at Rochdale the resident birds simply made friends with it. So the Rochdale problem has been solved temporarily by putting down drugged food, the 'knocked-out' birds being released outside on recovery.

1985

# *Where are the Painted Ladies?*

Even in a fine August I am reminded of one of the great natural tragedies of modern times – the decimation of our butterfly population through an unending chemical monsoon and destruction of habitat. In my view these two factors have been far more significant than the cooling of our climate over the last two decades.

Like many other schoolboys in the 1950s and 1960s, I collected butterflies just as avidly as I tracked down British Empire postage stamps and matchbox labels. Now few people lament the independence of the colonies which gave budding philatelists such fireside adventure, but most admit great sorrow at the loss of both wild flowers and the butterflies they supported.

Of course nostalgia clouds the view. Yet I have revisited most of my old haunts and there the meadows and glades I loved have been either buried beneath urban sprawl or become almost devoid of all life. Britain in the 1980s certainly is a tough place for butterflies.

Even gardens are not the havens they once were as almost every shed has poison on the shelf. We can only be thankful for the proliferation of nature reserves where *all* plant and animal life receives sympathy.

There are exceptions, of course, and here and there particular butterfly species are revived through the fortuitous manipulation of habitat – on motorway verges perhaps, or even across the increasing acreage of refuse tips where weeds invade the margins. Increasing afforestation has also allowed a few more specialist species to make a comeback. For example, now there seem to be many more white admirals dashing boldly along rides and woodland edges.

When named in the eighteenth century, the white admiral was uncommon in well-managed English woods, but in the mid-twentieth century its population exploded, spreading from Central Southern England into the West Country and the Midlands. The increase followed warm summers in the 1930s and the neglect of coppice woodland where trees were regularly trimmed and the undergrowth kept in check. Neglect allowed honeysuckle to take over, and this is the sole food plant of white admiral caterpillars. Since then the species seems never to have looked back.

But what of our more familiar butterflies? Where are the red admirals, peacocks, painted ladies, coppers, blues, heaths, whites, browns, hairstreaks and fritillaries which once filled the garden in high summer and swirled about the heathery heaths from harvest to the Feast of St Grouse? Each a gem, each a mobile mystery luring the curious ever onward, always one flutter or dart ahead;

but also, each a character, a conjurer recalling times and places which sleep snugly in the more pleasant parts of the memory.

Whenever I see red admirals I remember those golden days of late summer and early autumn in favourite orchards. There, in less clinical times, these velvety insects enjoyed the juice of rotting fruit allowed to decompose slowly in the dewy grass. Also in this untroubled company were drunken wasps, eyed peacocks and commas.

But usually, when I see the brown comma, whose ragged-edged wings look like leaves munched by caterpillars, I remember my old friend John Povall, sadly departed this life at the age of forty-one. His knowledge and love of butterflies were great, as they were of all wild things, but when he captured a comma with exceptionally large black spots, and had the variety named after him by the British Museum, his satisfaction was complete.

Coppers, heaths and skippers remind me of the thistledown scrub where I first walked-up partridges – all wild English birds, and where finches were as numerous as gnats. These small butterflies are mostly shades of brown and orange and well camouflaged among the baked grasses and parched flower heads of late summer and early autumn. Their once great number was only apparent when I moved among them, disturbing their resting and feeding places as I went after the skulking coveys, causing them all to take wing. But the small skipper is exceptionally alert and difficult to follow in flight as it darts about at great speed.

The small copper is still common in suitable places, though it is the last survivor of the British coppers, following the extinction of the large copper in fenland in 1865. Often on the wing into October, it is commonly in the company of blue butterflies. Each lives for about a month, as do white admirals, but some species, such as the small tortoiseshell, can hibernate and survive the most severe winters to lay eggs in the spring.

Small blues conjure up clifftops, refreshing breezes, the sparkling sea to my side and the apparently unending coastal path of the South Downs before me. Speckled woods paint a picture of farmland shade, cool bowers where I have lain in wait for evening rabbits, and secret glades with only deer for company.

The oft-maligned 'cabbage' whites, of course, are the constant companions of the vegetable gardener, their caterpillars fattening on both wild and cultivated members of the cabbage family. The small white seems to have fared better of late than the more handsome large white, so common before the last war. Then they were major pests, destroying great numbers of cabbages. But the widespread introduction of insecticides ended this, and in 1955 they were stricken by a butterfly virus. They have never regained their previous numbers despite a regular influx of Continental migrants.

I have seen many of the butterflies on the British list and all retain special associations for me. But there is no need to dwell only in the past: there is much to be done to help butterflies today. Apart from the obvious, such as joining the public rebellion against unnecessary use of chemicals on the land and supporting a return to organic farming, we can take active part. If each of us left just one corner of the garden in a wild state, with nettles, weeds and long grasses, we would go a long way towards redressing the balance. Favouring ornamental plants of use to butterflies would help too.

1987

## Beware the Gardener

A country garden is a place of unending charm. There is no need to leave its reflective sanctum to go in search of exotics. Given sensible planting and reasonable position, here the whole range of English wildlife, so familiar yet largely unnoticed, will pass before the quiet observer.

Perhaps the riches are greatest now, in the second half of August, as the fast colours of high summer begin to fade with the first gentle touch of dew. In the cool of morning, the year's second flush of roses, brought on by judicious pruning, glistens with beads of moisture, yet by hot midday its glories are again wide open.

High above, the swallows play tag, frequently returning to base on the rooftop television aerial, where they forever overbalance in the turbulent air. Excited in company, their incessant twittering is everywhere – one minute high up among the drifting cumulus boats, the next in mad concert about the trees and houses. Certainly if I had to choose ten 'desert island discs' to remind me of home, the swallow's soliloquy would be one.

Far below the swallows' sky dance, butterflies throng in wobbling profusion along the herbaceous border. There goes a blue, but which one? I call them the waders of the insect world because, like the shorebirds, they rarely keep still long enough to be identified. Oh yes, you can say that X does not normally occur in this area and that Y is only occasional so, given its size and blurred colour, it is probably Z. But there is always the feeling that it could be that rare A!

The brimstone is no problem – he is a blown leaf of lemon

meringue sent to sweeten a world of green. Then comes the stately peacock, with eyes wide open on emperor's robes. Gracefully he works the highest flower plates while – quite five feet below – the humble gatekeeper checks entry to the perfumed jungle.

Suddenly the little orange tip dashes past, white wings dipped in gold. He's as restless as the house martins which draw invisible arcs on the blue wash above. But while they still play, the snub-nosed swifts have already charted the route south. They might have used the splendid maps on the comma's wings.

No flight of fancy for the pheasant though. He will eke out his few seasons here, forever walking in search of a meal. This morning his red cheeks flashed among the runner beans, wide eyes peering to see if the coast was clear, head cocked in permanent question. When tired of pecking at the salad hors-d'oeuvre and the sun was high, he would return to the nearby stubbles to get down to some serious scratching with his associates.

But the rabbit is not welcome here. I have no desire for crinkle-cut lettuce. He is wise to thump the ground at my approach as I still have the patience for half an hour in the hedge with the old BSA air rifle. And what better than wild rabbit and mushroom pie! Fortunately, it's usually the young bunnies which raid the kitchen garden, for they are as tender as the plants they covet.

Traces of other banquets are here too – the wreckage of snails about the thrush's anvil, and a circle of bloody feathers where the sparrowhawk has had finch for breakfast.

Others are more welcome at the August garden table – the Velcro hedgehog which snuffles by night on the trail of slugs, and the brigadier toad whose incredible tongue is the scourge of all juicy pests. He, in turn, must watch for the grass snake, whose hungry glide parted these grasses long before fences were first built.

But for all these creatures my country garden boundary exists only in law. Our sky is open to all with wings, and unhindered is the progress of seeds which bring the surprise and variety we love. No gates are closed to the fields and woods, and the rickety hedges are little barrier to even the largest with four feet. Fox, deer, badger – all have visited, and the natural aspect of self-sown herbs is much more pleasing than the regimentation of bedding plants.

In addition to the continuing element of surprise in variety, there is the uncertainty of success in an unpredictable climate. Not for nothing did the old keepers have so many sayings such as 'Good roots, bad birds!' Yet in every year at least one vegetable and one flower seem to thrive, and there is always some species of wildlife on the up and up.

These then are the elements of largely unappreciated wildness and uncertainty which make the English country garden far more exciting to me than that of hotter but more stable climes.

But now the pigeon are bunching about the hedgerows and my trigger finger is really itchy. This evening I will remind these plump pillagers who really owns this land. Yes, we might all live in one big garden of England, but the whole shooting match is governed by man and I suppose I am just as hypocritical as anyone.

1986

## Helping the Hedgehog

It seems to me that the drier the weather the greater the interest scavengers show in road casualties. Of course, this is always more noticeable in summer anyway, as there are then many more road deaths with naïve young mammals and birds in abundance and an increased volume of traffic. But the highway plundering seems to go way beyond that, and I would suggest that it is at least partly due to the relative scarcity of other foods and the moisture derived from carcases in drought conditions.

One mammal which seems to have fared particularly well on motorists' handouts is the hedgehog, a creature which itself is so common a victim of our helter-skelter existence it is almost dismissed as of no consequence. Yet this is one of the most fascinating animals which tread the paths about man's habitation.

The hedgehog is a great opportunist and there is no doubt its nightly depredations often get it into trouble with poultry keepers, game preservers and wild-bird lovers as it is partial to eggs and chicks. However, its usual diet consists almost entirely of ground-level invertebrates, some of which will have been exceptionally scarce this year. One study from a variety of habitats showed scarabaeid beetles and caterpillars to be the most frequent (each 21 per cent by weight) prey, followed by earthworms, flies, carabid beetles, centipedes, spiders and harvestmen. Slugs, too, are important, but difficult to evaluate. Anyway, one hedgehog's nightly total intake is believed to weigh some 70g.

The validity of persistent tales of hedgehogs deliberately carrying fruit (mostly apples) on their spines is always disputed, though perhaps not quite so strongly as those involving taking milk from resting cows. But there is no doubt that hedgehogs will regularly travel a quarter of a mile or so to sup a saucer of bread and milk left out for them.

Because it has such an effective armour of spines (some 5,000 on an adult's back), the hedgehog can afford to eat noisily. For the same reason, it has no need of long legs for running.

A foraging hedgehog holds its body close to the ground as this is the best method for nosing out grubs in the leaf litter. Other large mammals which hunt for invertebrates cannot match this method. For example, you may have seen how clumsy a fox is, coming down on the potential food from above but generally ending up with only a mouthful of leaves.

Some of the fruit taken in autumn is fermenting and frequently makes a hedgehog quite tipsy, just as it does butterflies such as red admirals and peacocks. Affected animals wander about the garden bumping into fence posts, trees and bushes. But with a clear head that same animal is surprisingly nimble and will not hesitate in scrambling over tall fences and other barriers with only the slightest purchase. Sadly, their confidence often leads to their death when, for example, they become entangled in netting.

At other times, strategically placed wire netting can be used to save their lives, for example as a kind of ladder in garden swimming pools, where otherwise they frequently drown. Ornamental ponds with smooth sides should be similarly equipped.

It is thought that hedgehogs are less afraid of falling than most other mammals because they are well cushioned by their spines. Unfortunately, this often seems to lead them into danger, for they frequently fall into deep holes, such as those beneath cattle grids, from which they cannot escape. But now many thoughtful owners are providing their grids with ramps, ideally covered with netting for a good grip, to help stranded hedgehogs escape.

Another way in which we can all help this mammal is avoiding use of poisons in the garden, as the hedgehog is soon affected and often dies after eating prey which has taken even small amounts of toxins, such as those commonly used in pesticides.

Providing a healthy environment in which to get fat is most important for the hedgehog as it depends on its reserves during hibernation. With insufficient 'stores' it simply won't survive, and during a time of exceptional stress the population may tumble. Even in its hibernaculum the hedgehog can suffer through lack of moisture; the nest of leaves and grass is as important in preventing the mammal drying out as it is in avoiding freezing and the eyes of predators. But why the hedgehog anoints itself with masses of frothy saliva, plastered all over the body, including the spines, no one is sure.

1989

## My First Shotgun

All this summer rain has reminded me of when I (or rather my friend, as I was just fourteen) bought my first shotgun, a single-barrelled Webley 12-bore. Before that I borrowed from the largely motley collection of mostly hammer guns belonging to what was, on reflection, an equally motley collection of boys. There was, however, a revered Joseph Manton (gun that is), the name whispered among us as outlaws may have said 'Wyatt Earp'.

Anyway, with my own gun at last I was free to stalk the lonely trail, to hunt as I wished. But on the day the gun arrived, and fivepenny green Russian, orange Czech and yellow Wizard cartridges were brushed aside in favour of the seven or eight penn'orth (£ s d that is) of venom vented from the Hymax, it rained and rained and rained. The deluge showed no sign of abating, so with Graham and his Canadian Cooey 12 and John with his Turner 10-bore we plodded up the foreshore. I shot six tin cans thrown under duress, a sheet of corrugated iron, and a pied crow lunching on the mudflats. I was totally drenched but a barrel never felt smoother and powder smoke never smelt sweeter than on that first day I used my own gun.

1980

# September

## Gossamer Days

Now there is a chill to the night, the days are distinctly 'closing in', and over the water-meadows the moisture evaporated during the day distils after sunset in level layers of mist. Such 'vapours' bring down with them the numerous small insects on which the swallow tribe feed.

Suddenly the world is full of spiders. At dawn their lacework sparkles like jewelry about every fence, bush and tussock, and their lifelines of gossamer drift across the fields, glinting in the early rays. They descend in droves, at the whim of the wind, and instantly the countryside is magic-carpeted.

But even more prominent in September is the birdlife – the excited gathering of species destined for warmer climes, the advance parties of winter visitors, and the flocking of finches which must stock up against the lean times ahead. Woodpigeons assemble to gobble up the last of the stubble grain, owls have a new note of earnestness in their hoot, and sparrows noisily brush wings with starlings in the hedgerow roost.

In favoured corners, the partridge turns his rusty key at close of dusk, and teal wing into the flightpond with newfound fervour. There is an air of excitement and urgency which infiltrates every being abroad in the countryside, and the hunter yearns for coastal excursions after wildfowl.

1988

September

# Wells and Dew-Ponds

While the drought continues we reassure ourselves with the fact that even during the heatwave of 1976 our private water supply did not dry up. But what will happen to us, and many thousands of other rural dwellers if we now have an exceptionally dry winter? Should we dig a well?

I have been fascinated by wells since childhood – not that there were many left even then. The one we had in our garden had not been used for decades, but it was a constant source of wonder to me as it gobbled up garden refuse with an insatiable appetite. Year after year my father filled it to the brim with greenery and year after year this offering to the gods of the underworld soon disappeared.

In his *Natural History of Selborne* (1789), old Gilbert White wrote: 'Our wells, at an average, run to about 63 feet, and when sunk to that depth seldom fail; but produce a fine, limpid water, soft to the taste, and much commended by those who drink the pure element, but which does not lather well with soap.'

White also noted how the water supply can vary greatly within a relatively short distance: 'At each end of the village, which runs from south-east to north-west, arises a small rivulet: that at the north-west end frequently fails; but the other is a fine perennial spring little influenced by drought or wet seasons, called Well-head. This spring produced, September 14th, 1781, after a severe hot summer, and a preceding dry spring and winter, nine gallons of water in a minute, which is 540 in an hour, and 12,960, or 260 hogsheads, in 24 hours. At this time many of the wells failed, and all the ponds in the vales were dry.'

In those days country people were not too particular about their water supply; if they saw a dead mouse floating about in the swirling well bucket they were not generally perturbed. And until quite recently, unless they thought the water was actually poisonous, many folk would never bother to boil it specially. But now the bureaucrats soon pop a cork into any outlet that fails to conform with 'rules and regs'. There will be no returning to the days when many villagers took water from ditches and contracted typhoid.

Shallow wells – those down to about 28ft – usually tap what is generally known as surface water, that which falls as rain, sinks through the soil and rock and accumulates in underground pools and lakes, in the folds of impervious strata. The surface of this underground supply is known as the 'water-table', and the depth at which it occurs is much the same over considerable areas, within

163

which a well dug almost anywhere taps water at the same level as neighbouring wells.

However, the depth of the water-table varies greatly with the season, reaching its highest in February and March and receding to its lowest in late autumn. Occasionally, in the spring the water-table reaches the surface and appears through rills – springs coming out of the ground.

Many old legends surround such springs. For example, at Turville in Buckinghamshire they say that when the springs come out in the village street there will be war in the following year, giving examples of the year before the Boer War – 1898, 1913 and 1938. But no doubt the villagers conveniently overlooked years of peace which followed those when the springs also appeared.

There can be little doubt that many country people have developed a tolerance to polluted water, for many wells which were once relatively pure have been tainted by nearby development. Some have attracted the seepage from house drains, while others have been the recipients of the run-off from stockyards. Stories abound of how well owners have lived with such problems all their lives without suffering any dire consequence, but in more than one case, once they learned of the problem they mysteriously acquired symptoms – no doubt psychosomatic – such as a sore throat. Just ask any of the old plumbers or drain men.

Of course, most people living in sterile urban environments, with very clean mains water, are very susceptible to the mildest water pollution, as many know to their cost after trips abroad to more backward countries. Similarly, at home there was a real problem during the last war, when children were evacuated from the towns to the countryside. These youngsters often developed a tummy ache, or worse, and in return they passed diphtheria and scarlet fever to the country children.

By World War II, well-digging by manual labour was already a dying craft, but a few old boys retained the skill. First they would simply mark a circle on the ground, then dig round and round with a spade, pick and crowbar, for which tiresome work they received about £1 a foot. It was not at all easy to keep the hole both round and vertical, and swinging the tools in such cramped positions was extremely difficult. Also, a 'top' man was needed to haul up the excavated earth in a bucket.

Well-diggers used to tell many hair-raising stories of collapsing walls, being overcome by foul gasses, and of exciting rescues. Some were knocked out or injured by falling rocks, and others nearly drowned when their picks broke into standing water, which could flood a well within minutes.

Today the old well-digger has long since hung up his pick; engineering and drilling have developed at an incredible pace, and man can bore down for miles if he so wishes, usually in search of the black gold that lubricates society.

Nowadays, a sight almost as rare as a working well is a dew-pond, though some are retained to supplement water supplies for stock in high, dry country. Some of these large, bowl-shaped depressions still exist on the downs, their working principle being very simple: they collect more water through rainfall and condensing dew than is lost by evaporation.

However, it is said that the making of a dew-pond was a highly skilled craft, the recipe of the mixture used to make the watertight linings being kept a secret. Basically, clay was mixed with coarse materials to minimise cracking and shrinkage in dry weather, but today there would be little problem with waterproof cement and other materials to hand.

Sadly, now there is little need for dew-ponds, with water easily piped from place to place, but there is no doubt they are extremely attractive elements of landscape and a great help to wildlife on some nature reserves.

I wonder what old Gilbert would have made of water privatisation.

1989

## Muddy Memories

For many folk the stench of tidal mud is an abomination, but others, including myself, find that this is not only an acquired smell but also a highly evocative one. Just one whiff is enough to conjure up whirling memories of wind, wings and weather. Thus it was good to return to the Sussex saltmarsh during September's first week of the wildfowling season, even though a temperature in the seventies was scarcely reminiscent of prime fowling days.

In the afternoon we were entertained by water-skiers and the continual passage of yachts over the sparkling ripple of the main channel, while mud banks dazzled like snow. Entrenched in a gully, with the chance of curlew, there was plenty to see. Mullet cruised among tiny fish rising in steadily filling creeks where cockles spurted. The tall summer saltgrasses now energising in bright sunlight would soon be as forests to the ranging bass. Bold, twisting redshank mobbed Mike's Irish setter, Misty, and the garbled instructions of yacht crews carried on the salt breeze. A lone sandwich tern beat low over me, his tilted head alive to every opportunity, repeating that *kirrick* call which, to me, is synonymous with summer fishing.

With dusk approaching, the wind steadily increased, bringing vast columns of starlings curling in on murmuring wings. A nightjar passed high up in his last month with us, and a kingfisher buzzed the shoreline, his plumage surprisingly dull in the failing sunlight.

It was a short flight, consisting of one teal and four mallard which arrived in the murk at the height of our expectancy, to leave two of their number behind in exchange for four shots. What more could we ask? Testing shots in wild surroundings, a duck apiece and ample incentive for next time. The easy rhythm of tides and a timelessness on civilization's neglected margin. Twilight on the marsh in the twilight month of the year.

1980

## Sting in the Tale

When the window cleaner said 'Oh, by the way, you have a wasps' nest in the roof' we pretended surprise. It had been interesting to watch the striped predators zip past the bedroom window, sometimes carrying other insects of considerable size. Admittedly their excited droning has been a hindrance to early-morning slumber and they have bumbled into the house a few times. Indeed, one evening we were alarmed to find a cluster of nine around a bedside lamp, and one morning I was stung on the bottom of the foot while dressing. But wasps are not officially classified as pests – in our district at least – and I didn't consider the intrusion serious enough to warrant paying the local council £19 to 'do for 'em'.

Common wasps usually build their nests underground, in the burrows of small mammals, where the papery cells are built up in horizontal tiers rather than the vertical combs of a beehive. In my youth, any ground nests which occurred in local gardens were filled with paraffin and set light to, though I am not sure how effective this was and I suspect that some people were primarily interested in being vindictive.

Britain has seven species of social wasp, the black markings on the yellow face of the common wasp distinguishing it from other species. Unlike the honey bee, it has an unbarbed sting which can be used several times to kill insects for food, and to provide a deterrent against larger animals, such as lizards, as well as birds and man. A colony of drones and workers, headed by a queen, contains up to about 2,000 wasps – a tiny number compared with a typical gathering of 50,000 bees.

In spring and early summer, worker wasps do a lot of good in killing large numbers of pests such as sawfly caterpillars and aphids, which they feed to their larvae. In return, the wasps feed on a sweet saliva produced by the larvae.

The queen wasp stops laying eggs in late summer, and then there are no more larvae to produce saliva, so the wasps have to seek out other sweet foods such as windfall fruit, cakes and jam cooling by the window. But with the coming of autumn all the drones and workers die, leaving the fertilised queen to hibernate. And it is not unusual for a queen to tuck up in a little-used curtain.

Wasps are very much part of the early-autumn scene, especially when they clamber drunkenly over fallen fruit, their 'feelers' apparently waving haphazardly 'under the influence'.

1988

## Hints for Holidaymakers

Recently we rented a black-beamed, seventeenth-century farm-house for a holiday in a remote part of Herefordshire. The building was charming but, to say the least, far from clean and orderly. Therefore it was not surprising to find some most amusing comments in the guest book, entitled 'Hints for happy holidaymakers'. Two of my favourites were: 'Beware of switching off the fridge in mistake for the light' and 'The milkman visits the farm in a white van on Mon, Wed and Friday (sometimes Sun, Tues, Thurs and Saturday)'. There was even an index, though 'The cat and where to go for a good meal' seemed an unlikely grouping. Other advice concerned comfort, such as 'The bed in the main bedroom tends to roll occupants together. Not advisable to be slept on for your own safety.' 'There is a noisy crow's nest over the large double bedroom – which makes for a very noisy night in the breeding season.' Also: 'It is very advisable to get to sleep before 10.30 otherwise you will find it difficult because of the noise from all the mice, squirrels, owls, etc, in the loft and cellar.' Quite obviously some of the guests were used only to a spick and span existence.

1982

## My Secret Apple Store

I always loved sitting in a September orchard, watching the insects make use of the sugars in fermenting fruit. When I was a boy, one of our garden trees was a splendid, high and ancient Victoria plum, with dark, fissured trunk and cracked branches where tits and even tree creepers nested. Its foliage was sparse, yet the faithful tree still fruited well. Some plums dropped into our little pigsty and were immediately consumed, but more littered the path, attracting wasps and red admirals by the score. I loved those plums so much I even ate ones partly chewed by wasps!

Another favourite autumn pastime was laying the apples out in long rows in the large loft over the outbuilding. With just a glimmer of light from the tiny gable window, I carefully placed the different types of apple – eaters and cookers – onto spread newspapers on the bare floorboards, all precisely one inch apart and carefully staggered in size. My aim was to eat the small ones first and work upwards towards the prize fruits around Christmas. This was my store alone, where never a breath of wind stirred, where not even the mice could reach and all my little secrets were stashed so carefully along with my collection of feathers, skulls and old nests.

Sometimes I crept out at night and climbed up the steep, open, wooden steps with the hurricane lamp, just to sit and admire my store of apples. On a clear night I would snuff the flame and watch the moonbeams search among my silver fruit. Then there always seemed to be an owl hooting, and below I could hear the rats scratching and racing about father's grain store. My September fruit was safe, but I still set a trap for good measure.

Sometimes today, when I think hard enough, I can still smell that paraffin lamp and the maturing apples. Nostalgia it may be, but I don't think I've ever tasted any fruit to compare with the Victoria plums, long-matured russets and unidentified apple varieties of my childhood.

Sadly, that outbuilding of my past is gone: it was demolished long ago to make way for a car park. Perhaps one day, someone excavating there might come across a few of the old bones I gathered and then falsely proclaim that here was the camp of primitive man. I would not describe myself quite as this, but at least I was, and still am, a hunter.

1986

## Ozone Friendly

How pleasing to report that relatives and friends are seeking out and using the new 'ozone-friendly' aerosols and shunning those charged with CFCs – those dastardly chlorofluorocarbons blamed for that great, growing hole in the ozone layer. Certain supermarket chains are applauded for leading the way, especially in the officially designated 'Green Week' that has just ended. However few customers are naïve enough to believe that the shop owners' actions are anything other than commercially motivated. It took years to convince Mr and Mrs Average that a mere squirt of hair lacquer or furniture polish within the confines of their near draught-proof house could have any effect whatsoever on distant layers of the earth's atmosphere – to them virtually outer space.

But there it is, the movement has started and it doesn't really matter that the impetus is fuelled by greed; the underlying pressure is public concern for the environment. The ozone trail merely follows in the wake of terrestrial anxieties such as that over excessive crop spraying, which gave rise to the revival of organic farming. Again, public pressure paved the way and profit-motivated entrepreneurs turned dreams into reality when the number of people interested reached a level to make marketing viable. No one has any doubt that concerned individuals will pay the premium for chemical-free 'health' foods and 'safe' aerosols as long as it is not too much. However, the degree of acceptance will vary greatly with the prosperity of the region.

In this country the Government has left the phasing out of CFCs to the whims of commerce, but at least it has made a positive contribution to air purity in another direction. Its recent decision to commit many millions of pounds to the eradication of acid rain is long overdue and welcomed both at home and abroad. The installation of plant at power stations, to prevent sulphur dioxide and other nasties getting into the atmosphere will do much to help regeneration of dying forests and 'dead' waters, both in Britain and those countries downwind of us which have been the unhappy recipients of our 'fall-out' for decades.

1988

## Hope for the Partridge

The last of the corn is coming in exceptionally late. Some fields have lain half cut for weeks on end, ears have sprouted in contact with the earth and what promised to be a good crop is now a salvage operation. Yet out of the mire comes hope – partridges seem to have made good use of fields retaining stubble for much longer than is usual. Today's quick-turnover agriculture prefers to plough in stubble at the earliest opportunity, in preparation for the next crop, and as a result partridges and other birds have lost much of their traditional foraging ground. But this year it's different.

1985

# Tough Times for Toads

One night recently I discovered that a toad had taken refuge in the very narrow gap between the bottom of the front door and the threshold. Fearing that the amphibian might be squashed by less vigilant or occasionally intoxicated members of the family, I carefully placed it in the nearest flower bed, where there are always enough juicy slugs to make a toad positively froth at the mouth. But this is obviously a toad with a will, one scornful of manhandling, for on every one of the eight nights since that first encounter he has returned to claim that threshold.

The owner of a healthy garden soon gets to know that the toad spends the brighter hours in shelter, often in some sufficiently moist hole in the earth or among stones. Unlike the frog, it has dry skin and does not lose water readily, but still needs to avoid very dry places which might cause dessication.

When it has grown larger than the entrance hole to its daytime quarters, a toad may be imprisoned, leading to many press stories about toads emerging alive from stones, rocks or even coal, in which they had been 'embedded'. The animals were noticed only when the lumps were split in half, and unfortunately the observers had not spotted the holes through which the toads had entered. Toads are known to have survived in such chambers for as long as two years, provided that there was a crack sufficiently large to enable prey food to enter.

Toads will continue to drift towards their hibernation holes during this month and next. Some go into mud at the bottom of ponds, but larger numbers lie up together on dry land. However, I don't think our doorstep toad was after early hibernation. It is much more likely that he had been attracted by the odour of temporarily abundant prey. Experiments have shown that, after feeding for a day or two on a particular species, toads are soon attracted by the smell of that prey, which also causes them to lower their snouts and put out their tongues.

Fortunately, Sam the cat, who is particularly active at 'toading time', keeps well clear of all amphibians, having had the usual distasteful lesson long ago. Skin secretions of both adult and immature toads protect them against a variety of predators, including dogs, which salivate violently and show clear distaste if they attempt an amphibious retrieve. Only a few grass snakes will eat them, but hedgehogs have no inhibitions, and crows and rats often kill toads without eating the meat.

Other toads meet their end with a sickening crunch beneath our car tyres, but to me the most hideous toad mortality is that caused by greenbottle parasitism. The fly lays a cluster of eggs on the toad's thighs or lower back. When these are moistened the larvae hatch and make their way up the toad's back to the eyes, travelling across the lachrymal duct into the nasal cavity. The host is then eaten alive, beginning with the head, so that the toad dies within two or three days. It's certainly tough being a toad, even without man messing up the environment.

1988

## 'Food for Free'

Harvesting the fruits of field and hedgerow has generated considerable renewed interest in recent years. Indeed, in an age when gardens are mostly cosmetic and do not easily facilitate self-sufficiency, there is growing awareness of long-neglected crops. In our house at least, it is difficult not to experiment as I am surrounded by a very inquisitive family. Why, only last week we had spicy chanterelles lightly fried with onions. Yet I couldn't bring myself to try the fillets of beefsteak fungus which my son deposited in the larder. Good it might be but, when sliced, this type of fungus really does look like old liver past its sell-by date.

It is most important not to eat any wild fungus whatsoever unless you are certain that it is edible. There is nothing clever in taking a gamble. Remember, Britain has the world's most poisonous fungus in the death-cap, and the destroying angel is just about as lethal. Even inhalation of the spores of these fungi can bring a slow, painful death.

Most people are happier with blackberries, and what sweeter smell is there than blackberry and apple stewing in the kitchen? Blackberry wine is an old favourite of mine and bramble jelly is like nectar on fresh bread and butter.

Long ago, blackberries were known as bumblekites or scold berries and they have been used medicinally since early times. Although they have been part of the kitchen garden hedge since the sixteenth century at least, serious cultivation did not start till the 1840s, and then in America. The juice was used for swollen tonsils and gum ulcers, and the plant's young, peeled shoots were put in salads, being thought useful for tightening loose teeth. Pulped leaves were used for ringworm, scalds and leg ulcers.

Blackberrying is one of the great joys of the British countryside. Many's the time when I have deliberately arrived too early for an evening flight on the foreshore in order to collect a few pounds of 'blackies', though those near the sea are generally of the small, seedy variety. Much better are the big, luscious berries which abound in the semi-shade beneath the pigeon roost. Mind you, the fruits stain your hands so easily I wouldn't be surprised if you could black your gun barrels with them. After all, bramble shoots were once used to produce a black dye widely employed for staining mohair, silk and wool.

A better wine is produced from elderberries, now largely neglected compared with ancient times. Greying Romans used to dye their hair black with elderberries, and even into the eighteenth century the green bark was used to make a black dye. A purgative was made from the leaves and the young branches were used to whip fruit trees and garden crops to prevent attacks by insects. It is said that the leaves were also effective in making moles leave their burrows, and that when pounded with beef tallow they eased the pain of hot swellings and tumours.

Among the wide range of uses for elder wood was making the tops of eighteenth century fishing rods and butchers' skewers. Elderflowers, too, make an excellent wine and give a fine flavour to gooseberry jam. Medicinal uses for the elder have been legion and ranged from an elderflower tea laxative to berry jelly for catarrh. Now the elder is not usually cultivated, but it is quite difficult to keep this invasive plant out. We always like some nearby to make a delicious cordial from elderflowers with oranges and lemons.

Crab apples have only rarely been grown in the kitchen garden, though their use in giving additional flavour to tarts and pies has been considerable. For cidermaking they were usually stored till December, but then only used to strengthen the flavour of cider 'washings'. The bitter flavour was thought quite suitable for labourers, rather in the pompous way that elderberry wine was thought suitable for rustics but not for those with sophisticated tastes. Of course, it is idiocy to compare fruit wines of this nature with fine 'table wines', which I dearly love. All have their place and moment.

One plant which is having its moment now, in my neck of the woods, is the raspberry. In the last few years it has suddenly decided to rampage across the farmland in the manner of the bramble, so that now we can go raspberrying as well as blackberrying. Always difficult to remove from gardens, raspberries are truly invasive.

Our particular delight is 'freezer jam' made from raspberries mashed with sugar, lemon and 'Certo'. Its freshness makes it far superior to any jam made in the ordinary manner, though a whole variety of fruits can be used in this way.

Collecting hazel nuts – mostly the wild cobs rather than the cultivated filberts – is another activity which always gets me in wintry mood. These, too, have always been associated with superstition, but I am more interested in a good crunch rather than a cure for jaundice or malfunctions of the bladder.

1986


## Exploded Myths

Now, traditionally, we study the abundance of wild fruits and the behaviour of wild creatures to make bold predictions about the mood of winter. In so doing, St Michael's Day (29 September) has been regarded as critical in much of Europe, but just how much of the lore has any credibility and how much is mere myth?

Sadly, it seems that science has dismissed most of the old saws, but most of us don't want to delve too deeply into the truth for we appear to harbour a deep-rooted love of natural mystery. In a world where man can demolish an empire at the touch of a button, and where most of life is so predictable, we secretly relish

174

the uncertainty of the seasons and the prospect of all men bowing to superior natural forces.

There is certainty, too, of course. We know that swallows will now be restless in their roosts. Reed-beds will quiver with the expectancy of their departure and wires will sag with the weight of their longing to be up, up and away on the first favourable wind. But hedge fruits and nuts are far less predictable, in quantity at least, and it is largely into this variation that man inserts his crystal ball. Only this year many people have remarked on an exceptionally large wild harvest, but what does this mean, and is there any uniformity in the phenomenon?

Rustic poet John Clare (1793–1864) seemed to have little doubt when he wrote:

> The thorns and briars, vermilion hue,
>     Now full of hips and haws are seen;
> If village prophecies be true,
>     They prove that winter will be keen.

But at least one Victorian country writer had the sense to remark: 'If the crop be a heavy one, it points rather to the favourable season for flowering that has gone than to anything in the future; but our simpler-minded ancestors had a firm belief in a law of immediate compensations in Nature. If one year was wet, the next would be dry; if winter was keen, there would be a liberal provision of berries for the feathered folk, and so on; a simple creed hardly supported by records of the Meteorological Office.'

Yet the arguments go back even further. In the reign of Henry VIII, a proclamation was made against the almanacs which transmitted the belief in saints ruling the weather. Hardly surprising in a country which is still world-renowned for being weather conscious, though we do have the excuse that, while our climate is relatively free from extremes, it is more variable than most.

An old Scottish proverb proclaimed: 'Mony hips and haws, mony frosts and snaws'. It suggests that kindly nature will always provide, but sadly this is not the case. In fact, studies of records have revealed that there is no truth in this at all. Today we are told that not only do plants merely react to *present* weather but also may even give a completely misleading indication of the weather to come.

Similarly, there seems to be no scientific basis in the suggestion that animals are able to 'read the signs' and react to approaching weather. Of course, here we are only concerned with long-term forecasts and not short-term behaviour. For example, there is no doubt that wildfowl will and often do move to frost-free feeding areas, but *only* when severe conditions have set upon their traditional haunts.

However, when it comes to migratory species the situation is more complicated and, like everyone else, I love to speculate about the cold to come in relation to the arrival of migrants. Have the geese left their northerly breeding grounds earlier than usual because great snowstorms are impending? And thus will our winter be exceptionally severe because we tend to get the weather which follows the birds? Unfortunately there seems to be no certainty in any of this, though bitterly cold winters have generally been shared by the whole of North-West Europe rather than confined to Britain.

It is the availability of food which is crucial, and if it so happens that ice or snow make particular foods temporarily unavailable then even normally sedentary species must move to find alternatives. Because Britain lies at a 'weather crossroads' and is such a key staging post for migratory birds, even in an average year our bird 'supply' is erratic.

None-the-less, belief in the old law of compensations continues. Of late, everyone (even the BBC) has been looking for an Indian summer, but why I do not know. On the contrary, a glimpse at records reveals that dramatic changes are unusual in this country, and quiet reflection will remind you that poor autumns and winters tend to follow poor summers. This is at least partly due to Britain being a relatively small land mass surrounded by sea. Compared with that of the air, the sea's temperature is slow to change and thus, when it is already exceptionally low in summer it will tend to chill autumn winds more rapidly. There will then be a knock-on effect into winter. For example, that great-grandaddy of all hoary winters – 1962–3 – followed a rotten summer. The mean temperature of every month from March to September 1962 was well below average, in South-East England at least. October hiccuped with +1.2° F above the mean, but the plunge returned in November.

Yet, despite the language of satellites and computers, I still listen to the old wives' tales, and this autumn I will be out there looking for the first fieldfare as keenly as ever. If he comes early and brings all his relatives then . . .

1985

## Dream of a Flight

The god of hunting blew strongly across my chimney, calling with hollow sounds just like those created by blowing over the tops of large bottles. He cast his spell about my cosiness and smothered the sunset with a mizzling rain which surged and sank in eddies of greyness, washing all colour from the September landscape. A twig tapped repeatedly on the window, drawing my attention to the arrival of the 'duck wind', and the trees rocked and nodded in whispered agreement. It was time to prepare.

The 10-bore felt good in my hands again, the breech snapping shut as sweetly as ever, the old brown barrels gleaming as I oiled them in the soft fireside glow. Yet clean as it was, the fowling piece retained that unremovable patina of adventure and the whiff of seasons past. There still were all the dents and scratches from days when blood ran hot and pursuit of quarry swept away all cares of self or possessions. Then the wilderness and chase were as drugs.

But now came a new season and fresh opportunities. As I sat and dreamed by the hearth, I wondered what the gamebook would record for tomorrow. Would the old enthusiasm be there, and would success come my way?

I need not have worried for, true to form, I awoke instinctively ten minutes before reveille, when the alarm would have sounded. How much more satisfying and less taxing to be awoken naturally by excitement rather than shaken out of insensibility by some god-awful, klaxon-loud timepiece.

Yet years before, such had been our youthful ardour, we tied strings to our big toes and dangled them out of the window for summoning friends to tug. It was a good system and avoided the wrath of disturbed parents but occasionally went wrong when calling angels got carried away. Once a chum pulled so hard and long I winced with pain and in my rush to the window clambered all over my brother in the next bed, and he, being older and bigger, rose up to deliver a good thump.

Thus I was smoothly underway and this day there was even time for a wash and coffee. And for once the milk didn't boil over onto the stove in preparing my favourite flask of hot chocolate for later.

It was only a five-minute drive to the marsh, but a thirty-minute tramp beyond that to my favourite station. During the walk there was no light at all, no glimmer from distant towns or roads, no moon, no stars and no sea-wall to follow: only the faint gleam of mudflats and a receding tide.

How creepy these solo, nocturnal jaunts are, with the wind sucking at your ears, dropping now and again so that you can hear the 'super rats' and other beasties rustling through nearby bushes and reeds. Then there's always a skitty moorhen to shake you with its call and rush, or an unseen gutter to fall in, to jolt the head and wrench the gun away as you attempt to save yourself from the abyss.

This morning was no exception and, while I knew the way well, the ground was forever changing under the wash of tides. Thus, when I jumped a small creek, I faltered and the gun, already out of its sleeve in readiness for a shot, hurtled away from me and nosedived into the thick mud.

Of course, like a fool I had no pull-through with me and the only recourse was to take the barrels off and wash them in the briny. I had done this before and got away with it as long as I cleaned the gun promptly and thoroughly on returning home.

Despite the mishap, I was well entrenched in the forward line quite fifteen minutes before the first wave of duck were due over. It was pleasantly warm and my 'Ready-Brek' glow was only spoiled by the faulty puncture repair on my left wader, which allowed the ooze to squelch between the toes.

Then the rain returned and visibility was just about zilch through my specs. However, I plugged the chinks in my armour as best I could and held firm like Roy of the Rovers. Fortunately, the ebb coincided with dawn and I could expect a good turnout of fowl. But first came the burbling of curlews, rising and falling with the wind, uneasy on their temporary roost. Then the haunting cry of distant peewits and a sudden rush of wings as a squadron of golden plover hurtled past, mere shadows without colour or shape.

At last the veil lifted, slowly and gently, with never a trace of sunlight to fire the sky, only an almost imperceptible lightening of the grey. However, the gale was erratic and in a lull I caught the first quack of prospecting mallard. Then it stopped, only to come again between gusts, this time to my left and much closer.

I slid round just in time to see their familiar silhouettes heading straight towards me, with unwavering intent like bombers on a mission, but it was difficult to assess their range. On they came till at last I saw they would be 'tall' birds, yet well within the grasp of the 10-bore. When their undercarriage was square on overhead I rose to crack the dawn with both barrels, parting the gloom with tongues of flame.

The gods were certainly with me for I had taken out the entire squadron. One was winged but three were dead in the air, cartwheeling and carried on the mighty wind for quite fifty yards. Yet I could hear the thud as they struck the mud and marked them well as my labrador Tiger went after the parachutist.

Hardly were the birds gathered when the whistle of wigeon drifted over. In an instant they were before me, wheeling about and searching for safe quarter along the tideline, the white patches on the drakes' forewings winking against the gloomy sky.

Again the 10 spoke and Tiger made short work of a right-and-left from the waves. There was a tremor of excitement in my fingers as I dropped two more 'shells' into the still-smoking chambers.

Back came the 'goldies', jinking and weaving, hugging the contours of the shoreline, and this time I was ready. Here indeed was a favourite meal. The first shot downed four in front and the second six more as they veered broadside on, yet hardly deviated from some pre-ordained pattern. Would there be enough room for all these birds in my humble gamebag?

However, there was no time to answer this question. Suddenly there was a crick in my neck and it was totally dark again, save for a faint red glow – from my fire! I had fallen asleep in the study, with the cleaned gun on my lap, and the entire flight had been one of fancy. But there was yet time to reach the marsh before daybreak!

1987

## Successful Sweep

Tomorrow the sweep is coming to clean the chimney, for within weeks the first logs will crackle in the hearth, to blush our cheeks after a day of early frost and pheasant shooting. He always complains about the twisting inners of the stack, but his rods get there in the end, and after putting the soot on the compost heap to weather he drives off in his new van with another £6. It seems only yesterday that his predecessor came on a bike and worked for five shillings and a cup of tea. Like the farrier with his shoeing, in a country that has never had so many horses, the sweep is not doing too badly with the trend towards log burning accelerated by woodland clearance and Dutch elm disease.

1982

# October

## Ensuring Survival

October is a wonderful time for birdsong, especially that of wren and robin. Even though the month is characterized by decay and the general withdrawal of nature, the wren especially seems to have unbridled energy, singing as enthusiastically in the pre-dawn twilight as he does in May, with the days lengthening.

October is also surprising in that it is a time of courtship for some species. The red deer rut is hard to miss, but one could easily be forgiven for overlooking the lovemaking of spiders, now pairing in every hedgerow. The females are easy to see as they alone spin the webs. The males are relatively hard to find but easy to recognise, with their longer, leaner bodies, and pair of curved feelers with club-shaped ends.

So, far from being merely a month of harvest and slowing down, October is also a time for consolidation and ensuring the survival of species.

1989

## Cider and Sheep's Blood

What magical places orchards are – especially those which moulder gently in the old-fashioned way, where maximising profits is unimportant, chemicals are banned and machines virtually unknown. Some, especially in the cider country of the West, are very, very old and wonderfully dilapidated, festooned with soft-grey lichens and moss and thickly clustered with mistletoe. They are little use to the new, perfectionist breed of grower, but what a joy to the naturalist or wayfarer. Yet even out of this apparent chaos an amazingly prolific crop can emerge.

They say that an old cider-maker could follow his nose home blindfold, and I think it fair to say that autumn orchards are truly heaven-scent, each with its own very individual character. But it is not only differences in the fruit which have brought variety to our traditional ciders. The old recipes show an extraordinary degree of imagination in the cider-making.

In the Devon valleys, tradition called for the addition of milk, eggs and cream, while Cornish miners used sheep's blood. In Kent, cherries, blackberries and spices were added, along with the gum that oozed from the trees, as a natural substitute for isinglass.

How sad it is that we have lost, and are still losing, so many of our apple varieties as eco-efficiency rules the roost. Fortunately we still have people devoted to apple rescue and preservation. The names alone are worth saving. Take, for example, the resplendent fruits preserved forever in the Victorian lithographs on my kitchen wall, including Ecklinville, Duchess of Oldenburgh and Ribstone pippin. To some folk, no doubt, these are little gems of mouthwatering history, but to most they are little more than curios.

A few people, apparently, still collect rotting crab apples for cider making, though I know of none. And further back, other country folk made a vinegar, called vargis or verjuice, from crabs. Even crab-apple jelly is rarely made nowadays, and the only activity I see about the crab trees is the desultory pecking of birds.

Some of the old crab trees produce fruits to tempt hungry children, but these apples' abundance of malic acid soon halts their munching. A few supposed crabs are really 'escapees' from nearby orchards and these may produce reasonable apples. Their pips are easily passed by birds, and some may have germinated when rustics discarded their cores.

1990

## Fruits of the Forest

This year's World Conker Championships have been plagued by a split decision – the organisers have struggled to find sufficient nuts of uniform size and quality because so many have cracked through drought and erratic water supply. Yet the prize seed is set for another year, thudding down on roads and pavements, drives and dark alleys, parks and playgrounds, to delight small boys with their glistening promise. How eagerly the green caskets are cracked open, like Fabergé eggs revealing exquisite jewels.

Some nuts crash down on cars, frightening occupants; others score direct hits on passing heads, including my unshielded pate, and a few even manage to startle woodland animals as they descend through the canopy, ricocheting against trunks and branches as if in a pinball machine, before crunching into the leaf litter.

Acorns, too, plummet with a vengeance. Only last week one delivered a savage blow to my unprotected skull, and another hit my car with such ferocity I immediately pulled over to see if the roof had been dented. Thank heavens we don't have coconuts to contend with in this country.

Now the leaves are in full flight before a grey wind bent on washing every vestige of colour from the countryside. Here they come, blustering up and down like smuts from a bonfire, carrying hundreds of yards from sylvan towers to block our roof gutters and set overflows spouting in the next storm. On damp days they lay flabbily about lawns, mantling the worm-pimpled surface, or stick to pavements and steps, waiting to upend unwary feet. But, when dry, their vigour is restored, tracing the wind's currents, peacefully sailing with puffed spinnakers in the upper air or madly swirling in drifts about courtyard corners.

When the autumn underworld is bone dry even the blackbird sounds like a boar foraging in the leaf litter, flicking over the parched pages of summer, searching for nourishment. How often I've stalked such a grubber in the belief that at least a rabbit was there for the taking.

Now the leaves have performed their main function for another year, having manufactured chlorophyll to nurture the trees. Gradually the green colour disappears, allowing autumnal tints based on trace minerals in the tree's nutrients to take over. Where leaves and twigs join we find barriers of a corky substance being formed, to cut off the supply of sap. Then the leaves die and flutter to the ground, adding to the humus for recycling. But on some younger trees – notably oaks – the gum which fastens the leaves to the twigs is too strong, holding them fast throughout the winter. However, you will never see this on old oaks because their annual rhythm was perfected long ago.

But there is another reason for autumn leaf fall. Even a tree as strong as an oak, with its deep anchor of roots, could not withstand the gales and blizzards of winter with such a heavy cloak to carry. Conifers, on the other hand, can cope because their conical shape and thin, glossy needles enable them to shed heavy loads of snow and to filter gale-force winds, while their habit of huddling provides further protection, rather like emperor penguins in the Antarctic.

In the old days schoolmasters complained that classes were small in the acorn season because many of the children were out gathering the nuts for pigs. Furthermore, even as late as the 1860s, in some poor rural areas acorns were also ground for mixing with wheat flour to make bread.

The ancient feudal right to allow pigs into the forest for the autumn harvest of acorns and beechmast was known as pannage, and few lords of manors can ever have denied the right. However, they had other than charitable motives. First they were concerned that their young cattle roaming the forest should not gorge upon the acorns and poison themselves. The green, unripe acorns which start falling in September affect ruminant animals in the way that small, green apples plague boys. When taken in large quantities, without adequate corrective of grass, hay or other fibrous food, they remain in the animal's first stomach instead of passing to the second for proper digestion. Death often follows as the stomach wall is inflamed.

Even more important was the landlord's concern for his deer because, being ruminants, these too can suffer in this way. If the peasants removed the acorn threat, the lord of the manor was more than happy. Thus the right of pannage was usually exercised from 25 September to 18 November, after which remaining acorns were generally ripe and therefore relatively harmless, so they had to be left for the deer.

When we were kids we used to gather acorns for other reasons. One was to use them for catapult ammo in gang warfare, the other to turn the largest acorn cups into pipe bowls. A stem would act as a mouthpiece and our baccy was dried grass or herbs. What little horrors we were!

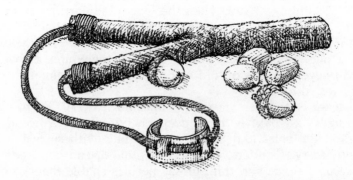

Another important English rural pursuit of past centuries was autumn truffle hunting, using dogs to sniff out those undistinguished but valuable lumps of fungus which grow underground beneath forest trees, especially oak and beech. Indeed, the search for these culinary curiosities, ranging in size from a walnut to a small orange, continued into the early years of this century. Small dogs were specially bred to hunt the truffles. When puppies, their food was smeared with truffle so that they came to think of truffle and food as one and soon developed a keen appetite for finding the fungi. Legend has it that a Spaniard introduced the truffle hounds in the seventeenth century.

Abroad, in more gastronomically interesting climes, truffles remain important. In France and Italy, for example, the fungi are still used for flavouring chocolates and pâté de foie gras as well as other delicacies. There the hunting is generally undertaken by pigs and goats, which need little training. In Perigord some hunters maintain that they need no animal assistance because they are so experienced. Perhaps that is why their noses are so long.

1989

## Gin, 'Brains' and Beans

Tired of many seasons of slurping other Guns' sloe gin without being able to offer my own concoction in return, I have at last bottled up the relevant wild fruit and liquor in a marriage of hope. My wish is that the ensuing brew is half as good as all those original blends which have materialised from car boots and pockets to pass my lips on so many days to remember. From hip flask or vacuum flask, from coarse mug or finest silver beaker, the slugs of sloe have never failed to please.

Ignoring all the tenets about picking fruit only when dry and with the bloom off, and much more, I did at least bother to prick every berry before drowning the fruit in a cascade of gin.

Just last week my curious palate attended a brew of eighteen years vintage! Rounded and mellow it certainly was, but that son of a Gun who made it confessed to the addition of 'just a tincture' of almond essence. Sadly, I fear my cellar is not that patient or inventive, and if the season closes before my first tasting then I will have acquired new will-power. Yet I know the stuff can be excellent after just three months.

Also recently, I had my first taste of giant puffball. With much mycological pride, my younger son brought the great 'brain' home from its birthplace on the edge of Heron's Pond. Lovingly, he

185

washed and skinned it in the kitchen, proclaiming: 'It must be a young one as once the spores develop the flesh is useless'.

That day, each time I passed through the kitchen I glanced at the 'head' under a cloth with considerable apprehension. But when it was served up that evening as 'fritters' in a savoury batter I was pleasantly surprised. It was much milder than I had envisaged but we all agreed that its richness called for modest portions.

Now, as we tuck into hedgerow goodies, much of the garden's produce is going over. We have just had the last few runner beans, but I must recommend something we 'discovered'. With all those runners which have got too big and stringy, remove the actual seeds (assuming you have left some for next year's sowing) and cook them in the manner of broad beans: they are delicious.

Yet some things remain to be nursed along for winter and spring. And in so doing a funny thing happened to me the other day. At last I got round to thinning out the purple sprouting broccoli and, after a spot of replanting, had need of the watering can – at the beginning of October! I took the said receptacle down from a shelf and went to fill it in the kitchen because the outside tap was still broken (yet again!) after last winter's big freeze. As the water entered the can drowsy gnats came flying out the top and spout, like genies from the lamp, until dozens were about the room. Unusually, throughout the summer that can had lain unwanted and thus became the haunt of insects.

1985

## Garden Visitors

The early part of this month brought the usual procession of small migrants through the garden – chiefly relatively inconspicuous warblers apparently investigating every bush on their way down to Africa – and had us reaching for the field guide at every twist and turn. How leisurely is the autumn migration compared with spring's urgent influx, when feathered frames are charged with the drive to breed, and the need to regain condition after a long journey.

In the fall these travelling birds seem to adopt a temporarily high degree of tameness and often come surprisingly close when picking about the garden. Indeed, they bring me great delight on October days with axe and spade. It was only last week that a lesser whitethroat presented itself for my scrutiny as I broke off from log splitting to mop my brow.

Minutes later I was suddenly aware that all the small birds had 'shut up shop' for the day. My bonfire smoke curled up into the mauve dusk sky and in the sudden peace I was more aware of the thud of the axe. A squadron of Canada geese drifted quietly over at tree-top height, like bombers returning to base after a successful mission. Briefly, I paused to admire the satisfying stack of oak logs that would fire next winter's hearth, drew deep breath on the earthy air and made tracks in the dew as I headed towards the porch light and supper.

1988

## Nut Nicker

I was drawn by an advertisement offering 25p each for 'large, bushy grey squirrel tails, winter coat, any quantity', for at the time I was watching two of these rodents pilfering nuts from the garden hazel. For some days they had methodically worked their way through the yellowing leaves to find their winter food supply. But they were entertaining little varmints, scampering away to bury each mouthful around the garden, and I decided that 25p less the cost of a cartridge and a stamp was not only a loss in cash terms but also in enjoyment. Of course, if I were a forester or gamekeeper I would sensibly be removing them anyway and even 25p would help reduce costs.

The squirrel's tail hairs and ear tufts are moulted only once a year – before the autumn moult in July and August. The second body-fur moult takes place between September and November and may last six weeks. Interestingly, this proceeds from back to front, but the spring moult (March to May) works from front to back. Pelage characteristics of the winter tail and coat can be used to distinguish age.

Now the grey squirrel is at its heaviest – up to 800gm – as it stocks up for winter, with peak activity at four or five hours after dawn. The hazelnuts are nibbled at one end until the lower incisors can be inserted to prise off pieces of shell, and a skilled adult can quickly nick and split a nut in half lengthways.

Along with acorns and chestnuts, the hazels are buried in the soil about one or two inches deep or placed in tree hollows, clefts and dreys. It is thought that memory is significant only in recalling the general storage areas and that scent is used for precise location, so that damp conditions are required. Bark stripping mostly occurs when the squirrel is after the sappy tissues beneath for nutrients and food, but bark gnawing is also of social importance.

1986

## Strange Encounters

Recently, when we were driving home in the small hours, we saw a totally white badger rooting at the roadside, along a nearby lane. And, although albinos are supposed to be weaklings, there was no doubting this Brock's fitness as, the moment we slowed the car for a better look, he lifted his snout from leaf-mould matters and ran full tilt into adjacent woods. Apparently albino badgers are not that rare, but this was the first anyone in our family had seen.

The following day, I had another unusual encounter. After spending the morning working on my new book about birds of prey, I decided that aching limbs needed limbering. So off I went for a roadside jog, and to my amazement found a tawny owl road casualty in the village layby. It was the very species which I had just been writing about! As it was in perfect condition I gathered it up and ran back home to make a few notes. How odd I must have looked, jogging along the highway with a dead owl tucked under my arm.

1990

# No Time for Tea

Bramble jelly – two simple words which, for me at least, encapsulate the luxurious bounty of autumn. However, I had forgotten just how good that king of jams can be, until a friend recently gave me a jar. Immediately I thought of all those far-off days with sumptuous teas by the fireside. Crumpets and cake, of course, but especially thick slices of fresh bread with equally thick layers of butter and bramble jelly. Now the tea meal is no more. I, and most others, must conform to a life of lunch and dinner, with no time for magic sweetness in between.

1989

# Colourful Sport

The man who saves all his energy for November pheasants misses a great deal indeed. Gameshooting never was and never will be *only* about birds in the bag or difficulty of target. It is a whole way of life that demands attention in every season, and the genuine sporting countryman needs no telling what treasures October has to offer, for then the country scene is often at its very best.

Many of us have heard some privileged hot-Shots disdainfully declare that they never touch their pheasants till the leaf is off the trees and the birds are well grown. Others offer the excuse that October should be devoted to the partridges which needed 'warming up' in September, and some insist that early-season grouse shortfalls (dreadful word) must be October's priority while the weather holds. But why are they so hidebound by custom and achieving targets, and are they so devoid of discretion they cannot recognise a good bird when they see one?

When gameshooting was primarily the pursuit of country gentlemen there was more of a natural scheme of things. Most Guns could afford to limber up on August grouse before tackling September partridges and then moving on to mixed skirmishes in October. In the days before gross habitat destruction most estates had good numbers of wild grey partridges to provide sport well into autumn if required. Thus there was less pressure to get on with the main pheasant days. And with greater numbers of wild birds in countryside generally more hospitable to game there were more mature pheasants about early in the season.

Today we have very many more people chasing an ever-increasing total bag on land which, collectively, simply cannot accommodate much wild game. Commercialism seems here to stay, the emphasis is ever more on rearing and release, and there is a growing tendency to 'shoot right out' in every year, with little incentive to leave a 'surplus' of pheasants which hardly know how to fend for themselves let alone raise a family. Paying Guns demand their money's-worth and, not surprisingly, greedier individuals often shoot birds straight out of nappies.

Now if the recent trend towards more modest bags accelerated and became wider, and put-and-take gave way to better habitat control, many newcomers to shooting might get the chance to adopt the more laid-back approach of our forefathers. And I am not talking about the most inappropriately named 'Golden Era' of gameshooting, when Victorian/Edwardian big Shots were obsessed with huge bags. I mean earlier, walked-up days, and the later period between the two world wars, when we had a fortuitous blend of optimum game habitat in many areas plus the keen interest of many new syndicates before the general advent of let days.

Despite all, there is no doubt that we do still have favoured areas where good wild pheasants may be found in an average October. Even on many estates still dependent on rearing and release, through unsuitable climate or habitat, we still have keepers skilled enough to put on a good early show.

Unfortunately, there are many Guns who lack the motivation to set forth for very small numbers of testing birds, and commercial shoots have no desire to arrest the trend as big bags mean 'big bucks'. For many people, basic overheads such as accommodation and travel, plus the allocation of precious, limited holidays, do not justify the total outlay and general hassle of organisation when bags are relatively small. Sadly, the greater the cost, the more bag numbers seem to come into the reckoning. With some people it is as if ambiance, atmosphere and comradeship count for nothing.

Thus it is that anyone who does a lot of shooting really savours that bright October day when he is the guest or regular on a private pheasant shoot, where the surroundings and company are more important than the total bag and there is no pressure on anyone to shoot a bird not considered to be up to the mark.

October's country scene is rich and vibrant with colour and movement whereas November paints a drear portrait. While woods are still aflame and hedgerows heavy with fruit there's always a creature or two to entertain the waiting gunner. Rides and airways bustle with life and the observant sportsman is always in the 'pound seat'. How could he ever be bored with a constant procession of birds and mammals charged with the urgency of winter's imminence?

Whether walking-up or standing, the October Gun is surrounded by action. The countryside stands ready to deliver its natural harvest and the hunter is truly at home. What contrast with November, when so many mammals and birds have slunk away to winter lairs, others have migrated and the deep, dank coverts echo only to the sounds of beaters.

Men with particularly barren shoots devoid of wildlife might argue that even in October they have little natural interest, but I have yet to see the patch where the full flavour of every season was not apparent.

October's landscape has a softness quite unlike the ethereal vision of November. The clouds are different, the earth's aroma is different, the sounds of the countryside are different, each lungful of air is different and the wind moves across your cheek with distinctive delicacy.

Standing at your peg, you relax as at no other time, enjoying the redbreast's simple song of autumn, watching the weak sun dissolve the early frost. On these first excursions the mature cock pheasant always seems bigger and brassier than at any other time and the thrill of renewing the old acquaintanceship is especially intense. Old Longspur presents a mighty and colourful challenge as he bursts from the copse and crosses the valley where you line out far below. His cries of protest serve only to emphasise his presence and no one is in the least bit interested in the stumpy trainer jets which shudder past in the shadow of his bomber wings. Should you manage to bring him down you will be happy indeed for you will have exercised both skill and discretion while at the same time savouring the most colourful month of the year.

1988

## The Ooyah Bird

An old boy I met recently wrinkled an eyebrow in disbelief when I said that guillemots laid eggs with a tremendous variety of patterns so that the parents could recognise their own in large colonies. He said: 'Obviously you've never been on a seabird cliff, or you would 'ave seen that nearly all the eggs were covered in white crap that nobody or nothin' could see through.' I suppose he had a good point, but then I did take his remarks with more than the usual pinch of salt, especially when he said that the guillemot is also called the 'ooyah bird' because its enormous egg is hell to lay!

1993

## Pupa Hunting

October is a month of contrasts. Every vestige of summer is swept away and by the end winter is staring us full in the face. The beginning of the month is often fine, as it was this year, but soon the chill descends. Most of the gales which follow the equinox are over by the middle of the month, when there is often a rise in day temperature, a southerly or south-easterly wind, a sky flecked with a few cirrus clouds and we are into St Luke's summer, named after the festival on the 18th.

But St Luke is short-lived. The first fires are lit. However, I always leave mine as long as possible for it seems to me that once that warm glow returns to the hearth it is indeed hard to forego it on subsequent evenings, even with a rise in temperature.

On the 27th we say goodbye to British Summer Time. It is

certainly useful to have the light stimulus in getting up in the morning, but oh how dreary that long drive home in the dark is.

Autumn leaves still glow with a deceptive semblance of warmth, but after an October downpour their dank decay will only tell more clearly that the time of bare boughs is at hand. Snails tire of their garden raids and retire into winter quarters among the ivy leaves, beneath old cans and rubble in hedgerow bottoms, and in sinister clefts where ancient walls have fallen into disrepair.

Caterpillars, too, have ended their endless munching. It is time for pupation – that remarkable, death-like quiescence. The chrysalis swathed, as it were, in swaddling clothes, suggested to the early naturalists a child's doll – hence 'pupa'. The term chrysalis actually relates to the pupa of a moth or butterfly and derives from the Greek *khrusos* for gold, from the golden colour they often exhibit. However, in my youth we generally referred to the pupa of a butterfly as a chrysalis and that of a moth as a cocoon.

Many years ago I used to get really excited about chrysalis hunting and well remember many happy days of tree climbing in search of something special. But most productive were the undersides of window sills, and in and around old buildings generally.

Pupa digging is particularly good for the entomologist in October, when they abound before the moles, mice, birds and floods take their toll. Most are 1–3in (2.5–7.5 cm) down near the food plants of their larval stages, shallow in gravel, deeper in sand and close to the surface in clay. Some larvae merely crawl under leaves, where the tough 'mat' provides both camouflage and protection from temperature extremes. Others, such as the wood leopard, goat moth and certain clearwings, bore into the wood as larvae. Still more knit themselves into a silken cocoon.

Pupae should be stored under conditions as natural as possible, out of sunlight and not too warm (certainly not in a centrally heated room). A wooden box half filled with sandy loam and with a loosely fitting lid (to permit 'breathing' but keep scavengers out) should be stored in a cool place such as an outhouse or garage. Insects 'hatched' in this way might be kept for collections and the remainder released to help the conservation effort. In the right conditions the survival rate will be higher than in the wild, and thus no criticism could be made of this practice.

Adult insects are to be seen a-wing throughout October in the last flashes of fairly powerful sunshine. The round clusters of ivy blossoms bend back their yellowish petals and, in the general scarcity of more attractive blossoms, butterflies, moths, flies and gnats crowd to the nectar and quickly become intoxicated. And how intriguing are the golden lights of the moths' eyes at night, like those of the cat on his stealthy manoeuvres.

Just before November throws her veil upon us a few 'lost' butterflies will be found about attics and bedrooms with windows left open, where they flutter in search of winter homes. Gnats continue in dizzy dances along the riverbank but overall the chill dusks and dawns will decimate the insect world.

1985

## The Disappearing Ale

We have huddled around our hearths during a cold and tempestuous month which opened with thunder and reminded me of an amusing incident which happened in October 1976.

One evening I took my brother to the Hampshire Bowman, a pub at Upper Swanmore, because he particularly likes the 'real ale' brewed by Gales of Horndean and served 'out of the wood'. After a few minutes lightning caused the electricity to fail, so that we stood in the middle of the packed bar with many other unseen imbibers, like penguins in a rookery on an Antarctic night. When light was restored we rested our pints on the counter alongside a few others.

Only a mouthful or two was gone from our second round when we were plunged into darkness once more. When the light came back on yet again we reached for our glasses, only to find that they were both virtually empty. This might have been a mistake by thirsty hands groping in the darkness – but both mugs? More likely it was country cunning from those with previous experience of such mysterious happenings.

We left the real ale and the jostling for the comfort and conviviality of what was then my local, the Bold Forester at Newtown. Very soon their lights, too, flickered and died, but this time, despite being on 'home territory', we did not put our glasses down!

1980

194

# The Great Storm

The tangle of earth-caked roots rose quite six feet above the torn earth, no longer anchoring the mighty trunk which lay utterly still, its shattered limbs strewn about the undergrowth. The proud conqueror of over three centuries of frost, drought and tempest had been laid low by a storm without precedent in rural England.

There, still lodged in the bark fissures, were the hazel shells wedged by hungry nuthatches. In a once-secret hollow was the old, white egg of a tawny owl, miraculously unbroken, and the twig platform of a pigeon's nest was surprisingly intact in the oak's crumpled crown.

Many were the occasions these knotty branches had shielded me from sudden downpours and countless were the times I stood beneath them to ambush woodpigeon. In summer they had given me welcome shade and in winter the massive trunk had offered protection against bitter easterlies. For me at least, this great oak had been a living temple of memories, but now it was merely a ruin. Yet this was but one of a million or more trees which had been toppled by 'The Great Storm' of 16 October. And, just like 'my' oak, most would have had special places in the hearts of men.

Overnight the country scene had been transformed, but so too had the lives of many rural communities such as mine. Yet even now as I write, ten days after the hurricane and still without electricity, I am heartened by the fact that most of the people inconvenienced regard the loss of the trees as the greatest tragedy of all – apart from the loss of human life, of course. Neighbours and friends who had buildings and vehicles squashed by large trees take refuge in their insurance policies, but nothing can compensate for the many decades it will take to restore our landscape.

The loss to the shooting community has been enormous. I hear of entire coverts blown down and most others in the area will certainly have to reorganise many of their drives. On the other hand, there is no doubt that some shoots, even those with sufficient finance, had allowed their woods to grow way past their best and had they already started the long process of systematic tree replacement then their losses would have been far less significant.

Also, local keepers have picked up scores of dead pheasants, blasted from their favourite roosts, to which they had clung obstinately, to be exhausted and crushed by a maelstrom of branches. Others will have been hopelessly disorientated, never to return, and we can only guess at the casualties among the rest of our wildlife.

On the plus side, removal of many mature trees from some over-wooded acres has let substantial light in for the first time in centuries and this will enable many species of wild flower to re-establish. That is providing that landowners resist the temptation to rush into re-planting with quick-growing conifers which have relatively little value for wildlife compared with native English hardwood trees. With luck some of the fallen trees will be left to decompose naturally, providing further valuable habitat for both plants and animals. Man should never be so conceited as to deny nature a hand in shaping the countryside, for her softer lines are always more soothing than vistas concocted by the planner's pen.

For a day and a half we were effectively cut off from the outside world, the roads blocked by countless trees and the telephone wires down. People wandered about in astonishment – 'It's like World War Three' – and in their search for chainsaws encountered folk they 'hadn't seen for years' and 'didn't know they were still alive'.

But at least we have had water, for our supply is not on the mains, but gravity-fed from nearby hills. Many folk – even in towns – have been without water for long periods because generator-dependant pumps are off. We have been able to cook on the hotplate of our woodstove, which also provides heat, and for a while we were gluttons in the rush to use up the meat which had been stored in the deep-freeze. However, a litre of Wall's Soft Scoop ice-cream was just too much in one go.

The children think it's all a bit of a hoot, especially as the schools were closed for some days. But lack of hot water is not at all funny. For a start it takes so long to get ready in the morning, boiling up kettles on a camping gas stove, as well as the Jotul woodburner, and trying to shave by candlelight. And we soon ran out of candles as local suppliers' stocks were exhausted. Gas canisters were quickly sold out and then the rush was on for paraffin power, while the more affluent invested in generators costing from about £300 upwards.

But the real answer has been to make best use of every daylight hour going so that when darkness closes in again one can relax with a dram, attempt to revive the art of conversation or even see what the crystal set has to offer. If the torch batteries are still functioning one can perhaps tiptoe up to the Dog and Pheasant, only to stumble across the fallen wires and branches on the way back.

Driving has been decidedly dangerous, of course, as long after the great blast weakened trees and branches have been falling across previously unblocked country roads – usually at night and inevitably just around a bend. Some minor roads still remain impenetrable.

Accidents have been much more common than usual. For example, people have been killed through traffic lights being blacked out, and in many homes the very young, elderly and frail have been at special risk with naked flames and matches all around them. The blue lights of police cars and ambulances have been flashing up and down the black road much more frequently than usual – often in the small hours.

All over the region, less afflicted friends and relatives have been visited for the mere sake of a hot bath or the chance to reduce mounds of unwashed clothes.

Now everyone has time to talk, but as soon as the power is restored I bet we'll all return to the usual rat race and mostly ignore each other. But at least my newly-acquired solar-powered calculator should be able to work out the bills of a winter's evening. It thrives on strong electric as well as natural light but candles have proved just too dim.

Of two things I am now certain: I'm glad that I live in 1987 rather than 1887 and anyone surviving till 2087 will still be talking about the day the trees fell down in 1987.

1987


## Death Moths

Earlier this month our attention was drawn to a large moth flapping on the lawn, and close inspection revealed one of those gory episodes of insect life rarely witnessed by us giants. A persistent wasp had worked its way under the moth's body and proceeded to chew away until, within a few minutes, the thick abdomen was detached. Then, as the wasp flew off with the juicy food parcel as big as itself, the moth's wings remained flapping feebly, still attached to the head and thorax in the grass.

We did not see whether the moth had first been stung. It could have been waterlogged in the wet grass or perhaps partially disabled by a passing bird. I have seen birds of many species snap at flying moths, and sometimes they do not bother to follow up and eat the insects, rather like a salmon unable to resist snatching a fly which it has no intention of eating.

Few people realise that one British moth is as big as a small bird, and quite intimidating. It is the death's head hawk-moth, which I

197

have seen just once, in an aircraft hangar where a schoolchum's RAF father took us.

This huge, fat-bodied moth gets its name from the bizarre skull pattern on the back of its thorax, and when its wings are open the yellow bands on the body look like ribs. To add to the frightening effect, the moth can utter a high-pitched squeak if it is touched. The five-inch horned caterpillars, too, are alarming and they often used to scare potato pickers in the days before mechanical harvesting and widespread use of insecticides.

Death's heads are regular migrants to Britain and may be found anywhere in the country between May and October, even around the lights of North Sea oil rigs east of the Shetlands. As well as taking the sweet sap of various trees, they lap the honey from the combs of honey bees. Their squeaking mimics the piping of the queen bee and apparently deters the bees from stinging them. Nonetheless, some are attacked and killed.

1988

## Fires for Fertility

Once bonfires blazed across the land at Hallowe'en. In later days they were luck-bringing and fertility fires, but in dark, pagan times they were part of rituals to strengthen the sun at the beginning of winter. The bonfires which burn now, on 5 November, almost certainly have their true origins in the Hallowe'en period, for this saw many lit centuries before the failure of the Gunpowder Plot in 1605.

For the last few weeks children have been active in the dusk after school, gathering all manner of combustible rubbish which they haul feverishly to every village common and town waste in the land, to build *the* bonfire to outshine all others. But gone are the days when a boy's trousers bulged with forty 'bangers' done up in an elastic band, when ash and smoke filled the air in every street and field, and 6 November dawned with rocket sticks on every pavement. Today, in most towns we have yet more regimentation – elbowing for space at great public displays and unreasonable entry fees. Thank goodness many villages still keep the local spirit alive with torchlight processions and pumpkin candles so that the inevitable drizzle is tolerable.

I still prefer a Guy Fawkes night with just family and friends in the garden – eyes twinkling with starlight and sparklers, cheeks burning while bangers sizzle and tatties char 'neath the guy; breath billowing in frosty air, columns of spark-filled smoke and a sky full of colour and 'oohs' and 'aahs'. It's quite possible to have all this and safety, and you might be assured of a good crop next year. Mind you, I'm glad I don't have a thatched roof.

1980

# November

## All is Safely Gathered In

Of all the months, November is the most deceptive. Beneath her calm, aging face lurks not just a landscape ticking over but a countryside pulsing in preparation for winter. Come rain or shine there is excitement in the air and no one has greater reason to venture forth than the country sportsman.

Winter steadily asserts itself now as a strange feeling of emptiness and loneliness descends into almost deserted woods and valleys where warblers whispered not so many weeks ago. Yet a touch of yellow ochre, gold and even oak-green clings defiantly to the quietening trees as sap retreats and winter tugs with icy fingers.

In soft Surrey our first real frost came on 27 October, the day before the clocks went back, plunging evening rush hour into darkness and turning commuters into moles from now till spring. Yet at least that first frost brought approval to try the first parsnips. I wonder why this alters their flavour so.

Almost everywhere our arable farmers sit contentedly astride bumper mountains of corn, next year's crop already shooting satisfactorily after an ideal sowing period during early autumn. Barns bulge with bales and great flapping sheets protect the surplus from rotting rains. Some poorly protected stacks sprout green across the top, and everywhere farmyards promise a record winter for rat hunters. The collared dove, too, appears to be thriving as the grain mountain grows.

1984

## *Foreshore Fireworks*

We all have our special visions of every month. My picture of
November is one of garden bonfires, muffled children scurrying
home through the damp dusk, and estuaries enveloped in grey.
Perhaps I am unduly influenced by one memorable day when all
these ingredients came together.

It was one November in the mists of childhood, and the 'gang'
planned a crack at the wigeon before more traditional bangs
around the 'bonnie'. Prospects were excellent all round – cold
north-easterlies had persisted for a fortnight, bringing plenty of
duck to our south-coast harbour and an abundance of dry wood
to fire the guy.

With all the enthusiasm of youth, we set off for the foreshore on
foot, attracting inquisitive glances from less adventurous chums as
they hurried towards hearth and home, cocooned in tweed overcoats
and balaclavas, clutching the biggest rockets they could afford.

Of course we were early – we never did things by halves in those
more carefree days. If we were going to walk that far it had to be
worthwhile. We knew every inch of every path, and on the way
there was always the chance to pick up a couple of rabbits and
a pigeon or two. Then, nearer the ducking place, would come
chances at redshank, snipe and plover, and still there would be
ample time to let the estuary settle before the weak sun closed its
red eye on another day. And thus it was, all to plan.

We three musketeers moved to pre-chosen positions, each content
that his was the prime mark, the place proved most productive
by personal experience. My lonely outpost would be the first to
disappear beneath the incoming tide, which on this occasion was
due with the first stars.

It was freezing as I crouched in my mud hole, and the multicol-
oured starbursts of early fireworks were especially brilliant over
the nearby town. I could even hear the crackle, whizz and whistle
of festivities way across the water. To my right, facing east, John
was virtually invisible in a clump of marsh grass, only occasional
puffs of cheap Craven A cigarette smoke revealing his position.
To my left, Derek floundered like a beached whale as he tried
in vain to make himself invisible. Finally, he lay still, a hunched,
black dinosaur silhouetted against the sunset.

I turned to watch the display of pyrotechnics and relapsed into
a dream world, my mind half on our cache of rabbits at the bottom
of a nearby bank. It was that magic moment of total readiness and
anticipation, of utter peace and contentment, which few hunters
have the opportunity to enjoy so fully as the wildfowler does.

Boom! Boom! My reverie was split asunder as John's old hammer Manton poked two tongues of flame in the vague direction of a bunch of teal. The birds' only response was to engage afterburners, taunt with a belly roll or two and jink away into the gathering gloom. The shots echoed around the harbour, a 'shanker' scalded, a curlew bubbled and peace returned to the saltmarsh.

True to form, we hung on to the bitter end, each hoping that the others would not express any desire to return to civilization. We trusted our 'night eyes' and attuned ears to make the best of any chance which might come our way. But sadly, no wigeon whistle came as we had so very much hoped; only the muffled explosions of more and more rockets broke the increasing stillness as the first ripples washed around my wellies.

But then, oh so faintly, I heard two voices, and turned my head this way and that, trying to home in on the broken sound. Silence. Then they came again, a man and a woman, two sad souls apparently adrift at sea. But I could not make out what they were saying.

Suddenly I could just discern a large, rounded object moving towards us, speeding up the main creek in the flood tide. Then, plainly, I heard the woman call out, surprisingly strongly, 'Are you all right Nigel?'; to which came the rather uncertain answer: 'Yes, I think so darling'.

In the next instant I saw them briefly, white faces photographed by moonlight as they clung desperately to the side of the upturned yacht. 'Ahoy there,' I called: 'Do you need help?' What a silly question I thought to myself, but then you never know what takes some people's fancy.

'Of course we bloody well do,' shrieked the haughty woman. 'Can you get help – capsized you know. Put up a flare just before she went over, but seems all the silly buggers in sight thought it was only another firework. Stupid clots. Oh do hurry up, pleeeease!'

'OK, hang on,' I replied. So off we raced to the nearest house – some two miles away – to phone the police. And that was the end of that. We knew the couple would probably be all right because they would soon make landfall with the strong tide running them up the harbour into the shallows. The only real risk was that they would perish through exhaustion or hypothermia.

Later that evening we joined a local fireworks party, where we embroidered our tale with deeds of daring. Burnt sausages and spuds never tasted so good.

Next day we raced back to recover our stashed rabbits. They were gone – foxes, of course. Neither were there any washed-up bodies or wreckage. The incident didn't even make the local evening paper – what a let-down for a trio of schoolboy musketeers. But how that vision of November has haunted me ever since.

1989

## Romantic Lights

In these dark country evenings light bulbs sparkle within the steamy mystery of the milking parlour, while in town bank-weary clerks summarise the day in hard cash beneath characterless fluorescence. Trains of car headlights snake through suburbs, filtering down amber-lit avenues. Some, like me, press on to relatively deep countryside where, once the last tractor has droned into the yard and the opening farm door has momentarily released an orange glow, utter darkness descends.

Yet it is for only a few generations that our society has been so well lit. Just recently, my neighbouring town of Godalming celebrated the centenary of their introduction of the world's first public electricity supply, and this conjured up romantic images of nights of old.

I was a child when I last visited a farmhouse without electricity, when winter dusks brought Sunday tea within the bewitching glow of a paraffin lamp that threw such shadows as to make the cakes appear even larger. But today even the most remote dwellings have 'juice', many of them with their own generators. Now the only inkling we get of life without power is when lightning or flood knocks out the lines. Then even the 'goggle box' is extinguished and men must resort to the ancient method of communication known as conversation.

1981

## Sounds I Have Loved

As I sat dreaming into the dusk the other day, the black silhouette of an old 'prop' aeroplane droned over. With slow but unwavering flight it moved out of the dark wings of the world where the first stars blinked, across that mauve and yellow sky which jigsaw makers love to copy, and eventually crossed the red giant itself. It took me with it, back through the rushing decades, transporting me all the way to the time when I was first allowed out alone. This gentle

203

engine sound is the first I can remember and, though man-made, remains as magical to me as the calls of migrating birds moving unseen through the night.

Always I wished to be on that little plane, and always I wished to be up with those redwings or geese, thrusting across sea and mountain to new adventure and unfamiliar wildness. I reclined in suburbia but my heart was up the Amazon. I've never really grown out of this yearning and remain primed for activation by a whole host of sounds I have always loved.

Sometimes I wonder which sounds a city soul can recall from early childhood. The screech of bus brakes perhaps? The chuggity-chug of the 6.30 out of Euston, the clink of milk bottles while men are still abed? Or perhaps the gate slamming as the paper boy leaves? But it could be the wind's hollow moan in the chimney, or the pattering of rain on the window, for even in the heart of town there are clear signals that this remains a nature-dominated world.

Probably it all depends on association with experiences and the fact that we remember most vividly those sounds which came to us at times of great pleasure. For example, I cannot help but think of bitterly cold weather whenever I hear the haunting whistle of wigeon, simply because I saw and shot my first in that great freeze-up of 1962–3.

On the game-shoot the whole day is punctuated by evocative sounds which we subconsciously link with past outings, and this always heightens anticipation. Perhaps the one to make the adrenalin flow most freely is the steady tap-tap of the stops as they dissuade birds from breaking out the sides of the drive. Then there is the excitement generated by unseen beaters crashing through the undergrowth, and finally the explosive whirr of pheasant wings as birds make a bid for freedom.

At the end of the day comes the crunching of boots in the early frost as we trudge back to the vehicles, the reverberating hoot of the wood owl anticipating supper, and the crackling of a log fire as we thaw out back at the shoot hut. Later, when we hear any of these sounds in other circumstances, our shooting hearts are tugged back to those satisfying times with fellow Sports.

The fowler will become restless merely at the sound of a gale in the thatch or the alarm call of the redshank on the foreshore. Even in summer these will remind him of foreshore magic. And if a skein of geese should happen to fly over, calling and conjuring up wilderness as only wild geese can, he will be taken by a kind of fever from which he will never recover until he gets down to the saltmarsh one more time.

But whereas the fowler is mostly taunted by sounds only in

winter, because the majority of his quarry are migratory, the poor pigeon-shooter is tantalised by 'woody talk' all year round. His is a sport without season and any time he hears a shot over the hedge he wants to know what's going on and whether or not he can get in on the action.

Whenever our pigeon-popper goes for a summer stroll he hears his quarry cooing enticingly in the greenwoods, and in autumn he is aroused in his walk beneath the colourful beech trees by the clap of pigeon wings as the birds take off in alarm. I guarantee that this sound will make the woody-shooter halt in his tracks as certainly as the crow of the cock pheasant will induce restlessness in the game-shooter.

The stalker paints whole pictures of fond memories every time he hears the roar of the stag in the glen, and the fox-hunter dashes to his cottage window whenever the hounds of the neighbouring pack give tongue to the hills. Even the supposedly placid angler is stirred by the gentle ploop of a rising fish. And the splash of a jumping bass in the harbour is always enough to send me scurrying off to dig for ragworm.

In the countryside – or even sometimes in suburbia – the start of day is addressed by cock-crow, a natural alarm clock to satisfy even the sternest soul. But there is much to hear even before that hour. The fox barks on his way back to base, shrews squeak in the hedge beneath the window and an owl's claws can be heard scratching on the chimney pot. Through the open window the cries of curlew and peewit drift over from the heath.

The dawn chorus itself is loved by all and must be the most wonderful unorchestrated concert of the natural world. But how much better it is when the listener is out there among the performers. Some birds can be heard only at close range, while others dominate from lofty platforms. Together they lift our spirits into the realms of the immortal.

Whether countryman or sporting Gun, you would be hard-pressed to decide on a set of 'desert island discs' of sounds which you have loved. Even your gun talks to you sweetly with the crisp metallic closure of a well-made breech or the wind sighing across the muzzle as you wait in silence for duck to come. All these I have loved and all never fail to stir distant memories of red-letter days.

Perhaps my favourite sound in all nature is the full, unbridled melody of the blackbird on a soft summer evening. It is a dream which at once takes me back to that childhood idyll, but also forward in preparing my spirit for eternity.

1986

## The Maligned Month

A frosty easterly winnowed the quiet woods, shaking spent oak cradles down onto the brook which gurgled strongly at winter level after recent storms. The leaves skimmed across swirls of shining black water each side of the little wooden bridge, then glided away to gather in frothy eddies and backwaters. Eroded banks tilted trees with chaotic roots which are favoured picking grounds of the wren.

Out on the blanched stubbles, where manure had been spread, slowly restoring the compacted, mossy soil, the air moved with wintry power and the cold was in my bones again. Then, as if to confirm the message, two fieldfares towered from the nearby wood and winged high over with economical flight, their white underwings winking and chestnut backs glowing in the thin sunshine. These were my first of the winter, but they denied me their exciting wild cry of the north.

Along the more remote and sunnier hedgerows, with a noon frost in the shady bottoms for the first time this year, showers of finches rose before me to scoot nervously down the wind. Leaves and birds flew together, twisting and tumbling in all directions to speckle the new face of winter.

There were no woodcock to be seen but I sensed that their leader had arrived, his bright eyes unmoved but intent and aware of my unpredictable passage through dappled sunlit coppice and marshy brake, where his long bill probes for worms among the rusted bracken.

Later that day I was thrilled to see several flocks of twenty to thirty fieldfares and a great gathering of over 100 which banked and *chack-chacked* over me in that typically bewildered manner. This was early for such sizeable flocks in this area, but hardly surprising given the low temperatures which Scandinavia has been having of late.

This is an unpredictable month and Thomas Hood was rather uncharitable when he penned his clever poem *No*. His words – 'No sun – no moon! No morn – no noon – No dawn – no dusk – no proper time of day . . . November' – certainly help perpetuate the popular image of the month. Yet the netherworld of November has so much to offer. Quite apart from sport, the rambler has the way to himself and that is far from dull with the translucent red berries of guelder rose and glossy holly to brighten hedgerows where hazel catkins have already set.

Now nature is seemingly in retreat, retiring into its rootstock. Fish become sluggish, seeking the deeper swims, and birds retire to their roosts well before the ochrous sun has set long shadows in the wood. After the hurly-burly of summer and the mellowing of autumn, bird, beast and flower adopt the tempo of survival. To understand all the moods of this natural harmony is to appreciate the wealth of intrigue and beauty which the maligned month of November has to offer.

1980

## Fire and Brimstones

One of the joys of living in the countryside is that the garden is constantly invaded by a wide variety of colonising plants and trees. Some seed is borne on the wind, others hitch a lift on or in birds and mammals. But all are welcome because they set themselves where nature sees fit, achieving that enviable informality which even the greenest fingers cannot emulate. In contrast, most town gardens are places of sameness and sterility.

Of course, many of the colonists must go because their presence is too incongruous or growth too vigorous for more benign bedfellows. Nipping that taproot or searching sucker in the bud can save much work and November is a delightful time to go about this business. Few tasks beat putting the ground to bed for the winter, especially when the sun shimmers across the damp loam after days of grey skies.

In particular, I like a good bonfire, trading woody roots and disease for soft, grey ash, but not before extracting every single item which will rot down in the compost heap. Yet I am conscious that in this green age the garden bonfire is gradually being extinguished as man worries about pollution. It is unfortunate that he often substitutes with new shredders which devour energy as well as vegetation, and in so doing creates atmospheric pollution elsewhere.

The Oxford Dictionary tells me that the word bonfire originates from 'bone-fire' – 'a great fire in which bones were burnt in the open air', or a funeral pyre, or 'a fire in which heretics or proscribed books were burnt'. It dates the use of the word with these meanings to the sixteenth and seventeenth centuries. But another suggestion follows a completely different tack, offering bonfire as a derivative of 'bonny', 'bonhomie' and 'Boniface', simply meaning a jolly good fire of sticks and anything else to make a cheerful blaze on a winter's evening.

Few smells capture the essence of countryside as does that of garden refuse burning, just as the whiff of coal smoke is redolent of town; both friendly and reassuring aromas, scents of memory which transport me back to childhood.

Sometimes I come across butterflies and moths lurking in my bonfire and, even if it has just been moved, always try to give the debris a good shake before putting a match to it. One spring I was amazed to discover several brimstone and comma butterflies in the heap I was about to burn. In any case frogs and toads are usually lurking in the damp bottom and I certainly do not want to cook these friends.

1990


## Rebuilding our Forests

I find great comfort in November. As the damp wind drives the last few dried leaves from the covert's ceiling the land reveals its framework. All around us the great trees, which earlier had concealed our game in its daily foraging, are now skeletons rattling to the tune of winter. It is a landscape which haunts me, a landscape of decline and death, but it brings me immense peace.

This year's leaf fall is particularly poignant because we are better able to see the destruction caused by the hurricane on 16 October.

Wherever we wander, tired old trunks lean at crazy angles, uprooted but prevented from toppling by sturdier neighbours. In some places whole acreages are blitzed and flattened. The roadside view is but the tip of the iceberg: if you want a true impression of the damage then join a beating line.

After coping so well with immediate dangers, the council gangs are busy about their cosmetic exercise in the lanes, like ants swarming to repair a damaged nest, removing the debris and striving to restore the customary quietness and order of rural England.

For now the whine of the chainsaw is an everyday sound and the men in hard hats and fluorescent safety colours are a familiar sight around their blazing brushwood bonfires. Mighty is their task and bewildered their expression. I sympathise, knowing how long it takes to clear just one small garden.

There is no denying that England is an exceptionally tidy-minded country and sometimes I hanker after a little more disorderly wilderness about our countryside. Why, even our nature reserves are fanatically manicured, all trimmed and shipshape, criss-crossed with gravel paths or planked walkways and plastered with neat signs declaring where you can go and what you can do. I know this is necessary if we are to channel the masses through the gates. It just seems a pity to interrupt the flow of natural lines.

Already the boffins are planning the systematic replacement of every tree and bush lost to the hurricane. But are British foresters obsessed with numbers rather than quality? Of course we want our children to grow up with the idea that planting trees is good, but it is so essential that they plant the right trees in the right places.

The current comprehensive policy for forestry in Britain has its origins in the early years of this century, when the woodland resource, decimated during the Middle Ages, the early Industrial Revolution and the First World War, began to be restored. Island difficulties of timber supply during the Great War led to the creation of the Forestry Commission and a far-seeing initial programme of afforestation.

Initially, the Commission was given the target of a state forest covering 715,000 hectares by the end of this century. They also had to encourage private owners to repair the wartime ravages and then maintain in a productive state some 1.2 million hectares of their own woodlands, so that neither war nor national emergency should ever again inflict the desperate timber shortages of the First World War.

At the outbreak of World War II, the Commission had in its care 176,000 hectares of woodland and the private sector had restocked some 500,000 hectares. In 1943 a Government White

Paper proposed the establishment of an effective national forest estate of 2 million hectares by the year 2000. This target was achieved in 1983.

Today 10 per cent of Britain's 22.7 million hectares are afforested, 77 per cent is devoted to agriculture and 13 per cent to urban and other use. This may be compared with 28 per cent forestry in France, 30 per cent in West Germany, 45 per cent in Greece, 68 per cent in Sweden and Japan and an almost choking 76 per cent in Finland. For the whole world the figures are 31 per cent forest, 36 per cent agriculture and 33 per cent urban and other use.

After World War II the Government's main concern was still to establish and maintain a strategic reserve of timber, but in 1957 it accepted the recommendation by the Zuckermann Committee that the Commission's future objectives should be of a *commercial and social nature*. Since then environmental and ecological interests have been given increasingly significant consideration. The importance of recreation, including shooting, has been recognised too, and it is an important aspect of amenity planting policy.

Policy statements in 1973–4 set out a framework designed to ensure that forestry formed 'part of an effective pattern of rural land use, in which it is harmonised to the best possible advantage with agriculture and the environment'.

Thus we have plenty of fine words and apparently good intent. Hopefully, shooting interest will continue to be increasingly significant in rebuilding our countryside, especially now with alternatives to agricultural land use in the spotlight. We can move forward confidently in the certain knowledge that what's good for game is good for wildlife generally.

As we explore the shattered pheasant coverts this month, which in a normal year should bring the biggest days, we might look at them in a different light. This land remains wild because the shooting interest has dominated, but the recently created spaces are not merely for filling, to prevent ingress of development or agriculture. All planting needs very careful thought concerning tree species, density and position.

1987

## Smash Hits

Last week my elderly neighbour was sitting quietly in his room of rustic retirement when a cock pheasant smashed through his window and fell in a heap on the floor. It soon recovered and pecked around the room for a while before flying back out through the broken window and thence to forage quite happily in a garden close by. No shooting had been taking place nearby and children playing outside had seen the bird glide across the field, through a thin belt of trees, and rocket into the window. Why?

Over the years I have seen many small birds crash into windows, frequently being terminated on impact, but always into fairly large panes with further glass in the background giving sufficient light to deceive the birds into believing that they could fly right through. But this particular pheasant flew into a room with no light beyond, though there is a possibility that light reflecting off the glass had outwitted our 'comet'.

The episode reminded me of a true shooting story which never fails to make me chuckle. An acquaintance had cast a longing eye at a small party of Canada geese as they beat a regular and most predictable flightline over his house every evening.

Eventually 'R' could not resist the 'Flying Fortresses' any longer: he licked his lips with relish each time he saw these potential roast dinners fading into the sunset. So one evening he had his trusty fowling piece at the ready.

The squadron appeared on cue. The gun swung sweetly and a mighty gander nose-dived heavily at 45 degrees – straight through R's very large and expensive picture window! He had his dinner, but the price was indeed high.

1985

## St Martin's Goose

It is hardly surprising that the modern wildfowler regards the goose with a strange mixture of awe and superstition as both wild and 'tame' geese have been associated with magic for many centuries. In olden times this month was especially significant in the goose world, for St Martin's Day (11 November) was traditionally celebrated by eating a goose washed down with lashings of wine.

The old saws also tell us that with the arrival of St Martinmas winter is truly on its way. From then on we can expect storm and tempest at any time. Indeed, one of the most ferocious gales ever recorded in England was on 27 November 1703, when 250,000 trees were blown down in Kent alone! These same strong winds can blast large numbers of wild geese way off their normal migration routes to deposit them in surprising places.

Yet November is also renowned for quiet weather which, in the days of the old professional goose-hunter, brought the killer smog. As he took his carted bag to market, the gunner saw how London's million chimneys converted the white river mist, that drifted up on the almost stagnant east wind from the Thames marshes, into a dense, yellow, sooty smog through which the gas lamps glimmered in faint, lurid patches of red. In the end the marketing of wild geese was outlawed and smoke-free zones were created, made all the easier through wider availability of gas and oil.

I can still remember the pungent smell of coal smoke filling the town air as dusk fell, and I must confess that – in moderation – I found it to my liking. For me it marked the passage of the year as clearly as the arrival of winter wildfowl, and the deep fogs of November seemed to accentuate the mystery and expectation enveloping the season of frosts ahead.

Out in the country, the curl of woodsmoke still marks a nest of cottages as it has done since time immemorial. And with the present vogue for old times, old ways and self-sufficiency, the rush is on for every log in sight.

Although, traditionally, we expect a short return of warmer weather – St Martin's Summer, about Martinmas – most of the old associated ceremonies were of an indoor nature. However, few people now bob for apples on a string with their hands tied, roast apples and burn nuts in playful divination.

Martinmas was a time when geese traditionally came to market in great numbers, for there was no deep-freeze and winter's cold made difficult the keeping of all stock. These were the stubble-fed geese which started to come in from Michaelmas, whereas the 'green goose' of Shakespeare fattened on lush May grass.

Our common-or-garden goose is descended from the wild greylag. One suggestion as to the derivation of its name is that it was a bird that grazed the fields or 'leas' – 'lea goose', turning with usage into 'lag goose'.

The worldwide magico-religious significance of geese goes back millenia, the two strongest themes being solar symbolism and fertility. Later, the Greeks and Romans attached more of an explicitly sexual meaning. The fertility aspect continues in parts of Europe, and even in Britain it is not so long since November was a popular marrying month, with geese central to the festivities. Many people still innocently teach their children the nursery rhyme:

> Goosey, goosey gander, whither shall I wander,
> Upstairs and downstairs and in my lady's chamber.

Today sportsmen look to the wild geese for signs of winter chill, but associated traditions go way back. In 1455, Dr Hartlieb, physician to the Duke of Bavaria, wrote of the way the goose was consumed on St Martin's Day. Always, the breastbone was retained, dried and scrutinised. It would reveal what kind of weather was to follow. Teutonic knights in Prussia went even further and were said to wage war according to the state of the goose bones. And even when eating goose lost popularity the augury continued in weakened form. As we started to eat more duck, and later chickens, we continued to 'pull the wishbone' and put our future in the lap of the gods. Men also looked at the way geese flew, the nature of their formations supposedly indicating the length of frost.

On one of his campaigns, Caesar noted that the goose was taboo in Celtic regions of the British Isles, where it was kept in enclosures for sacrifice but never eaten, but elsewhere the goose was important in festivities. Also, ever since they roused Rome, with the Gauls threatening at the gates, geese have been renowned for their vigilance.

In some parts young, wild greylag used to be rounded up for eating or to provide breeding stock, for they were easily tamed and their flesh was much esteemed. Old geese were shot, plucked and sold in the market as tame birds, and the buyer would not be aware of the coarser meat until the bird was on the table.

Most geese were reared in the fens of Lincolnshire, where many gozzards (goose-herds) each had 1,000 geese, rearing an average brood of seven. Many of the birds were left to their own devices in the marshes and on the village greens during summer, but in autumn they would be put onto stubble to fatten on the scattered grain.

Thereafter they flooded the market, multitudes being driven in by road to the great metropolis. They were also taken into every market town in bags and panniers. In 1799, Thomas Bewick wrote: 'To a stranger it is a most curious spectacle to view these hissing, cackling, gobbling, but peaceful armies, with grave deportment, waddling along (like other armies) to certain destruction. The drivers are each provided with a long stick, at one end of which is tied a red rag on a lash, and a hook is fitted at the other; with the former, of which the geese seem much afraid, they are excited forward; and with the latter, such as attempt to stray, are caught by the neck and kept in order; if lame they are put into a hospital cart, which usually follows each large drove.' In this way they travelled about eight to ten miles per day from 3 a.m. to 9 p.m., those fatigued being fed with oats, the rest with barley.

Old geese were called carmags and were, according to Bewick, 'bought only by novices in market-making for they are so tough as to be utterly unfit for the table'.

The palatability of geese has been widely debated in recent centuries. Hawker stated that William IV 'esteemed brent beyond other wildfowl', but in 1846 Craven thought barnacle was by far the best, 'especially those of Ireland where the country people cook it by all conceivable and inconceivable contrivances'.

Friends who have eaten barnacle and brent, quite legally, tell me that the former is delicious but the latter varies from 'not bad' to 'vile'. My own experience is limited to greylag, pinkfoot and Canada, all utterly delicious and with thrice the flavour of the market geese which are the greylag's descendants. But, with the sale of wild geese rightly forbidden, only the lucky sportsman will be fortunate enough to have a wild grey goose on his table at Martinmas.

1986

## Service with a Smile

In Victorian times a host of poor folk went about the countryside peddling a very wide range of goods and services. How very different from today, when few traders arrive, unsolicited, at the door. A relict brush salesman perhaps, or a bright lad with the spirit of yesteryear offering to clean the car. Now they all flee before the stark message 'No hawkers and no circulars', and the only sales pitch comes telephonically in the infuriating form of a double-glazing salesperson.

Yet we still have the 'postie', the dustman and 'milkie' to bring full measure of news along with their important goods and services. Through storm and tempest, drought and drudgery, most whistle on with reliability I could never match. But how they vary from place to place.

Recently, our local dairy stopped supplying our scattering of houses because we were deemed 'uneconomic'. It took too long for the milkman to weave his way around innumerable tracks and up rutted, often icy drives, to make the relatively small sales worthwhile. As a result, some more mobile neighbours now rely entirely on the supermarket, where the milk is considerably cheaper. But another roundsperson – an enterprising young lady – has stepped in with a franchise from another dairy and the improvement in service is marked. I have already seen the franchise system work well in other areas. Where the delivery person stands to profit, service and courtesy seem to improve overnight. It is much the same in any walk of life I suppose – good, old-fashioned incentive.

Do you remember those little third pints we were given at school to make sure that we all grew up into bouncing bombs? It was OK most of the time, but when the weather was hot or the crate was left near a radiator – aaargh! Not surprisingly, some children never touched it, but I developed quite a taste for the stuff, commonly bagging several unwanted bottles. The fad was to shake and shake until your wrist ached, whereupon a delicious buttery lump would form. No worries about cholesterol then.

Later, those flavoured straws came into fashion and the school corridors echoed with the sucking and slurping of us infants turning plain spoils into treasures of strawberry, chocolate and banana.

1990

## Shocking Ignorance

It was sad and ironic that in the same week I received literature from both the British Dragonfly Society and a cosmetics company which displayed a dragonfly on the front of a leaflet promoting insect repellant! What an unfortunate indication of widespread public ignorance when it comes to so-called 'low life'. Not only would a dragonfly never trouble even the most fragrant of people, but also it is one of the many species in special need of a helping hand from mankind.

1989

## Bringing Back Flavour

With today's sophisticated fridges, cold rooms, irradiation and suchlike, most people take for granted the storage of perishables. But while these technologies may be good for hygiene, health and economy, they rarely do much for flavour. It is also sad to see the disappearance of so many skills that once promoted self-sufficiency.

In the old days, in the month or so before Christmas, a lot of stock had to be killed because the owners had insufficient feed left for the lean times ahead. The meat thus sacrificed meant a temporary abundance and fitted in well with the festive period which preceded Christmas. The pagan celebrations also brought luck for the new year.

Meat and fish that could not be eaten immediately or before it rotted could be preserved by drying, smoking or salting, or a combination of these processes. Even before man became conscious of the need for a balanced diet, with the correct intake of vitamins and minerals, a lack of fresh food often jeopardised health.

Nowadays we do not have to hang game, though most of us do in order to enhance the flavour, especially as much chainstore meat is so bland and boring. If more people patronised the small, independent butchers, who generally ensure that meat is hung properly, then we might see the return of real flavour to British meals.

In the eighteenth and nineteenth centuries rich estate owners often had ice houses for storage. These outdoor stores varied a lot in shape, but many had conical brick roofs covered in mounds of earth and small doorways leading down to tiny, round rooms. To keep the temperature constantly low, the walls were very thick and generally below ground level, and ice was laid on the floor between layers of straw. One theory was that the ice house idea was imported into Britain by travellers who had seen similar constructions in Italy, where peasants stored food in caves with ice which had been collected from the mountains. British ice often came from the estate's own frozen lake.

In the early days of gameshooting it was grouse which caused the greatest storage problems because when the season started the weather was generally still warm, or even hot; and when there was a glut of birds the problem was considerable. There is no doubt that the arrival of commercial cold storage in the late nineteenth and early twentieth centuries had a significant impact on grouse availability.

Almost without exception, older people now say that farmed meat is not what it used to be. 'It's the chemicals they use' is but one of many stock phrases. One of their greatest laments is the degradation of ham. Now you have to pay a huge premium for 'home-cooked' ham or 'ham on the bone' rather than that plastic excuse for meat primarily sold as a cheap sandwich filler.

In the 'good old days' every country house kept a pig or two, every kitchen sported at least one bacon hook and pig-killing day was a real social event, with beer on tap for all willing hands. Many households cured their own bacon, made their own sausages, and so on; and hams would be rubbed with salt over three weeks or so and then smoked for a further few. Indeed, it was nothing to eat one several years old. That's one for the EC commissioners to digest!

1992

# December

## Winter Ways

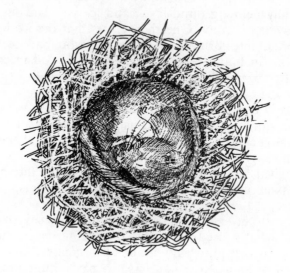

As the chill intensifies we may still hear snatches of favourite birdsong on those odd days of calm and softness when the grey shell encasing the land is pierced by ochrous sunlight. The bright chaffinch may quiver with full song in the cherry tree, as if convinced spring's blossoms are still about him. The bold mistle thrush may address the world from atop the mighty oak, as if convinced the spirit will always prevail. But now there is no denying the blackbird's note of sadness, reflecting his vulnerability as cold and hunger darken the northern horizon.

Throughout December there will be times when the sun fails to appear for days on end, at least a few nights of hard frost and days of deluge. Yet often, after all this dragging depression, the small tortoiseshell butterfly rises miraculously like Lazarus to illuminate the garden. A mere speck of life retaining whatever mysterious chemistry and motivation are needed to overcome the bitterness. And even on the darkest day of thick, encircling mist that master of survival, the woodpigeon, will dispel the gloom with his softest coo.

Disenchantment may now be about the camp of man, when faint hearts scarce move beyond the hearth, but wherever we look there is a lesson of survival in nature. Plants and trees wind down for winter while the dormouse curls up to idle in neutral; and those animals which do not hibernate are left to rummage about the emptiness as best they can.

In the garden the dankness intensifies all scent, as we fork out the last weeds, turning the tired earth to be purged by frost, and the robin's carol is on the wind. Leaves are raked, hedges trimmed, the skeletons of plants and vegetables gathered and all consigned to the burn-heap.

Bonfire smoke is the essence of countryside, a wisp of the past, a snatch of childhood harking back to the magic of that first remembered blaze. Through the blue, bitter smoke we again glimpse those days of woolly hats and mufflers, balaclavas and ruddy cheeks. Now, down the long years, we struggle to recapture such joy in simple things.

Walks about these Surrey lanes are especially pleasing in winter, for not only can we spy the wildlife more easily but also we can peek at the unending variety of old houses and gardens which had mouldered in secret before leaf fall. Here we may stop to investigate the hedgehog in his ball of leaves within a rooty hollow, and there towers the most wondrous chimney stack which has poured woodsmoke across these hills for centuries. I wonder how many jackdaws felt the warmth of its red brick and how many passers-by looked up at its yellow coronet before this highway was tarmacadamed and invaded by motor cars.

There goes old Tubbs the jobbing gardener, creaking up the lawn, hoping for a dry spell to enable him to trim the grass for the last time this year. Now his weathered, wooden barrow is brimful of trash, which he trundles away to burn in a quiet corner of the kitchen garden. Close behind him is the familiar robin, but equally attentive is the opportunist magpie, now skulking in the thickest hedge after Tubbs' antique airgun took out a tail feather last spring.

Next door a goldcrest works the hedgerow honeysuckle, a tiny blob of olive feathers systematically jerking up and down every twig like a clockwork toy, and quite unperturbed by human presence. His thin bill probes for insects and spiders while the much stouter beak of the visiting redwing plucks berry after berry from the glistening orange and red harvest.

Through a gate marked 'Tradesmen only' we spy a curious meeting of centuries – a disused, green-painted water pump from the eighteenth, an intriguing octagonal greenhouse from the nineteenth and a plush BMW with dark-tinted windows from the twentieth. Here is one of those orderly gardens belonging to someone who enjoys a touch of the old, but only as long as every blade of grass is just so long, every flower at the correct, boring distance from its neighbour and everything wooden is painted white: in fact even the stones around the lawn are painted white!

But the lane leads ever onwards, twisting this way and that, drawing the eye up and down, through nook and cranny, and occasionally surprising with a view right across the valley. Now we are very pleased for there, surely, is the scene our grandfathers saw, and their grandfathers before them. The hills and dales may be the same, scarcely altered by the rains of a millenium, but the detail is very different indeed. Overall this remains densely wooded country but the pattern of trees has never stopped changing. This glade where horses now idle the year round was once a coppice of oak and ash where redbacked shrikes found sanctuary, and that birch scrub soon replaced the elms destroyed by disease. Over there is a sunless spruce thicket, smothering the patch of England which was once commonland, where children skipped around the maypole; and beyond it a field ploughed to perfection marks the former village dump.

But the hanging roots are the same, festooned about the deep, sandy sides of the lanes with all the mystery of distant jungle. Tennyson must have seen this same natural ropework when he strode about these ways, then merely mud and stone.

On the whole, a winter walk hereabouts reveals a pleasing prospect. Yes, there is a considerable element of pretence and even vulgarity about some of the *nouveau riche* homesteads, but many gems of cottage life remain in unadulterated mellowness. About these oases our wildlife still clusters.

Yet I have no wish to wave my magic wand to protect this corner of England from all development, for no countryside should ever be regarded as a museum. All we can ask is that man makes his mark with sympathy.

1987

## Heaven Scent

They say that man has lost much of his sense of smell, and no doubt this is so as he has 'progressed' from hunter/gatherer, sticking his hooter close to the earth in search of prey, to sedentary farmer growing for the pot. No doubt biologists would tell us that our sense of smell retains some essential significance in sexual responses, but on the whole we smell for fun. And what great pleasure we continue to gain from matters olfactory. In our daily round, delicious odours assail us from every direction, but out in the countryside the best of them really are heaven scent.

It often amazes me that we seem able to 'remember' smells: perhaps this is as well as some people suggest that our nose-power deteriorates with age. I haven't noticed this yet, but I am convinced that the sense of smell can be improved with determined practice.

I have heard that a huntsman can smell success or failure as soon as he opens his door in the morning. Could this be true in a literal sense? Who among us would be brave enough to pooh-pooh such an idea when many insist they can smell such nebulous things as the approach of cold weather, or even Christmas?

Friends look at me askance when I suggest that I can date old books to within a few decades by their smell alone. Yet I know this to be true. For example, those of the early eighteenth century are ancient yet subtle whereas those pre-1700 are inevitably more pungent and 'churchy'. Late nineteenth century can be difficult, according to binding, but the generally inferior products of this century are mostly easier. In any case the feel of a book would give it away if one were blindfold.

Which chemicals – if any – are released when there is snow in the offing or a book to hand I know not, but they certainly seem to have the power to stimulate excitement. But where a smell is linked to a previous bad experience then apprehension is more likely to be induced. For example, that delicious, almost tangible smell which wafts up from the leaf mould of a damp wood always brings pheasant shooting to mind, but I do not like that strong, musky odour which hangs about fox dens and rabbit burrows.

What I do like on a shoot is the almost addictive whiff of powder smoke which hangs about you on a still day. When I first started shooting I loved it so much that I instinctively sniffed the barrels after every shot, just as some shooters are in the habit of blowing the smoke from the bores following each discharge.

When Guns assemble at start of play there is often a strong

smell of new rubber boots and waxproofs, especially early in the season on a smart shoot. Then there's the great smell of leather, especially that generated by the old cartridge bag when it's treated roughly. After a couple of drives and a liberal application of mud on a wet day, everything adopts a distinctive pong.

The wildfowler is not short of stimulation either. When the tide is up there is the magic of sea air, that memorable tang of the salt breeze that clings to the lips and cheeks long after the flight is ended. It is the flavour of the deep, the association of storm-tossed wigeon, boats rocking gently on the swell and waders jinking across the wild 'white horses' – all encapsulated in one taste of the open air.

But perhaps the best of all shooting smells is saved for the end of the day and is enjoyed by shooters of every description, except the rich man whose servants minister to his every need. A chore it may be when limbs ache and the brain is numb with tiredness, but there is no denying the wonderful smell of the gun-cleaning kit. I can't decide which I like best – the mineral lubricants for the metal parts or the erotic aroma of walnut oil rubbed sensuously into the stock.

At home yesterday I could smell that the dawn was frosty even before I creaked out of bed. For some reason this always makes me want to go pigeon shooting. But by far the best way to urge me from my 'pit' is to allow the delicious smell of frying bacon to escape from the kitchen, not that I'm allowed much saturated fat nowadays.

After stoking up on a good English breakfast, what better than taking axe and saw to the wood stack, where the real smell of the countryside lurks among ash, oak and beech? In an ideal world one would then stroll about the fields, taking in the delicacy of new-mown hay, especially after soft rain has unlocked all the scents of the earth after a long dry spell.

Perhaps, after all, when I'm next reborn I'll choose to return as a gundog, for with a nose of that calibre then surely everything must be heaven scent.

1986

# Language of Yesteryear

No sooner did I sit down to write than 'the electric went' and we were plunged into primitive darkness, an echo of yesteryear, the age of the candle. The wind howled wolfishly down the chimney, a hollow laugh at our helplessness after puffing the power lines down. It is always the same in the country – cuts every winter whenever a severe gale comes, and inevitably at night. No amount of cursing will stir the 'powers that be' (or rather the 'powers that aren't'!) into devising a more reliable 'juice' supply.

But the log fire crackled merrily. The wind sucked white plumes of woodsmoke erratically up the gusty flue and we were warm and dry. A good prod with the poker sent a rush of sparks up into the beastly night, the fire showed its red heart and we settled down to 'real' toast for supper, not those near tasteless squares which leap conveniently from the Russell Hobbs.

In the candle flame there is a language that we have ignored for too long, and a power cut provides ample opportunity for its proper study. It is a flickering peace, a slowing down and drifting back from the heartbreak hurry of the 1980s. Around the walls shadows dance in rustic mystery, their tempo dictated by the wolf-wind sucking at the door and stalking behind the waving curtain hem.

1986

## The 'Country Club'

It was past midnight when my neighbour heard a knock at the door last week. Not surprisingly, she responded to the summons with great caution for we live well off the road and even Jehovah's Witnesses and double-glazing salesmen are *rara avis* hereabouts.

Silhouetted in the soft porchlight, and almost ghostly against black garden trees, stood a smartly-dressed, middle-aged woman whose first words were: 'Do you have some shape?' Her demeanour was not that of an escaped lunatic so my neighbour was understandably puzzled. Who on earth knocks on some stranger's door in the dead of night, apparently to enquire about the occupant's voluptuousness? Or had the mysterious visitor unexpectedly run out of the popular butter substitute and could not bear to breakfast without it?

But even before the aroused lady could utter one word the rather refined stranger spoke again, this time with greater urgency: 'Do you have any shape? – they're all over the road!'

'Oooh, *sheep*!' exclaimed the enlightened householder, 'they must be from Orchard Farm, just up the way. I'll phone Bob Giles immediately.' Which is just as well as itinerant A-road mutton would soon have provided Sunday joints for the entire county.

The incident emphasised just how caring a few people remain in a society increasingly without time for public-spiritedness. In this case the concerned lady was also quite brave in venturing down a strange, lonely track late at night.

Loose livestock have given me a fright on numerous occasions, especially when I have been tearing through the dark to catch dawn flight on the foreshore. Big as they are, cows and horses are not the easiest things to see through bleary eyes in unlit lanes. And they are always where you least expect them, often blocking the way around a blind corner, for they commonly wander long distances when mankind is asleep. Only last week I had to swerve to avoid a calf virtually imprisoned by the steep banks of a local lane some two miles from the nearest farm.

In my experience, horses frequently present danger on modern roads. OK, I know they came before the internal combustion engine, but is it really necessary for pleasure riders and even professional trainers to be about the highways in the late dusk without lights? Surely this is extremely irresponsible with today's volume of fast traffic penetrating every byway!

Sadly, most people who complain about lax country ways get labelled as busybodies or do-gooders, and the accused are only too ready to blame interference on mass immigration of townies. Yet nothing could be further from the truth. Most townsfolk I know love the countryside for its contrast and vitality and would do almost anything to protect it. All too often it is the man for whom the countryside is a factory floor who abuses it.

Ignorance is the common enemy, not accident of birthplace, and the sooner press-promoted barriers to rural-urban harmony are dismantled, the quicker conservation, fieldsports and other amenity interests will be able to move forward. The 'country club' needs all the members it can get, to protect habitat and wage war on unscrupulous developers rather than squabble in the ranks.

1988

## Weather Eye

With ever-increasing public interest in environmental matters such as the 'greenhouse effect' and acid rain, it seems that more people than ever are keeping a weather eye open for significant climatic change. Now there are three 'weather bores' for every one ten years ago, and instead of hanging up seaweed or noting the arrival of geese they pore over graphs, talking about occluded fronts and computer predictions.

Down at the Dog and Pheasant old Joby White gently places his pint on the table, slowly wipes his lips with the back of his hand, takes the deepest of breaths and declares: 'Bet none of you can remember the winter of 1928–9. That were a real bone-cracker.'

'Oh yes, that was undoubtedly a severe winter,' says smart Nigel Snodgrass, 'but in fact the mean temperature was 35.6°F, whereas that of 1946–7 was 34.3°F and 1962–3 was even lower at 33.0°F.'

'Don't give me that,' says Joby. 'I were twenty in 1928 and I remember it as if it were yesterday. You couldn't blink without a tear freezing, and the poor ol' birds wuz lyin' feet up in the lane all over the place. '62–63 were nuthin' like that.'

So it goes on, each of us remembering certain winters for particular incidents or circumstances, not necessarily for the lowest temperatures or deepest and longest snows. But what we can be sure of is that in the old days, when poverty and hunger were rife, severe weather had a much greater impact on the lives of men. Also, the further back we go, the greater was the incidence of severe winters.

In the nineteenth century there were no fewer than fourteen

winters in which the mean temperature was 36.0°F or less, over three times the number of twentieth-century chillers so far. Of those, nine were in the first fifty years. The winter of 1829–30 was as cold as 1962–3 in many areas and 1813–14 was even colder, with an estimated mean of 32.5°F. The five successive cold winters 1837–8 to 1841–2 included two with a mean of only about 34°F, and eight cold winters occurred in the nine years 1812–13 to 1820–1.

Spells of cold winters also occurred fairly often in the eighteenth century. For example, there were thirteen in the seventeen-year period 1770–1 to 1786–7, including the record cold winter of 1784–5, with an estimated mean temperature of only 32.3°F. The high frequency of cold years and the almost complete absence of warm years during the period 1763–1842 is a clear indication of what came to be known as the Little Ice Age.

Today all we ever seem to hear about is the greenhouse effect, and with the melting of polar ice one boffin recently predicted that by the year 2030 most of the Essex marshes will be sunk without trace and the mainland will be basking in a tropical climate. Bad news for wildfowlers yes, but even worse for sunbathers, who will be hard-pressed to find a beach on which to enjoy the new heat.

What really matters is the mean temperature for each entire year, not our obsession with 'good' summers and 'bad' winters. Only that can provide a reliable yardstick in assessing trends as one exceptional *season* may be rapidly 'cancelled out' by the next. It is the steady increase in mean annual temperature that has been worrying scientists.

The two coldest years on record were 1814 and 1816, with estimated mean temperatures of 46°F and 45.9°F respectively. The winter of 1813–14 was the last in which a frost fair was held on the Thames, when there were a great number of booths for the sale of gin, beer and gingerbread, and sheep were roasted over a coal fire on the ice. The meat was called Lapland mutton and sold at a shilling a slice. At earlier frost fairs the merrymaking also included shooting.

During the 300 years or so from 1500 to 1814 the Thames was completely frozen in eighteen winters, but today a frost fair is most unlikely because, even if the temperature were so low again, sufficient freezing would be prevented by factors such as the greater movement of water caused by changes in bridges and dredging, and the heating of river water by industrial outlets.

For us robots, cocooned in centrally heated homes and air-conditioned cars, it is hard to appreciate the misery caused by intense cold in the countryside of olde England, going right back to AD 80, when 'Sic crwell cald was nevir sene beforne'. The frost prevented ploughing, all agricultural work was suspended, the winter seed was destroyed and famine was widespread. There was no pay for those who didn't work, travel by land was virtually impossible and, with most of the workforce on the land, there was widespread despondency. What little international trade there was brought little relief as bitter winters here have always tended to follow the pattern throughout North-West Europe.

Not surprisingly, down the centuries there have been many men like Joby White, offering sense from old saws to relieve the misery. One of the most famous surfaced in the severe winter of 1837–8, which came to be called Murphy's Winter:

> Murphy has a weather eye:
>   He can tell whene'er he pleases
> Whether it's wet or whether it's dry,
>   Whether it's hot or whether it freezes.

But like many other quack, long-range forecasters, Murphy never repeated his success and soon relapsed into obscurity.

This year 'Murphy's men' are pointing to the early arrival of Bewick's swans at Slimbridge. Will they be right and will Joby's pointing finger mean anything more than his beer glass is empty?

1988

## Mental Therapy

As December drifts towards a new year and most households are preoccupied with laying in supplies for the holiday hibernation, there is an air of calm in the countryside. Autumn has departed tamely and now, before hard January puts Britain on ice, we can ramble and reflect. There is a lull about the land, as though some wondrous event is about to take place.

In walking, just as the shepherd feels naked without his crook so the sportsman feels undressed without his gun. The chance of a shot might be slim but adrenalin is diminished without that armed preparedness. This is not greed for every sporting opportunity but a way of life akin to mental therapy.

1984

## Kubla Kahns of Conservation

I live in that part of Surrey which, in wilderness terms, is certainly manicured yet contains space sufficient to blow away the cobwebs which urban employment drapes around one's shoulders. Nearby my native Hampshire beckons with a heartache tinge of jumbledom. There the muck is just that bit thicker in the lanes.

All around me is the Xanadu of the mighty ones of the money market, where they most often decree their lordly pleasure-domes – those vast red-brick habitations of the Kubla Kahns of the city. Yet, in this odd world of the orderly and the magnificent the conservation movement has flourished in the voluntary hands of a middle class with the time and money to indulge their ideals. But this great green belt is not guarded jealously. Here too, betwixt and across the mini empires the footpaths are well signposted.

Footpaths are under close scrutiny now, among the various consultation papers relating to the proposed Wildlife and Countryside Bill, which the Government intends to introduce during the present session of Parliament (i.e. by July 1980). There is a tendency to think that here is more tinkering for idle hands, but between the lines there seems to be a genuine and commendable attempt to help everyone, not least the besmeared 'townie', to enjoy the nation's inheritance without upsetting rural communities too much. Even phrases such as 'promoting enjoyment by the public' are included.

To meet the schedule the Bill must be drafted this month, yet most of the discussion papers were only sent out towards the end of August, leaving little time for the ninety-one organisations consulted to study points adequately.

On a more general note, I am delighted to see the possibility of increased control of habitat. For example, with regard to designated Sites of Special Scientific Interest, landowners may be legally obliged to give twelve months notice to the Nature Conservancy Council of their intention to undertake practices which would be detrimental to the identified scientific interest. While this would marginally erode the freedom of the individual, in many instances enforced control of habitat is essential. In all cases it is understood that the landowner will not suffer financially.

On the credit side, many of the Bill's proposals are aimed at closing the gate before the vulnerable have bolted. Such legislation is fine in theory but fraught with financial restrictions in practice. Equally important, and possibly more effective, would be to promote a custodial attitude in landowner and visitor alike.

1979

# Bottle-Fed Birds

As December becomes more proficient at its ice artistry and the natural larder is laid bare, certain birds increasingly come to our notice, especially about the house. Inevitably, the quick-learning blue and great tits are among them.

In common with many other folk, we have had our bottles of ordinary, silver-topped milk pecked open over many winters as the birds obviously relish the cream and its considerable nourishment. But recent rapidly rising sales of skimmed and semi-skimmed milk, linked to the new interest in healthier diets, seem to have spoilt the birds' fun. It appears that they have already learnt not to waste their time on the proliferating bottles devoid of cream. Whether or not they can recognise the different colour or pattern of the foil tops or spot the absence of cream through the glass I have no idea. We always have several types of milk – ordinary, semi-skimmed and skimmed – delivered together, and there is no doubt that hereabouts there is far less pecking going on. Perhaps when the tits find no cream in some bottles they think all the others are the same and ignore the lot.

1987

# Celebrating Nature

There is little doubt that if we had never been introduced to the Christian religion we would still enjoy a great festival during midwinter and that the source of our joy would be the unfailing wonder at natural phenomena and the simple passage of the seasons. Long before the Christian influence 25 December was the approximate focus of pagan rites celebrating the winter solstice, the Yule and Saturnalia. Many pagan customs survived the swamping by Christianity and remain today in our culture. Whatever the motivation, the festivals should and have reflected a people in harmony with the environment and the seasons, or – if you prefer – 'at one with nature'.

In view of this it was hardly surprising that much of the old fun and family spirit faded from Christmas as the industrial revolution drove people into the towns, where they became increasingly divorced from nature. There they have been subjected to commercialism and the hard sell of material possessions which, for many, is as much an anathema as the doctrinaire ramming of

229

popular creeds down our gullible throats. In olden times, with little scientific knowledge, people replaced ignorance with simple trust in religion to explain away many natural phenomena. But now, regardless of our technological and scientific potential, I like to think that we can still marvel at natural 'creation'.

Today, with widespread rejection of excess and interest in the countryside accelerating, we are witnessing a major change in society. Now man sees more clearly his position (not 'role', which implies an overall plan) from an environmental angle, takes joy in the beauty of things *for their own sake*, and has far less need for the attachment of symbolism. Yet our roots are deep and I believe that even an atheist would admit to the desire to celebrate in the manner of Christmas at least once a year.

During the dark days it is easy to understand how early customs and festivals started. For example, during Saturnalia, which began with a feast on 13 December and continued with riotous life, banqueting, games and licence until 23 December, candles were often given away as charms to ensure the return of the sun's power after the solstice. Most important, however, was the mingling of all classes in common jollity.

The other great founding festival was Yule, the ordinary word for Christmas in the Scandinavian languages. Its origin is obscure but it is clearly the name of a Germanic season – a two-month tide from mid-November to mid-January. It is no longer thought that the old Germans held a Yule feast at the winter solstice and it is likely that the specifically Teutonic Christmas customs come from a New Year and beginning-of-winter festival kept about mid-November. These chiefly religious or magical rites were transferred to Christmas and were intended to secure prosperity in the new year while Christmas feasting derived at least in part from the sacrificial banquets that marked the beginning of winter.

Even our desire to feed the wild birds at Christmas and through-out midwinter is steeped in custom worldwide. At Loblang, in Hungary, for many years the last sheaf at harvest has been kept and given to the birds at new year, while in southern Germany it has long been the tradition to put corn on the roof on Christmas Eve.

1980

## The Holly and the Ivy . . .

This month wild game comes readily to the table, but so too do ancient symbols of man's association with the land. Urban man now makes one of his rare excursions into the sticks, to seek out the few bright evergreens which 'drear December' offers up. Holly and mistletoe, and to a lesser extent yew and ivy, are plucked from the bare woods to share strange, new quarters with hi-fi and video as gestures of caring – for nature and tradition.

Yet these plants are valued for very different reasons and the stories of their associations are both legion and controversial. Take holly, for example, *the* Christian plant. Its name originally referred to the pointed leaves but later was probably related to holy. As one nineteenth-century scribe put it: 'The spinous leaves and blood-red berries may be looked upon by the Christian symbolist as a mystic foreshadowing of the Passion at the celebration of the Nativity'.

But there was also non-Christian reverence for holly. For example, it is said that in the ancient Forest of Dean oaths taken in the verderers' court were once sworn on a twig of holly instead of the bible.

Today many people still do not put up any decorations until Christmas Eve itself, but on the other hand the earliest Christmas tree and decorations I saw this year lit up the street on 1 December. In some areas, such as Rutland, it has been considered unlucky to bring in holly before Christmas Eve. And Derbyshire people once believed that the type of holly gathered determined whether the husband or wife would rule the household in the ensuing year. Prickly leaves favoured the man but smooth ones suggested the woman's dominance.

Holly boughs cut from churchyards have been deemed especially lucky and in some areas and countries regarded as sure-fire protection against thunder. There is no denying its value as a game and wildlife refuge when icy easterlies blow snow horizontally through bare woods. Farmers have valued it too. As John Evelyn wrote, 'Glittering with its armed and varnished leaves, blushing with their natural coral . . . it mocks the rudest assaults of the weather, beast and hedge-breakers.'

Use of mistletoe as a decoration is perhaps even more ancient. Most people have heard of its association with the Druids, who had a liking for threes and took a shine to the plant's frequent clusters of three berries. However, it is more likely that the mistletoe's greenness and fruiting in a generally barren season were of wider appeal and came to symbolise a promise of renewed growth.

Today mistletoe is generally only an excuse for a peck on the cheek beneath the chandelier, but in the dim past its associated superstitions were considerable, especially with regard to its supposed curative effect. Growing 'head downwards', it was obviously a cure for dizziness and the 'falling sickness' – epilepsy.

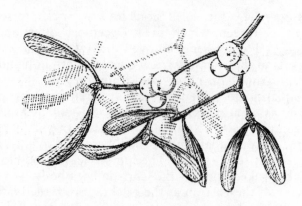

Less commonly used at festivals is yew, a more sombre decoration traditionally associated with Easter, but when it was more common it was too convenient to ignore as a decoration. Generally we associate yews with churchyard protection, but it is interesting to note that some specimens are even older than the churches in whose yards they guard the souls of medieval countrymen. Though valued for bowmaking, many of the trees were probably rooted out because of the poisonous effect of their leaves on livestock.

Because of the churchyard association, the yew has long been regarded as menacing. In 1664, in his 'Botanologia', Robert Turner wrote: 'The yew is hot and dry, having such attraction that if planted near a place subject to poisonous vapours, its very branches will draw and imbibe them. For this reason it was planted in churchyards, and commonly on the west side, which was at one time considered full of putrefaction and gross oleaginous gasses exhaled from the graves by the setting sun. These gasses, or will-o'-the-wisps, divers have seen, and believed them dead bodies walking abroad. Wheresoever it grows it is both dangerous and deadly to man and beast; the very lying under its branches has been found hurtful.'

The common ivy, too, can be an effective decoration. Twining of the vines around pictures and along mantelpieces used to be very common, and today we can brighten them up with white sprays and glitter to create displays infinitely better than the purely artificial and expensive kind.

1985

## *Christmas Spirit*

I would certainly welcome a return to many of the old ways and a clear move away from the commercial pantomime that masquerades as modern Christmas. Let's have far more of the spirit contained in the earliest-known carol, from the thirteenth century. Written in Anglo-Norman, it was discovered on what had been a blank leaf in the middle of a British Museum manuscript. Today few people would understand it, but a translation clearly calls for 'only mirth' and a house full of 'many a dish'. It also urges us to 'kick and beat the grumblers out'. As for a tipple, it advocates:

> To English ale and Gascon wine,
> And French, doth Christmas much incline –
> And Anjou's too;
> He makes his neighbour freely drink,
> So that in sleep his head doth sink
> Often by day.

It seems that even then there were too many office parties!

In fact most early carols were a mixture of scriptural allusions and invitations to hard drinking, and were mostly sung by the tribe of professional minstrels during the periods of feasting into which the day of the Yule was divided.

In later times, too, music and singing were held 'in greater account than devotion', and eating and drinking were rated far above all. This is confirmed by the accounts of the Stationers' Company for the year 1510, which include the following entry:

> Item payd to the preacher: 6s 2d
> Item payd to the minstrell: 12s 0d
> Item payd to the coke: 15s 0d

1992

## *The Great Escape*

My guess is that more people walk for pleasure in this last week of December than at any other time of year. The attraction is plain to see. As we stagger from one festive meal to the next, wallowing about like bloated sea lions in a breeding colony, the great outdoors beckons as never before.

233

Some people manage a high-octane sniff of fresh air when they shuffle to the door to refill the log basket, but most are so locked into an endless round of megalomanic partying that all they can do is stare wistfully through raised wine glasses out of the window. Even Uncle Charlie's bold suggestion that we all walk to the pub is greeted with great disdain.

But eventually enough is enough, and when I think that all the visitors are slumbering soundly by the fire, I am off and running, like a newborn lamb. Why should I feel guilty? After all, yet again I missed the Boxing Day shoot. It's all very well if you live in one of those households which eat, breathe and sleep shooting, but if yours is an average one, like mine, then obviously there are other things to consider. For example, there is eating, and drinking – and eating, and drinking . . .

Don't get me wrong. I am not saying that I look down on anyone who majors in Lucullan living. On the contrary, I believe that I have a certain renown for gastronomic and bibulous enjoyment. It's just that – well, there is a limit to one's elasticity and after the third pud and umpteenth port my inners start to scream for mercy.

Best of all, I like creeping off in the late afternoon when there is snow on the ground and it is so quiet that it seems as if the whole of Britain must be tucked up at home, probably prostrate before the hearth. I think of all that stale, hot air they are sharing, in such contrast to the scintillating freshness which marks my trail. And my high is even higher for having been party to that claustrophobia myself.

It is at times like this you realise that the precise day of the week, let alone yearly festival, means not one iota to any wild creature or plant. Call it Christmas Day, Good Friday or St Hubert's Day, the birds and beasts are still out there, sometimes freezing or starving to death, but mostly getting by through incredible resilience or adaptation.

One of my favourite walking places, which always helps to clear my befuddled brain, is nearby Blackdown, that great National Trust estate which towers above Haslemere, on the Surrey-Sussex border. Rising to over 900ft, this jewel in the countryside sparkles through every season, beaming many miles to the south across one of the most spectacular views in southern England. To sit awhile there, and contemplate that apparently unchanging and unspoilt patchwork landscape, is to believe that there is nothing wrong with the world. Saddam Hussein, HIV and European Monetary Union might as well be on another planet.

1991

# Of Seasons Past

The few days between Christmas and the New Year are always a time for reflection. Fat with excess, we cogitate by the hearth, occasionally stirring to prod the fire in eternal search for that spark of inspiration. There is a lull between parties and pantos and a rare chance to reminisce on missed opportunities as well as make bold commitments to our future.

The bright sounds of carolling drift away into the long night, the glass of port is laid aside and out comes the old gamebook to prove what might have been, show how 1988 compared with those long-lost days of plenty and emphasise how age mellows our activities. Did I really shoot only one snipe in January? Was that a reflection of reduced numbers or more an indication of premature dotage? How can it be that I had just one pheasant day in December? Did I always have some paltry excuse for not getting out? Was I genuinely too busy or, horror of horrors, could the truth be that the people had given up inviting me because I always had too much on?

Whatever the truth, there is no denying the attraction of a gamebook and I do urge those who found one in this year's Christmas stocking to start scribbling right away. Even better, take up the old fountain pen and recapture the style which won you an A for calligraphic excellence. Give as much information as time will allow and always detail various 'pest' species separately, never consigning them to the anonymous humiliation of 'various', as in the old days. Try to add a note or two on wind and weather, the strange gun that Bob Laughingstock brought along for the first time, the rabbit with three legs and the swallow which astonished everyone by sweeping past in a snowstorm. This – the social history and observations of natural history – is the essence of interest, not the bare statistics, which do little more than provide fodder for analysts trying to assess trends.

This week you may well record relatively insignificant outdoor happenings, such as the first flowering of the wych hazel or aconite, or the song of the thrush. But in so doing you will come to learn much more about our wildlife and countryside, especially as the years roll by, emphasising what is unusual in your area in each week of the year.

1989

## Green Explosion

As far as the general country scene is concerned, I think the most important thing to have happened in the Eighties is the fantastic explosion of interest in matters green. Whether your main 'thing' is wildlife, landscape, ecology or outdoor activities such as fishing, shooting, birdwatching or rambling, no longer can anyone act in isolation. Everyone has come to appreciate how frail and finite both Britain's and the world's natural resources are. Suddenly the green movement is a major political topic and the country scene should be all the better for it. Now that, at long last, man seems to be getting his priorities right in ranking spiritual wealth higher than materialism, we ought to move forward rapidly. Hopefully, in another ten years time this really will be a green and pleasant land, and with the upgrading of countless acres of habitat there will be less reliance on museum-piece nature reserves. That done, we can sit back and talk about the weather.

1989

236